Carol Spindel's
IN THE SHADOW OF THE SACRED GROVE

"Reading *In the Shadow of the Sacred Grove* is like having one's ancestral home described by an unlikely outsider who has almost come to feel at home there. This book, a 'true' recording of a period in the author's life, is a justified companion to such novels as *When Rain Clouds Gather,* by the African writer Bessie Head.

"Carol Spindel learns how not to be a stranger among other women; how not to be merely a 'white woman from another place,' how not to be a 'foreigner,' left on the fringes of another people's life. Her integrity is warming; her fidelity to her own experience and faith in her own *womanity* very moving indeed."

—Alice Walker

IN THE
SHADOW
OF THE
SACRED GROVE

IN THE
SHADOW
OF THE
SACRED GROVE

CAROL SPINDEL

Vintage Books   A Division of Random House, Inc.   New York

VINTAGE DEPARTURES

A VINTAGE DEPARTURES ORIGINAL, AUGUST 1989
FIRST EDITION

Library of Congress Cataloging-in-Publication Data
Spindel, Carol.
    In the shadow of the sacred grove.
    (Vintage departures)
    1. Senufo (African people)—Social life and customs.
    2. Senufo (African people)—Rites and ceremonies.
    I. Title. II. Series.
DT545.45.S44S65 1989   966.6′8   88-40357
ISBN 0-679-72214-9 (pbk.)

Book design by Cathryn S. Aison

Author photo copyright © 1989 by Tom Bassett

Frontispiece: Taken from a mudcloth painted by Ganignigay Silue of Fakaha, Ivory Coast

Manufactured in the United States of America
10 9 8 7 6 5 4 3 2 1

CONTENTS

PROLOGUE

Why africa in particular, of all the places in the world, should have called to me I cannot say. Why I wanted to cross over and experience life in another culture is easier to tell. I had grown up in a home of two cultures—my father was born in Brooklyn to a family of Sephardic Jews and my mother in Arkansas to Southern Baptists who can trace their roots to the earliest settlement in the Arkansas Territory. All my life, I crossed back and forth from one of these cultures to the other, learning Jewish history in the synagogue and how to gig for catfish from my grandfather. As I ate *latkes* and homegrown collard greens, I studied the grown-ups, alert for clues that would show me how to pass as an insider in these two very different worlds.

When I finished college, the first thing I did was to pack a backpack and head for North Africa. A friend and I traveled for months third class, from Morocco to

the Nile and as far south as Tanzania. I came home from
that trip with one firm conviction: If I really wanted to
understand life in Africa, I would have to move into a
village, learn the language, and live there for a year. I
was determined that someday I would do just that.

When I met Tom, who is now my husband, he was
trying to decide whether to do his Ph.D. research in cultural geography on agriculture in California or in
Africa. "Africa," I urged. "Go to Africa." But he was
stubborn and chose California until somehow a professor
and a promise of grants turned him around, and the next
thing I knew, he was planning to move to a village in
northern Ivory Coast (Côte d'Ivoire) for a year and a
half.

Tom left for Africa on January 1, 1981. I joined
him seven months later, three months after he had moved
into a large village away from a main road. Choosing a
village from among the thousands of Senufo villages that
dotted the savanna had been the first trial of his fieldwork. Touring the area on his moped one day, anxious to
settle on a village and begin his work, Tom turned in at
Kalikaha because he liked the shady lane of mango trees
that led to the village. He was taken to an old man who
told him, "It is not the elders who control the young here
anymore. It is the young men who control the elders."
Tom, who wanted to study the effects of cultural change
on the local agriculture, was intrigued. The villagers
seemed willing to have him, and so he decided to live in
Kalikaha. Best of all, an educated young Senufo man
who had been visiting Kalikaha the same day told Tom
that he would be willing to quit his job and come work
for him as his interpreter and assistant. Tom wrote me
that night, elated that his research was finally getting off

the ground, and described his new assistant as jovial, open, and very friendly.

Before going to Africa, I read everything I could find about northern Ivory Coast. The Senufo, the main inhabitants of the area, are well known for their carved masks and theatrical funerals. Art, in Senufo society, plays an important role as mediator between the living inhabitants of the village and the power of death. Their religious philosophy, called *poro,* is centered inside a sacred grove, where ritual initiations are held and objects of power are stored. Their land is not owned privately but is held collectively, for their ancestors and future generations.

These ideas intrigued me. I had studied art, and at one time, I had painted seriously. But I had given it up because I did not feel that my painting formed what was for me an essential connection between me and my society. In a Senufo village, the role of the artist was clearly defined, and this dilemma did not exist.

In Berkeley, the people I saw around me were searching for something. Lacking an inherited cultural tradition, they were seeking to formulate one of their own. They sought identity in a group and talked about "community." They longed for ritual and a sense of the sacred in their lives. But in modern America these qualities are elusive. Rituals have to be borrowed or invented from scratch. Groups form and then dissolve.

In Africa, communities who honor beliefs that are generations old still exist in a cohesive and viable form. The existence of the sacred grove reassured me of that. The sacred grove became for me a potent symbol of all that a traditional African society offered: art and ritual, community, a different attitude toward death, tradition, and continuity. I journeyed to Africa to experience for myself a society where these values were still important.

This book is the story of a one-year sojourn in a single African village as seen through a single pair of eyes. I am not a scholar, attempting to analyze and explain. Many aspects of life in Kalikaha are never discussed, and many others are treated superficially. The names in the book are real except for Kalikaha, which has been changed. My African friends would not understand this American concern with privacy. "Have we done something of which we should be ashamed?" they would ask. No, I reply to them in advance. I am only being cautious.

In Senufo culture the best thanks are those that come months, even years, after a gift has been received. In true Senufo fashion, this offering has been long in coming. Six years after leaving Kalikaha, I have fashioned this portrait of the village and of my experiences there. In return for the hospitality I received there, I offer this book.

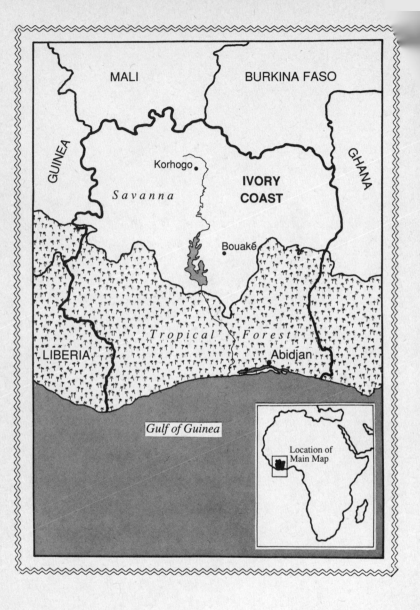

MALI

BURKINA FASO

GUINEA

Korhogo

Savanna

IVORY
COAST

GHANA

Bouaké

Tropical   Forest

LIBERIA

Abidjan

Gulf of Guinea

Location of
Main Map

IN THE
SHADOW
OF THE
SACRED GROVE

 ARRIVAL

FROM THE WINDOW OF THE SMALL PLANE, I LOOKED DOWN and saw the wooded savanna where I would live for the next year. The landscape was dotted with Senufo villages, like models we might have built in grade school geography, tiny and seemingly perfect. The orange mud houses were thatched with brown straw, arranged in tight clusters, and surrounded by tall cylindrical granaries topped with conical thatched roofs. Every brick, every wall, was the same pink-orange color as the mud the houses stood upon. At a distance from each village was a green patchwork zone of small fields crisscrossed with tiny trails. Just outside each village, clearly visible from the air, was a dense circle of trees—the sacred grove. From the air, I looked down into the groves and caught glimpses of clearings and small houses.

The groves were remnants of ancient gallery forests that had once been found along all the stream courses.

3

The other trees had been cleared; only these round groves had been carefully preserved. The groves had been there long before airplanes were invented, and the thick vegetation had hidden what was inside from curious eyes like mine. Although I peered down, it felt like cheating. I wanted to be invited inside, as Tom had been, and to enter as an initiate, barefoot. But sacred groves and their *poro* societies were the province of men. Only a few women ever entered, and they had to have passed menopause.

That the Senufo had chosen a grove of ancient trees as the symbol of their spiritual life was something I could instantly understand. Trees, especially large old ones, had always seemed to me to have a sacred presence of their own. I felt it as soon as I stepped under their canopy. All my life, I had run to the woods for refuge. There, in the shadowy calm, a dry, parched place inside me always turned moist again.

We left the town of Korhogo on our red Honda motorcycle late the following afternoon. The soft evening light gave the landscape a dusky glow. The sky was full of clouds with watercolor gray edges, and the valleys of rice fields were a bright, lush green. It was early August, the rainy season, and the vegetation was thick and growing. I couldn't recognize this as the hot, dusty place Tom had described in his letters a few months before. It was much more beautiful than I had pictured.

Each time we neared a village, the dirt road suddenly filled up with people returning home from their day's work in the fields. The boys and men rode mopeds or old bicycles wired together, which looked as if they would fall apart at the next bump in the rough muddy road. The women walked in single file along the edge of the road, carrying enormous bundles of firewood or the

4

empty pots from lunch on their heads. Bicycles, the men explained to me later, were very dangerous for women— they made them infertile. When we passed close to a line of women and they saw my face, they broke into surprised smiles and laughed and waved.

On the ground, I no longer had that sense I had had from the air, of villages made from, and therefore perfectly suited to, their environment. From the jolting back of the motorcycle, I was struck by the poverty to which the sameness of the mud houses attested. Each time we passed a village, I looked for the silhouette of the sacred grove, like a round green mushroom against the sky. At one village, the road had cut across the sacred grove, dividing it in two. The vegetation was thin, and I could see the small houses inside. "Everyone says their *poro* isn't very strong," Tom said over his shoulder, "because you can see right in."

We had been on the road for about an hour when we turned off on a much smaller track that led to Kalikaha. All around us, dark clouds were rolling in, and it looked like rain. This trail was rougher than the road, and we had to go slowly to avoid the rocks. Finally, we reached cleared fields planted in cotton and peanuts. "These are Kalikaha's fields," Tom called back proudly. "And this farmer is in my study."

As we rounded a curve, a road lined with mango trees opened up in front of us, and to the right of the road I saw a small wooden sign with the name KALIKAHA stenciled in blue letters. It was dusk, but lightning on the horizon lit up my first view of the village, spotlighting thatched roofs, orange adobe houses, and narrow paths. We turned down the small lane lined with mango trees as the lightning moved closer to the village. The sky was an eerie blue-gray, and the wind was cold on my bare arms.

Turning onto a path, we passed between houses and came out in an open area where a group of men were sitting under a mango tree around a bottle of wine. A shout went up when they saw us, and they all jumped to their feet, clapping and cheering.

Someone came running toward us, and I recognized Tom's assistant, Yardjuma, from the pictures Tom had sent me. Who else had a round belly like that one? He could have been pregnant. His round face, with the Senufo scars like cat's whiskers, beamed with joy at the sight of us. He came straight to me and hugged me, then gave me a kiss on each cheek like the French and then the third one that the Africans add. This was difficult because, in my excitement, I had forgotten to take off my motorcycle helmet. The group of men surrounded us, shaking our hands and yelling greetings loudly and drunkenly at Tom. *"Mbaaaa, mbaa, mba!"* answered Tom in an unfamiliar voice with an African accent.

Yardjuma planted himself in front of me and dramatically threw his arms into the air. "Now that Carol has come," he proclaimed to the stormy skies, "all my problems are over!"

Yardjuma's financial and family problems had been a recurring theme in Tom's letters, and so I was astonished to discover that I had solved them like that, just by arriving on the back of a motorcycle, my bottom very sore and the rest of me covered with red dust. I hadn't even spoken. But I had no time to wonder what he meant; the storm was nearly upon us. Twisting and turning through narrow alleyways, barely missing chickens, goats, and children, beeping the horn as we rounded granaries to warn anyone on the path, we crossed an open area and arrived at a passage so narrow that we had to climb off and walk the motorcycle through.

On the other side was the house where Tom had already spent three months. I had always thought of African houses as round, and in Kalikaha, the women's houses are round, but ours was a man's house, rectangular, with a roofed porch out front. It was adobe rather than bleached wood, and the roof was thatch instead of tin, but it looked familiar—it looked exactly like the weatherbeaten sharecroppers' shacks I had seen all my life as we drove from Memphis to my grandparents' farm in Arkansas.

As we crossed the Mississippi floodplain I crossed over from one culture to another. In Memphis, I left the urban Jewish environment of my father's friends; at the other end of that drive waited my mother's family's Christmas dinner of crumbling roast, homegrown collard greens, and Karo pecan pie. I had realized early that things learned in one of these worlds were not often considered important in the other. And the patched-together shacks I stared at from the car window were another universe altogether, one I never entered.

The small house, with its leaning porch roof supported by two poles, reminded me of the connections—the terrible threads of the slave trade that tied our continents together and made this architecture look as familiar as home. As the lightning moved toward us, I stood staring at the little house, and I suddenly understood, as I never had before, that history is not found just in books, but tucked in bits into every part of life, and that you can see it if you look in the way people build their homes and cook their food.

Tom unlocked the door with a large, old-fashioned key. We stepped into a small rectangular room, dark and cluttered and very dusty from the month that Tom had been away in Abidjan.

7

"This is it!" Tom said, pushing open the back door for more light. "The famous hut. What do you think?" But before I could answer, there were shouts behind me of "Tom! Tom!" and the house was suddenly full of men, shaking our hands and looking me over with open curiosity.

The crowd parted to let a young man through. He was short, with large muscular shoulders and a broad chest, and his stocky body seemed packed with compressed energy. His handsome oval face and shining eyes stood out in the crowd. Beaming fondly, he held out his hand to Tom and glanced over and smiled as if he knew me already. Tom punched his arm playfully. "Donnisongui, *ça va?*"

"*Bon, bon, bon!*" he boomed in reply, shaking Tom's hand vigorously and pretending to wrestle. "*Ça va, Tom, ça va? Bien, bien bien!*"

Laughing like two boys, they turned to face me. "This is Donnisongui," Tom said, smiling at both of us.

Donnisongui drew a deep breath, puffing out his broad chest. *"Dansi!"* (dawn-say!), he proclaimed, looking straight at me. "Welcome!" His voice was so warm, his happiness for Tom so apparent, that I felt no doubt about my welcome from our *jatigi*. The relationship between guests and their *jatigi* is an important one. It was Donnisongui's responsibility to see that we were comfortable, but more than that, he was responsible for our actions while we were in the village, and had we done anything to anger the villagers, they would have come to Donnisongui.

When Tom decided to do his fieldwork in Kalikaha, he asked the chief to find him a house. The chief, who had urged Tom to settle in the village, assured him it would not be a problem. But he had done nothing until

8

the morning of the day Tom was supposed to arrive with his things. Only then had he gone around the village to ask for a house for the next year. No one had wanted to give up his house for a strange white man except Donnisongui, who had moved his things out and was now living with his wife in her round house nearby. This was an unusual arrangement, since husbands and wives usually had their own separate houses.

Unsure what to do now, I sat down on one of our two straight-backed chairs. Yardjuma took a broom made of twigs from behind the bench and swept the dust out the front door. Tom found and lit the kerosene lantern and then bustled around, checking his books and papers to make sure the roof hadn't leaked. He reconnected the gas bottles to the camping stove and the small refrigerator. I was touched to see that there were two of everything—two cups, two plates, two sets of silverware, all piled on top of the small refrigerator and very dusty.

Donnisongui and the other men sat down on a long wooden bench along one wall. Outside, on the porch, a crowd of children fought for places at the door so that they could stare in at me. But the arrival of the rainstorm at that moment prevented any other visitors from coming. The huge drops landed loudly on the packed red dirt, closing us in together. The smells of the village suddenly became clarified by the rain, each distinct and strong: hay, wood smoke, and steam—as cool water met the hot earth.

"Come see the bedroom," Tom said, unlocking the other door with another large, old-fashioned key. We ducked under the low doorframe and went in. The double bed, covered with a mosquito net, filled the room. This room had one tiny window, the only one in the house.

"These are Donnisongui's medicines," Tom whispered, shining the flashlight on a wine bottle filled with a dark liquid, which hung just over the door in the bedroom. "Sometimes he gets it down and rubs some on his arms after he's tired from working in the fields."

I wondered why Donnisongui didn't take the bottle with him, or at least put it somewhere less precarious. But later I was to understand the importance of these medicines, all made of very secret formulas, and his need for a private, safe place to store them. Donnisongui had entrusted the house to us for as long as we needed it, but it remained very much his. He came and went freely and sat on the porch with his children or friends whether we were home or not.

A young girl arrived, ducking to enter because of the plastic bucket of water on her head. Donnisongui lifted the bucket down for her and put it on the floor near the refrigerator. "Fanta's come!" sang out Tom in Dyula and asked after her family, but she looked down shyly and wouldn't answer. She was dressed in a piece of cloth that looked like a long straight skirt when wrapped around her waist, and a blouse of the same bright butterfly print, her best outfit, I knew, because the blouse and skirt matched and the fabric was new. She was just a child, very thin with a pointed face, and it was hard to imagine that she was old enough to do the job for which Tom had hired her, to bring us water twice a day and to wash our clothes. From the corner where she squatted, she watched me with large, melancholy eyes.

"Did you see these?" Tom asked me in English, pointing to some pictures of me he had hung on the wall in a plastic frame. "Everyone who came in looked at them. Every day people would ask me when you were coming. The village has been waiting for you to arrive ever since I got here." He had also hung up some postcards I had sent him, one of the University of California campus and another of rice harvesting in Arkansas, showing six huge combines in one field.

"These are Donnisongui's friends," Tom said, pointing to another photo thumbtacked into the earthen wall. This one was black and white, and the six young men knelt stiffly in front of a painted background. "I just leave Donni's things here. He doesn't really have anywhere else to put them. And that bottle over the front door is more of Donnisongui's medicine. The round wrapped thing is a household fetish."

The inside space of this house was no longer purely Senufo, nor was it American. It had become a meeting place protected by Donnisongui's traditional household fetishes and filled to overflowing with Tom's books and field notes. There hardly seemed room in the little house for a third presence.

The line of men on the bench all watched me expectantly, waiting for a response to Tom's tour. I smiled self-consciously and realized that Yardjuma was watching us intently and that he looked surprised and upset. Tom turned around and saw his expression.

"We're speaking English," Tom explained to him in French. "You'll have to excuse us. I'm just so happy to speak my own language again."

Yardjuma had never heard Tom speak English. But now, he found himself in the same position Tom had been in ever since his arrival in the village. If he wanted to know what we were saying to each other, he would have to depend on our translation. If anyone knew the implications of this, it was Yardjuma, and I sensed that they made him uneasy.

The storm had ended suddenly and night had fallen. There were two small pools of light in the house around the kerosene lanterns; beyond them I could see very little. Tom called out to the children on the porch, and a little boy came in. "This is Little Bey" (Bay), he said to me in slow, careful French. "Little Beh goes to school and speaks French, so if you need anything, he can help you. He's a very serious student. He comes over at night to study by our kerosene lantern."

The small boy in ragged khaki shorts shook my hand gravely. Tom gave him our flashlight and some money, and he came back with three bottles of wine and a baguette of stale bread. Tom rinsed out the four glasses we had and served Donnisongui and Yardjuma and the two of us. Without thinking, I raised my glass toward Tom.

"To your arrival in Kalikaha!" he toasted. We clinked our glasses together and then reached toward Yardjuma and Donnisongui. The men on the bench all burst out laughing.

"It's a custom of ours," Tom explained to Yardjuma in French. "For good luck."

"Oh, yes. I've seen the French do that in Korhogo," he answered morosely.

Donnisongui clinked my glass again and laughed. *"Dansi!"* he said in Dyula. "Welcome!" Yardjuma's eyes met mine in the lanternlight with what seemed to me a challenge. I knew then that the prospect of change did not please him.

Donnisongui turned his glass bottoms up and gave the glass back to Tom to be rinsed out so that one of the other men could be served. By the time our four glasses had passed all the way down the bench, it was late and Yardjuma got up to leave. The others rose, too, at something Yardjuma said to them in Senufo, and after shaking everyone's hand again, we were left alone.

"We bathe in the back by kerosene lanternlight,"

12

said Tom, putting a pan of water on to heat. "I think you'll like it."

The air was clean after the rainstorm and quite cool; I dripped the warm water over my shoulders, one spongeful at a time, to make the bath last. The clouds had passed over and the stars were brighter than I had ever seen them. Light from the kerosene lantern reflected softly off the shoulder-high walls that connected one granary to another, like the walls between the towers of a castle. On the other side, I could hear footsteps and voices, but inside, the back courtyard felt cozy and almost private.

Officially, this was the "shower," and it wasn't intended to be used for anything but bathing and urinating. In the back of the small courtyard was a shorter curved wall, and behind this was our latrine, the only one in the village. Everyone else went out to the bush. Tom had, too, until he got his first case of dysentery. He had written me about having Malian masons come and dig the latrine and build the small wall.

"The house is small, I know," Tom said apologetically. "I work and cook and eat all on the one table, so we'll need another one for you to use as a desk. We can order one at the carpenters' shop the next time we go into Korhogo and have the transporter bring it the following Saturday in his truck. If there's anything else you want, we can try to get it made in Korhogo. The nice thing about this house is that it has cement floors. Most houses don't."

The house didn't bother me, but I felt unnerved by the way Yardjuma had watched Tom and me. I didn't think he was very happy about my arrival.

"Oh, no!" Tom said, surprised. "Yardjuma's been going on and on about how he couldn't wait for you to

13

arrive and how he would do everything possible so that you would like it here. I think he's pleased that I have a wife. It looked suspicious when I didn't have one. He's always worrying about my image in the village."

"He just seemed . . . taken aback. At seeing you speak English. At the way we talked to each other."

"He may be," Tom conceded. "When he thought about my wife coming, he probably imagined a young girl who would cook for us and never say anything if she wasn't asked. It may take awhile for him to get used to being around us. But I tried to prepare him. I told him you were my best friend and that we liked to do things together. He said he couldn't understand a marriage like that."

"That's probably what it was then," I said, not really believing it but wanting to reassure myself.

"He even said that he thought Siata would start acting more like a wife after she met you."

"But what kind of wife?" I asked. "Maybe not the kind he had in mind!"

We went to bed joking that a prerequisite for any couple desiring to live together in a house this small should be a seven-month separation like the one we had just been through. After all, Senufo couples didn't even attempt it and they knew a lot more about village life than we did.

 GREETINGS

Roosters crowed, and all around me, just outside our adobe walls, the villagers were already stirring—doors opened and closed, water splashed, voices spoke strings of syllables that I could not divide into words. I lay inside the green mosquito net and listened as the sounds increased in volume: wooden pestles thunked into wooden mortars, chickens squawked, babies cried, and goats wailed. Only the faintest gray light came through the window, but I had no doubt that it was morning. As Tom opened the back door, the room lightened slightly, but the light was still gray and the air was soft and cool. The sun had not yet risen.

We heated water to wash, and Tom shaved, standing in the back courtyard and peering into a small round mirror he had attached to the adobe wall of one granary. He never succumbed to the obligatory fieldwork beard; he said it wasn't his style. For breakfast Tom made pancakes, and we ate them with honey that Donnisongui had given us, dark and flavorful, with a few dead bees still floating in it.

"Koko!" Yardjuma strolled in and seated himself on the bench just as we finished breakfast.

"Koko!" came again a moment later as a tall, elderly man stooped to enter the low doorway. He arranged his loose cotton robe around his thin legs, leaned his cane against the wall, and settled himself on the bench beside Yardjuma. His eyes glowed with light and life. As they met mine they sparkled, as if we shared a private joke. I assumed that the chief of Kalikaha had come to call on us.

In fact, he wasn't the chief at all. His name was Beh Tuo, and he was the oldest Senufo man in Kalikaha, an important distinction in a society where social standing is traditionally based on age. The chief, I learned later, had been one of the drunken men who shook my hand when we arrived on the motorcycle.

"Tom, Tom, Tom!" the man called out in a cheerfully raspy voice. *"Bonjour,* Tom! *Ça va,* Tom? *Ça va?"*

As I was introduced his sparkling eyes darted all over me with quick interest, rested an overlong moment on the neckline of my T-shirt and then searched my face with lively curiosity. Then Beh Tuo looked at Tom and nodded his approval. Had Beh Tuo been younger, I probably would have held all this against him. But the young eyes that sparkled out of his lined face had charmed me the first moment they met mine.

Beh Tuo had asked Tom to buy him a hat in Abidjan, a red felt one with gold embroidery, and although we didn't realize it then, we had just procured the insignia of office for the new chief. Until Beh Tuo and the other elders presented the acting chief with a red hat, his position was temporary; they were holding off on a decision

16

because Kalenena was a weak, foolish man and because his descent in the lineage was not entirely without question.

"Yardjuma," Tom said very formally, "please tell Beh Tuo what an honor and privilege it has been for me to work with him in the past. Beh Tuo knows a great deal about the history of Kalikaha, and I appreciate how he has shared this information with me. We have worked very well together, and I hope that we can continue to work together during the rest of my stay in Kalikaha. This red hat is a gift to express my appreciation."

Tom handed the hat to Yardjuma, who turned and spoke to Beh Tuo. Yardjuma was doing more than translating Tom's French into Senufo; he was speaking *for* Tom. Speeches often went through a third person, even when two Senufo spoke to each other. The use of an intermediary lent the proceedings a certain formality. It was Yardjuma who thanked Tom, and had other people been present, they would have thanked him as well. But only the most peremptory thanks were given at this time. It was much better Senufo etiquette to wait and thank the person the next day. Better yet was to wait until that person was in need, perhaps years later, and then send a gift, when it seemed you had long forgotten. Not understanding Senufo etiquette, I thought that we had chosen the wrong sort of hat and that Beh Tuo didn't like it.

Tom had a side that adapted remarkably well to these formalities. He made speeches and received delegations as if he'd been doing it all his life. And I wondered, as I watched him in surprise, where this aptitude for public life had come from. He had made a life for himself in this village, and I could see that, although he might grumble about the heat or the chief's constant demands for money, he was excited about his work and happy to

17

be back in Kalikaha. But what would I find in Kalikaha, and how could I go about looking for it?

Beh Tuo turned to Yardjuma and said something. Then he walked to the doorway, spat red kola nut juice through it, and sat back down. Tom had forbidden spitting inside our house.

"Beh Tuo hopes that you can get back to work with him soon because he has no money left," said Yardjuma. "The prostitute who has been staying in his compound has taken it all."

"You mean she stole his money?" I asked.

"Oh, no!" Yardjuma laughed. "But the old man says that prostitutes are worse than thieves. Three hundred francs tonight, three hundred francs tomorrow night. Soon a man has nothing left."

"Worse than a thief?" I echoed in amazement. "But she didn't steal the money. Did he really say that?"

"Exactly that," said Yardjuma, grinning.

"But that's ridiculous! A thief comes in your house when you are gone or asleep. There's nothing you can do. But he chose to go and spend his money with this prostitute. I don't agree at all."

Beh Tuo looked at Yardjuma for a translation.

"Tom's wife has spoken wisely," he said seriously. His eyes sparkled, as if this exchange delighted him. "It is true that a thief is worse. Now that your wife has come, you should take her to greet the other elders," Beh Tuo said to Tom. He pulled his robe around him and left to go to his fields for the day.

Kalikaha is a large village of sixteen hundred people. Half of the population is Senufo, a farming people who are animists and whose religion is centered around the sacred grove and a men's initiation society called *poro*. The other half are Dyula, who are farmers but who also weave and trade and pray to Allah in a small mosque in their part of the village. Outside the village are several camps of nomadic Fulani herders who have recently migrated south from harsher, dryer lands. They are also Moslems who speak Dyula as a second language. No one spoke French except the older schoolchildren, a minority of the children in the village, and a few educated Ivorians who worked in the village—two agricultural extension agents and several schoolteachers. Yardjuma, who translated for us, spoke both Senufo and Dyula, as do many Senufo, since Dyula is the lingua franca of this region.

The village is divided into a number of Dyula and Senufo quarters, each of which has a quarter chief. Although we lived in a Senufo quarter, the quarter of the founding lineage of the village, we didn't learn to speak Senufo. It is an extremely complicated language with five different tones and a complex system of classifying objects by their physical properties. We had been told that it took five years to learn to speak Senufo, and so we had decided to ignore it altogether and concentrate on learning Dyula, which is a very simple language grammatically, with only two tones. However, for a tone-deaf English speaker, two tones are one too many. I could pronounce a word perfectly correctly, but if the tone was wrong, it meant something completely different. Not until I spoke Dyula better did I appreciate the comic opportunities this must have presented my listeners. "How are your fields?" I asked every day, but if I went down instead of up on the second syllable of the word *foro,* it came out, "How is your penis?"

19

It was just as well that I was innocently unaware of these traps as we set out from Yardjuma's house the second night on our tour of the village. At the compound of an important Dyula elder, we stopped. Yardjuma announced our arrival, and the man came out.

"Good evening," he greeted me.

To this, I gave the woman's response: *"Nnn-say!"*

This response is very musical in tone. The first syllable is low and the second several notes higher in pitch. As lovely as a chorus of chimes is the sound when you greet a group of Dyula women and they look up from their work and sing out, *"N-say!"*

But when I said it, the women, pretending to work nearby, burst into loud giggles.

The elder ignored them. "Have you spent the afternoon in peace?"

"Peace only," I replied, as I knew I should. I didn't mention the children who had stared in at me all day or the constant visitors who had come to greet me.

"Are you well?"

"I am well."

"And your husband?"

"He is well."

"And the people of your household?"

"They are well."

"And your children?"

"No children," interjected Yardjuma.

The elder regained his composure quickly. "May Allah give you one soon."

"Amina," I replied, tapping my forehead as Tom and Yardjuma were doing, to help the blessing sink in.

"And how are the people of Abidjan?"

"They are well. They all greet you."

"And your *jatigi* there?"

20

"He is well." I didn't know how to explain that Abidjan was a large modern city where we had been anonymous. We had lived in an apartment rented for foreign scholars by the university.

"And the people of France?" the elder asked me.

"They're not French, they're American," Yardjuma interrupted.

"And the people of America?" He didn't miss a beat.

"They are well," I replied, seriously. "They all send you their greetings."

"Dansi!" he sang out musically. "Welcome!"

"N-say!" I responded.

One woman nearly dropped the bowl she was carrying, she laughed so loudly. The man then made a long speech wishing us good health, long lives, a harmonious marriage, and many children.

"We have just come to greet you," Yardjuma told him. "We can't stay. We must go and greet the other elders." Before leaving, he invited the man and his family to the party that Tom was giving Saturday night in my honor.

But the people of America are not all well, I muttered to myself as we walked away. Most of them have no idea that Ivory Coast exists. Not only had they not bothered to send cross-continental greetings, they didn't even greet one another when they passed in the street.

"Dansi! Dansi!" I heard everywhere I went, a chorus of welcome.

"N-say!" I replied over and over, hopelessly off-key. The women laughed at me and then turned on Tom.

"Look at your wife," they called out. "She just got here and already she speaks Dyula! Why are you so slow?"

21

Behind me, they imitated my out-of-tune greetings. The children lined up to stare at me and then ran after us, yelling shrilly, "Madame! Madame!" until Yardjuma turned and frightened them away.

All through the village we marched, down narrow twisting paths muddy from the recent rains, from one quarter to another. Each elder gave me the same sequence of greetings, sometimes in Senufo, sometimes in Dyula. After the third time, Yardjuma no longer bothered to translate the fine points. "It's the same old thing," he'd say. "You've been given a lot of blessings and a lot of good wishes. Now, let's get moving."

To me, all the quarters looked identical in the moonlight. I couldn't tell where one ended and another began. I couldn't even distinguish between the Dyula and Senufo parts of the village. There were only two landmarks that rose above the thatched roofs. One was the minaret of the mosque in the center of the Dyula village. The other was the crown of trees of the sacred grove, just beyond our house. I could not possibly have found my way through the thousands of densely clustered houses alone. Until I learned the paths, I was dependent on Tom and ultimately, on Yardjuma. I couldn't even find my own way home.

I was very tired, and this thought made me irritable. I wanted to close the door to our house and go to bed. But Tom was determined to find some meat to buy. We had eaten only bread for lunch and rice with tomato sauce for dinner. Meandering through the village, we stopped at one hunter's house after another, asking for game. Finally, one held up a native West African guinea fowl with black and white feathers, called a *pintade* in French. The hunter's son plucked it for us at once, scattering black and white patterned feathers all over the ground.

As soon as we arrived at our house it immediately filled up with men coming to shake our hands. Except for Donnisongui, I still didn't know who these men were. Yardjuma took out our knife and began to strop it roughly against a sharpening stone we had bought in Abidjan.

"What's he doing?" I asked Tom angrily. "He'll ruin the knife like that."

"Leave him alone," Tom snapped back. "He's going to clean the *pintade* for us."

"We can do it ourselves! We're not helpless."

"Let him do it," Tom answered. "He always does it."

Everyone stopped talking to watch us. At this moment, some boys came in to offer another guinea fowl for sale. Yardjuma bargained for it, all the time giving me looks making it clear that he didn't like my interference. I felt like crying, but the house was full of men watching me. I wished that everyone would leave, Yardjuma most of all. I felt awful that we had quarreled in front of the others and particularly in front of Yardjuma. And I knew that Tom's sharp words were exactly what Yardjuma had been waiting to hear, the wife put in her place. The boys took the second guinea fowl outside and plucked it, Yardjuma cut it into pieces with fast, angry chops of the knife, and Tom wrapped the meat. I sat and watched them, and the men on the bench watched me.

The meat put away, Tom got up to walk over to Yardjuma's house to bring back the motorcycle. I said I would stay. I was utterly exhausted. But the men on the bench made no move to leave. They were going to sit there and stare at me. Even in my own house, I couldn't be alone for half an hour. I wanted to throw them all out and close the door, but I didn't dare. They would be terribly offended, and Tom would never get the answers he needed for his work. Hoping that sighs were cross-cultural, I gave the loudest, most exasperated sigh I could manage for the benefit of those on the bench. Then I got up and followed Tom.

It was Tom who broke the silence between us. "I'm sorry I snapped. I was feeling tense. I apologize."

"It's okay. I'm sorry, too. I just wish it hadn't happened in front of Yardjuma. I feel like he's trying to come between us, like he thinks it's him or me."

"Him or you?" Tom looked at me in surprise. "That's kind of strong, isn't it? I think he just wants to help you feel at home. You know, that Senufo hospitality he's always talking about."

"I don't want so much help. How will I come to understand this place if he does everything for me?"

"I don't know," Tom answered. "I guess I don't even try. I just try to get answers to specific questions that I came here to ask and for that, I need a translator."

"But he takes care of everything! We're not helpless. We could go around without him. Like today. We could have gone to that market without him. You knew the way. We could manage by ourselves."

"But we couldn't ask any questions. What's the point of being here if we can't ask questions about what we see?"

I didn't have an answer to this. I wasn't even sure what I wanted to learn. I only knew that depending so much on Yardjuma grated on me. I went over the night's events in my mind. It was true. Yardjuma had been very

24

helpful, but something else underlay all his actions, and I wasn't sure what it was. "So if you go back and you never learned to cut up a guinea fowl with a dull hand-made knife, that doesn't bother you?" I asked Tom, partly in jest.

"No," said Tom, grinning. "I have to eat so that I can do my work. My whole career rests on the data I bring back. But you're different. Maybe you want even more from this than I do."

"You're probably right," I admitted. "But I have no idea how to go about getting it."

"I need Yardjuma for the research," Tom continued. "When I first came, a lot of the villagers were suspicious and wouldn't talk to me, but Yardjuma convinced them. He was really good at persuading them that it would be all right to tell me things. I don't know how I could have gotten the census completed and the farm survey started if it wasn't for Yardjuma."

Soft melodic notes drifted toward us on the warm air of the dark village night. As we walked hand in hand along the narrow path, we came closer and closer to the source of the music.

"What is it? It's beautiful!"

"It's a *balafon.* Your very first sound of *balafon* music, isn't it?" Tom paused to listen. "It's Lasungo practicing. He lives very near Yardjuma. In fact, he gave Yardjuma his house, so he's really Yardjuma's *jatigi* although he's very young. He hasn't even graduated from the *poro* yet. He's the best *balafon* player in the village; his style is a little different from all the others." Tom smiled. "It was going to be a secret, but I'd rather tell you now. I've hired him and his group to play at the party Saturday night."

On the porch of the house next to Yardjuma's, a

25

young man bent over a large wooden xylophone, striking it with mallets that bounced off the wooden bars. He took no notice when we sat down in the dark to listen. The sound was at times delicate and melodic; at other moments, strong and rhythmic, with a fast, pounding beat. My body relaxed in response to the music. So far in Kalikaha, the only times when I had felt relaxed were on the motorcycle flying over the muddy roads and listening to the notes of this music vibrating in the moonlit night.

At dawn the next morning, we got up. My second full day in the village was beginning. I felt tired and groggy. I had been kept awake by the bats that swooshed in and out of the house all night long to perch on the rope that tied our mosquito net to the rafters.

When I pushed open the heavy wooden door, I nearly knocked over Donnisongui, who was waiting outside to present me with a guinea fowl as a welcome gift. In a few moments, the house was full of men shaking our hands.

"Have you spent the night in peace?" they asked me.

"Peace only," I replied. I knew that it would be bad form to complain about the bats. The greeting was a ritual, a miniature drama enacted between two people. This I was beginning to understand. Innovation counted for nothing. The sense of satisfaction, which for me was rather like hearing a childhood poem recited, came from following my part and hearing the expected answer return, always with the same intonations and the same pauses in the same places. Only after the ritual of the greeting was complete could any business be announced, and even then, a visitor had to wait to receive the cue, the question which came after a long pause: "What's the news?"

No matter how many words I memorized, it was not until I learned to wait just the right number of long seconds and then to ask, offhandedly, with the right amount of disinterest, "Well, . . . so what's the news?" that people in Kalikaha chuckled appreciatively, slapped their thighs, and said, "Eh, Carol! You really speak Dyula now!"

That morning, like most others, was spent doing interviews for Tom's farm labor study, going from compound to compound. If the family owned chairs, they brought them out for us. Modern desk chairs or folding yard chairs were the most prestigious, handmade African chairs like ours less so, and the little carved four-legged stools that everyone sat on were the bottom of the line. I hadn't realized how hierarchical an African society could be, but now I noticed it in every detail. We were always being ranked. Age came before youth and male before female, although as a guest in the village, newly arrived, I was given a special status.

"Before you came, I used to get the best chair," Tom teased me happily.

Yardjuma, making do with third-best, didn't look so amused. He usually ended up on a tiny, broken, three-legged stool. Even the "best" chair was often patched together. I sat down in one ancient canvas affair and went rolling over onto my back, my legs in the air.

Everyone commented on my arrival. I felt like the latest village entertainment, being paraded from quarter to quarter. The old women always came running when they saw me and examined me all over.

"Oh good, she's come just in time to harvest my peanuts!"

"I need a strong young woman to help transplant my rice."

One old woman with flattened, wrinkled breasts rubbed my arm and said my skin was too soft, too soft! For my part, I was shocked at the sight of her stomach, which showed above her wrapped skirt. I began to look closely at all the elderly women. The skin on their stomachs was like wrinkled leather from bearing so many children, with deep crevasses like valleys of eroded soil, and so loose that I could have gathered it in my hands.

When Tom did his census, he asked each woman how many times she had given birth. Ten to fourteen times was a common response. Then he asked how many of these children were still alive. Sometimes, a woman who had given birth ten times would have only one child surviving. The women became so upset by having to recall these lost children that Tom stopped asking them and began to ask the male heads of each household for the statistics instead. When we calculated the percentage, it worked out that a third of the children never reached the age of fifteen.

Everyone worked hard, even the children. But the women worked the longest hours. Before it was light, I could hear them all around our house, going for water, chopping wood with dull axes, pounding grain. I woke at dawn to the sound of wooden pestles striking wooden mortars and I fell asleep to this same sound at night. While we interviewed them they cooked or put down their pestles long enough to sit and answer the questions. Then, when the interview was over, they packed their things for the long walk to their fields and the long day weeding cotton or transplanting rice.

During the middle part of the day, from about eleven until about four, everyone was gone, and except for a few very old women and some children, the village was empty. Then, at least, if at no other time, I could be assured of an uninterrupted meal and a few hours of quiet to read or write in my journal. I had never been a particularly solitary or private person, and in general, I liked to be with other people. But I had never been in a situation where the notion of privacy was entirely discounted, where doors were never closed during waking hours. I found that I needed those few hours in the middle of the day when we were the only people in Kalikaha and I could be simply myself.

There were not only greetings for the four parts of the day but also particular greetings for almost every situation.

"Greetings on your way home from the well."

"Greetings at the market. Greetings on your return from a journey," and to the people coming from the fields, "Greetings on your return from the bush." To someone working, you could simply say, "Thank you."

What surprised me was that when anyone came into our house and found us reading or writing at the one table, they greeted us, *"I ni baara!* Greetings at your work!" or simply, *"I ni chay.* Thank you."

"If I were the one who went to the fields and worked all day with a short-handled hoe in the blazing sun," I said to Tom, "and then came home to see two people sitting in the shade at a table writing, I know I wouldn't have the bigness of heart to say, *'I ni baara! I ni chay.'* "

I pondered this often and finally decided that working as hard as they did, they had a tremendous respect for work itself—in all its manifestations. They weren't making a judgment on the value of what we were doing. What they recognized was simply the act of work.

Of course, in Kalikaha, where there were very few literate people, the ability to read and write took on added significance. For me, it was second nature, easier than whistling or pounding a straight nail. But in Kalikaha, I could no longer take this ability for granted. I began to see it as they did, a hard-won acquired skill, one that opened whole rooms of memory that otherwise would have remained closed.

Often the villagers said to me that Tom worked hard because he started early in the morning and finished late at night. But they had a harder life than anything I could have imagined. And if their harvest was small because the rains failed or cattle got into the fields, they would not have enough food for the coming year. August is called, in the Senufo calendar, "the month when everyone is hungry." As long as food remained, no one would go entirely without. This was the ultimate meaning of the concept of the common good. But everyone would have to make do with less.

Across from our house lived a woman named Sibatia, a young woman with large muscular arms and shoulders. In the evening, when she returned from the fields with her little boy on her back, she would bend her head and let her bundle of logs crash loudly onto the ground. Then, with a shy, almost mischievous glance at me, she would come over to retrieve her key from underneath the thatch of our porch, where she left it every morning. The first week, she never spoke to me. Her little boy, who was always on her back, had a large herniated belly button, considered a sign of beauty among the Senufo because it emphasizes the connection to previous generations and to the ancestors. He burst into a loud, terrified squall if Tom or I looked at him directly. When this happened, Sibatia glanced at me out of the corner of her eye and shrugged.

Sibatia was married to the man who lived to the left of us, Beh, the uncle of Little Beh, the schoolboy. Beh was a tall, thin, older man who greeted Tom in Dyula every morning and every evening from the porch of his house. He was one of those people who had the knack of conversing simply, so that we could understand.

"So your wife has really come?" he asked Tom every night that week.

"Yes, she's come." It was a phrase I must have heard a thousand times those first few days.

"That pleases me," he responded, touching his heart. "It is a good thing."

I liked Beh's gentle manner and his efforts at conversation. But he and Sibatia did not get along. If they passed in front of our house, they didn't even greet each other, a shocking thing in Kalikaha. And Yardjuma told me that she had a younger lover, a man her own age.

Once the villagers were home from their fields, the men disappeared into their back courtyards with buckets of water the women had heated for them and came out transformed. The ragged work clothes they wore to the fields were discarded for long flowing boubous or Western-style pants and shirts. Then, if we were home, the men came to greet us. They had nothing to do until the women finished making dinner—about nine o'clock.

It's an honor to be visited and greeted, I would remind myself, as one man after another came into the house. They greeted Tom and then shook my hand. Only Donnisongui knew my name. Then they took their places on the bench, stared at our possessions, talked among themselves, or simply watched us. "Benchsitters," we

31

dubbed those who made no effort to communicate with us. The high school students who were home for the summer came every night and stayed for hours, happy to be able to practice their French. From them, we learned the village news, although they were always several days behind Yardjuma to hear the latest gossip. At first, I thought the women didn't come because they were too shy, but later, I realized that they simply had too much work to do.

At this time, Tom and I were cooking dinner. If there were people in our house, we should, according to local custom, invite them to sit down with us and share what we had. In theory, this sounded admirable to us, but in truth, we wanted to eat our meal alone, in peace and quiet, talking over the day's events.

Some nights, our dinner sat warming on the two-burner camp stove for an hour while we waited for a solitary moment. When we finally dished it out and sat down hungrily, we were interrupted over and over by people coming to greet us. After they had left, we felt guilty that we hadn't invited them to join us and doubly guilty because our meal of guinea fowl and rice was such a feast in their eyes. The villagers rarely ate meat. They existed on rice or corn mush, called *toh,* flavored with sauce made from okra, tomato paste, dried fish, or cubes of bouillon. They ate this three times a day. Only the wealthiest villagers could afford meat in their sauce and then, just a few bits.

"Let's close the door while we eat," I said.

"We'd suffocate," he answered. "And besides that, people just wouldn't understand. You can close your door to bathe or sleep, but not to eat. They'd think something was wrong."

"We can't live like this. How did you stand it?"

"It's worse since you came," Tom admitted. "They had gotten used to me."

Finally, we had an idea. We would ask Donnisongui if we could cement the back courtyard and put a thatched roof over part of it, and we would put another table out there. This would give us a more private place where I could write during the day and where we could eat at night. People passing and looking in wouldn't see us, so they wouldn't be obligated to come in and greet us.

"Are you sure that would work?" I asked Tom. "What if they see our lantern in the back?"

"It's perfect," he exulted. "The door will be open so everyone will be satisfied, but the house will be dark so they'll think we're not home. Even if they see the light, we'll be sitting in the shower so no one will come to greet us there. It's the perfect compromise!"

Fortified by this possibility, we set our carved Senufo chairs on the porch, put the lantern on a desk chair between us, and prepared for the parade of late-night greetings as people passed by on their way home from other visits. Little Beh and his two brothers were sprawled on our porch sound asleep, too exhausted after their day in the fields to get up and go home to bed. They lay snoring behind my chair until their older brother came, shook them roughly awake, and sent them stumbling toward home.

LA FETE DE CAROL

YARDJUMA HAD JUST SETTLED HIMSELF ON THE WOODEN
bench and accepted a cup of Nescafé. He stirred in large
spoonfuls of sugar and turned to Tom. "Our most important work this week is the fête de Carol. We've invited all
the elders, and they expect true Senufo hospitality.
There is nothing worse, to a Senufo, than not to be hos-
pitable to a guest."

"Yes," said Tom. "But we have the farm study interviews to do and we have fields to measure. We'll have
to fit the preparations in between the other work. This
morning we need to go out to Bazoumana's fields."

"We could go to Bazoumana's this afternoon,"
Yardjuma said to Tom. "First we had better make sure
the party is in order. You have to realize just how important the party is for the future of all our work. If the
elders go away feeling as if they haven't been well entertained, the next time we come around asking questions in

34

their quarters . . ." Yardjuma rolled his eyes and drew his hand across his throat.

"How can we make it a success?" Tom asked him, worried now about those future interviews.

"Have a lot to drink," replied Yardjuma immediately. "That's number one. I think we should go over to Chez Mariam right now and reserve our drinks in case she sells out before Saturday. For the important Senufo men, we'll have beer and wine. If the Senufo don't drink well, it isn't real hospitality, and we Senufo take hospitality very seriously."

"What about the Moslems?" Tom asked.

"OK Tip Top Orange Soda," replied Yardjuma. "Lots of it. After we go to the bar, we should go see Zele and order two big pots of *chapalo.* She's a member of the blacksmiths, and they make the best *chapalo.*"

Zele was the mother of Lasungo, the *balafon* player, and *chapalo* was homemade corn beer.

"The best," Tom told me, "always means the hottest."

The first time I took a cautious sip, my mouth burst into red-hot flame. It was arson, purposely set, just like the brush fires that raced across the savanna during the dry season, snapping at the stalks of golden grass. Up, in one gasp of hot pepper flame, went all my ideas of sitting with the Senufo and drinking *chapalo,* an activity that was at the very heart of Senufo life.

Chez Mariam, Yardjuma explained to me on the way over, was owned by a city official in Korhogo who drove out once a week to replenish the stock. Mariam was his junior wife, and she and her two small children lived in the back room of the bar. The senior wife was in Korhogo with her husband.

"But just wait," Yardjuma said. "Each year, they

change positions. Next year, Mariam will be in Korhogo and the other will be here running the bar." Yardjuma's house was well situated, just across from the bar, on the other side of a hard dirt courtyard where men gathered under a mango tree to drink. This was where we had arrived on the motorcycle the first day.

Yardjuma settled himself into one of the big wooden chairs under the mango tree and turned to business, brisk and animated. How much beer, wine, and orange soda we would need was the subject of serious discussion between Yardjuma and Tom in French, and Mariam and Yardjuma in Senufo. When we had paid for numerous cases of each and seen them stowed away in the back room under Mariam's iron bed, Yardjuma leaned over to Tom and spoke in French. "This man here is a traveling musician, a Fulani come down from Mali." The man he indicated with his eyes was enormous, over six feet tall and broad-shouldered. "If we want to get to know the Fulani better, we should buy him a bottle of wine. It will make a good impression."

"The Fulani don't drink," said Tom.

"He does! Wait until you see this! This man is a giant among drinkers, *très, très fort!*" Tom handed over some money, and Yardjuma called to Mariam. In a minute she came out with a bottle of wine and presented it to the musician. The man called for glasses and poured a few inches for each of us. He stood up, held the bottle to the sky, and began to chant in a deep, rumbling voice. I heard *toubabu* several times, the Dyula word for white man.

"Praise songs," Yardjuma said to us. "About Tom."

When he finished, he turned the bottle up, downed

the rest of it in a single gulp, and then threw it on the ground.

"He knew my grandfather," Yardjuma said proudly. "They were friends."

Yardjuma went over to his house and came back with some smoked meat. The beef had been a gift from Beh Tuo for my arrival, and Yardjuma had offered to take it home and smoke it for us. "It's just now finished smoking," he said to me as he handed pieces around. The large piece of beef seemed to have shrunk considerably in the smoking process.

Yardjuma and the griot talked on and on, despite Tom's efforts to disengage Yardjuma and head for the fields. Finally, Yardjuma climbed on his moped. "Eat well, drink wine, and always be generous to guests! When I drink well, I eat well. It isn't good to be thin," he called to me as he pedaled furiously to start his old moped and roared off down the dirt road, still waving a rib of smoked beef.

That night, we went to see Zele, the mother of Lasungo, and the woman who had cooked for Yardjuma before he was married. She agreed to make one batch of *chapalo* for us and to deliver it on Saturday and to find a friend who would do the same. We had transacted our business sitting on stools just outside her door. It was night, but not completely dark. The moon was out.

"Carol's never seen the inside of a woman's house," Tom said to Yardjuma. "Would you ask Zele if we could come inside?"

She agreed, and we picked up our stools and followed her through the low doorway. The sense of space was very different from our house. Hers had only one room, but it was large and round and felt more spacious.

The walls curved around me and seemed to reach quite naturally toward the thatched roof, which was conical like those on the granaries. The high center point of the roof enhanced the feeling of spaciousness and gave a focus to the circle. Sitting almost exactly in the middle, I felt a rightness to this arrangement. It was satisfying in an inexplicable way.

The smoke and grease from daily cooking had created small black stalactites that coated the thatch and all the rafters like the inside of a blackened cave. On her three hearth stones, a pot simmered over a small fire. There was no chimney or vent, and my eyes watered from the smoke.

Zele turned to Yardjuma and spoke formally. "Never before," she said, "has a white woman come into my house, and I am an old woman. Probably another never will. Not only am I happy to show her my house. I am honored. This is a night I will always remember."

I thanked her. She seemed wise to me and womanly, the way she took my moment of discovery and turned it into history and gave it a speech just as serious as you would give to a chief. Zele was a Sando, a diviner, to whom people went to have events such as sickness and death explained. She acted as intermediary between the person who came to her and the bush spirits, ambivalent creatures that helped or harmed humans, according to their whims. That night, when I undressed, I smelled the smoke from Zele's fire on my clothes and hair.

How everyone knew how much beer and wine and orange soda we had put aside in Mariam's back room I don't know. But many people helpfully informed us that we had not bought enough drinks for the party.

"Don't worry," said Yardjuma. "I have a way to ensure that there will be plenty to go around." He asked for paper and scissors. "Written invitations will solve everything."

"But we've already invited everyone," I replied.

"Most of them can't read anyway," added Tom.

"This is the way we do it here," Yardjuma said firmly, having learned that this line worked wonders when we were being stubborn.

He cut typing paper into small squares and then slowly wrote, in a French-style script full of careful flourishes:

We beg you to honor us with your presence chez Monsieur Tom, researcher, quarter Pempoho, Kalikaha, on the 15th of August, 1981, from nine o'clock in the evening until dawn.

Soyez bienvenu!

Tom sighed as Yardjuma painstakingly rounded every curve and dotted every *i*. I could see Tom mentally counting fields that would go unmeasured this week.

"Why don't we just make them for the guests who can read?" he suggested. "That would be the four school-teachers and the two extension agents."

"No, no," Yardjuma responded. "That would never work!"

"But why not?" Charmed as I was by Yardjuma's invitations, this seemed like a reasonable compromise.

"The slips of paper," he explained as if to children, "are not to invite them. They've all been invited in person except for those Fulani on the other side of the swamp, and it's not our fault that the water is too high for us to reach them. If they would pay Lasungo for his work, he would finish the center of their bridge and then we could walk over there easily. But they won't pay him until he finishes the bridge, and Lasungo says he won't build the center section until they pay him. So, Lasungo has done all that work for nothing, and they have two ends of a bridge and no center." Yardjuma shook his head. "The Fulani are too stubborn. It is hard to do business with them."

"What about the written invitations?" asked Tom. "You were explaining why we need them."

"They're not really invitations," continued Yardjuma. "The slips of paper are coupons redeemable for one drink."

"But is that necessary?" I asked.

"Everyone will come to hear the music and because they are curious about the whites," he replied. "But only those with the papers will be given a drink."

Yardjuma looked surprised at our ignorance in these matters. But seeing Tom's expression, he offered to take the paper home and finish the invitations himself. That was the last we ever heard about them.

Tom had conceived of the party as a way to make my arrival a special event after the months of questions about when I would arrive. He had also seen it as a way to thank the villagers who had cooperated with him thus far, particularly the six families in the weekly agricultural study and the Fulani herders whom he interviewed periodically about livestock raising. What he had not envisioned were the political implications of giving a party. The list of people we "had" to invite, according to Yardjuma, kept growing and growing. And no matter where we drew the line, someone was going to be offended. Since every villager was a potential informant for future studies, this worried Tom. But short of inviting all sixteen hundred villagers and spending Tom's grant money on vast amounts of *chapalo* and orange soda, I didn't see how we could possibly get ourselves out of the situation without angering someone. Tom just hoped it wouldn't be anyone essential to further research.

By the time Saturday arrived, Tom and I wished that we could call off the whole affair. I was exhausted from the tensions of my first week in the village and lack of sleep because of the bats. Saturday, the morning of La Fête de Carol, I crawled out of bed sick. My stomach felt queasy, and my head ached.

That afternoon, the two pots of *chapalo* were delivered. The pots were so wide they wouldn't fit through the door, so we had to pass them over the wall into the back courtyard. When I lifted one of the lids, the air was full of the sweet and sour smell of fermenting corn, and the cayenne pepper vapor stung my eyes.

I quickly slammed down the lid and sank onto a stool. I was still feeling sick, and the idea of cooking for fifty people—not my own cuisine, but theirs—and entertaining them until late that night overwhelmed me. We couldn't possibly pull it off. We had only one small pot, one skillet, two forks, two knives, two plates, and two spoons. Everyone would be watching me. I hated to desert Tom, but I truly just wanted to hide out in the mosquito net and be left alone. We're courting disaster, I warned Tom. La fête de Carol would be a fiasco.

Tom tucked me into the mosquito net for a siesta. "You just haven't adjusted to the food and water," he murmured. "I was sick the first week, too. It won't last."

I had always prided myself on being a trooper who could travel anywhere. But as much as I hated to admit it, adjusting to Kalikaha was turning out to be harder than I had expected. As I lay in bed, sweating feverishly, a fog of questions descended, filled the mosquito net, and whirled around my head. Memories from the past week danced devilishly around me, and details from the million

41

and one tiny lessons I had learned raced around and around the room.

"When you lift down Fanta's washbasin of water, don't tip it, no matter how heavy it is, or you'll splash water all over both of you. Don't greet men who speak French in Dyula or they'll be insulted! Shake hands every time you greet a man and shake hands again when you say good-bye. When in doubt, shake hands again. But never put your hand out to a woman—she'll just stare and look embarrassed. Unless she's Fulani, then you should. Don't use your left hand for anything. Don't ever throw garbage into the pit near the path again! Donnisongui says it's sacred to women."

"Learn faster!" shrieked the voices. *"Don't be so slow! Learn the people's names, learn the village paths, learn how to say* 'N-say!', *so they'll stop laughing at you."*

"Stop trying to understand everything!" the voices shouted. *"Just ask Yardjuma what to do."*

But this was where I balked.

I had learned as a child to read the adults for the millions of tiny clues that gave away what they wanted; I knew how to direct and organize as if I were running a theater while remaining backstage myself. Women, I had learned as a girl in the South, were supposed to, above all, make "things" go "smoothly." Men, my mother had made clear, were like the blind. If you moved quickly you could avert them from the greatest dangers without them ever having to know that those dangers existed.

Accordingly, every day I went out into the village and stuck out my well-trained antennae, but the information that came back was garbled, as if some very important organ in my body no longer functioned. I, who had always known what unspoken words meant, now did not understand spoken ones. Even gestures confounded me. Ten, twenty, one hundred times a day, I had to turn to

42

Yardjuma and ask him what was meant so that I could respond.

For me, this was as difficult as letting him breathe for me. I had stepped off the edge of the earth into nothingness, like an astronaut walking in starlit space. Flailing, swimming in air but making no progress, I was weightless, and it was Yardjuma who was holding the other end of the tether that connected me to the African earth. Behind him stood the villagers looking out at me curiously. Would he cut the tube and let me float away, in lonely suspension? I suspected that he would have liked to, had Tom not been looking over his shoulder.

Everything about him irritated me. But I hated to admit this even to myself. I felt terribly guilty. After all, he was the African with whom I had the closest contact. Worst of all was the way Tom depended on him for everything.

You're too judgmental, I told myself sternly. Intolerant and narrow minded and still inhabited by tiny racist demons left over from your childhood. You want everyone to have the same values you do. But these self-administered lectures didn't change my feelings at all.

Tom and I had already fought about it several times. I wanted to do things on my own and suffer the consequences, whatever they would be. "But what is it you want to do?" Tom would ask. "Yardjuma could help you." I wasn't sure. I couldn't even answer. All I knew was that depending on Yardjuma stood in my way. I wanted to manage without him. Tom knew exactly what he had come to do, and he wanted Yardjuma beside him to help.

Ahead of me, as far as I could see, stretched an adobe maze of thatch-roofed houses, walls, and towers. Two beaten dirt pathways wound through the labyrinth.

43

I could follow Yardjuma down one path and depend on him, whom I did not trust, to guide me through. I would see what he pointed out, understand what he explained, and come out at whatever destination he deemed appropriate.

Or, I could take the other path alone. If I could learn to speak Dyula, perhaps I could find my own way to the people of Kalikaha.

It was this second path that beckoned to me in the feverish haze. I promised myself that I would learn Dyula as quickly as I could, and that I would stay on the second path as much as possible. Having made this resolve, the feverish whirling ceased at once, the shrill voices were quiet, even the midday heat felt less oppressive. I fell sound asleep.

Several hours later, I woke from a deep sleep feeling refreshed. Tom had cold orange soda waiting for me. A large pile of battered metal plates and bowls sat conspicuously on the table. Yardjuma arrived, already dressed in his favorite blue cotton pajamas and his best black leather shoes, almost dancing with excitement. As he looked around the house his eyes sharpened in disapproval. "Haven't you started cooking yet?"

Tom explained the problem of pots, and Yardjuma left and came back shortly with two large cooking pots he had borrowed. The round-bottomed pots, meant to be placed on three stones over an open fire, balanced precariously on our gas camping stove set on top of an old wooden mortar.

The menu was rice with sauce, standard fare in Kalikaha. However, our sauce would have meat in it, something many of the villagers ate only during funerals and weddings.

The recipe began with mounds and mounds of onions

sautéed in oil. "More oil," said Tom, dumping in another bottle. "You want the villagers to talk about what a good cook you are, don't you?"

All week, people had been saying to Tom what a good thing it was that his wife had finally arrived. It was really a disgrace that he had cooked for himself these past three months. I had my own replies to these comments, but I kept them to myself. In Kalikaha, I thought with satisfaction, they would know soon enough that Tom did as much cooking as I did.

It was already dark in the house, and the kerosene lantern was almost useless for cooking, so I shined our flashlight into the two pots, one for the Moslems and one for the Senufo, as I stood there stirring. It was a familiar enough feeling. Every cook knows that worry before the dinner party: Will the recipe turn out well this time? Will the guests like it?

At this moment, Siata, Yardjuma's young wife, arrived with an enormous washbasin of rice on her head, steaming hot. She had carried it all the way across the village. To spite Yardjuma, she left again immediately, although we tried to convince her to stay. They had only been married a few months, they didn't get along, and Siata was pregnant. I felt sorry for her, married off to Yardjuma at the age of fourteen because her mother thought that he was wealthy, an impression he did his best to convey.

Yardjuma complained about her constantly, saying that she was a terrible cook and hopelessly lazy, a Korhogo girl who wanted too many things. He had confided in Tom that he hoped, after she saw me, that she would shape up and become a proper wife. But he had said this before my arrival. Now I doubted that Yardjuma still thought I would provide the kind of wifely example he had in mind.

Yardjuma ran in breathlessly, tasted both pots of sauce, and dumped in the rest of the ground cayenne pepper, a large fistful. He tasted it again. "It's very good," he said, sounding surprised. "Usually it takes a lot longer to make a sauce this good."

He introduced us to the young man with him, who shook our hands stiffly. He was the son of an Islamic holy man and would serve the Moslems, lest they accuse Yardjuma of spiking their orange soda.

When Tom first decided to give a party, neither of us realized what a complex multi-cultural happening we were staging. There was no aspect of this party that was, in anyone's eyes, normal. First of all, it was being given by a white man who lived in a thatched-roof house. Clearly, he must be a little crazy because white people could afford to live in air-conditioned villas in Korhogo with lots of servants. Not only that, but he was throwing the party in honor of his wife, who went with him everywhere, so he was not only demented but probably henpecked as well.

He lived in a Senufo quarter but was inviting the Dyula and Fulani to the party. To invite the Dyula was one thing; they came and went often in the Senufo part of the village. And to see the Fulani in the Dyula part of the village was also normal enough; they had a common bond of religion. But to invite the Senufo and the Fulani to the same party was another thing altogether. They had just been enemies in a local "range war," and several Fulani had been killed. As a result of this conflict, most of the young Senufo men of a nearby village were in jail and would be indefinitely, it seemed.

These conflicts between herders and farmers over crop damages caused by Fulani cattle were one thing Tom had come to the area to study. He felt strongly that he had to remain neutral, and so he had invited his informants from both groups to the party.

"Maybe we'll have a peasant-herder conflict in our own front yard and you can study the problem first-hand," I told him pessimistically.

"Probably the Fulani won't come at all," he replied sadly.

But to our surprise, the very first guest was a young herd owner in Tom's study named Alaye. Although I could not yet tell the Senufo and Dyula peasants apart, the Fulani were unmistakably distinctive. Very tall, slender people, with relatively fair, almost reddish skin, they have finely shaped heads and long narrow faces. They are scattered all over West Africa and have the reputation everywhere of being extremely proud, even haughty people. Alaye was very handsome, with large dark eyes, long lashes, and a full, pouting mouth. Like all the young herd owners, he dressed well, and that night he was wearing an embroidered black boubou over large gathered pants of bright blue cotton. On his head was a brightly printed turban, and a scarf was draped gracefully around his neck. On his smooth hands, so unlike those of the Senufo and Dyula farmers, he wore several large silver rings.

For reassurance, he had brought a friend with him to this hostile territory, and the two young men stood nervously on our porch, holding hands. That morning, at the market, the Fulani men had surprised me by the unself-conscious way they touched one another. They wandered through the market holding hands or sat in groups talking, one abstractedly rubbing the nape of another's neck as he listened to the conversation.

And the Fulani women, among the sameness of the mud walls and the monotony of the earth-toned colors, had moved like a flock of yellow butterflies in a dark wood. They wore full, tiered dresses of bright prints, always yellow. The dresses had tight, fitted bodices decorated with rows of colored rickrack, and for the mothers, this rickrack ingeniously hid two zippers, which opened so that they could nurse their babies. Into their intricate hairstyles were woven coins and amber beads, and they also wore large gold earrings and strings of amber around their slender necks. They carried themselves with unusual grace, their gourd bowls of milk for sale balanced delicately on their heads.

That morning, they had surrounded me, giggling, as they filled my plastic camping bottle with milk. Next to them, I had felt dowdy and mannish in my plain khaki pants and T-shirt. I wore only a small string of turquoise beads as an ornament, and they all noted the beads with interest.

Using Yardjuma as an interpreter, they had interviewed me. "Why didn't your mother pierce your ears? Don't you have any bracelets or anklets? And your hair, don't you put oil on it?"

"We'll be happy to pierce your nose for you," one had offered, "and then you can make your husband buy you a gold ring like mine." My reaction to this must have showed on my face because they all laughed.

Yardjuma prolonged this female exchange for the vicarious pleasure of translating it. When we said goodbye, although they remained a careful distance from Tom and Yardjuma, each one shook my hand gracefully, the only women who had done this since my arrival in Kalikaha.

From the porch, I could hear Tom talking to Yardjuma in the "shower," where the drinks had been placed for safekeeping. "I thought all the Fulani were Moslems. But Alaye wants beer."

"These young Fulani are all spoiled rotten," replied Yardjuma, ironically puritanical all of a sudden. "They all drink. They're not like their fathers, who never touched a drop in their lives and are real men you can respect. It's too bad their sons are all ruined.

"Let me pour you a drink from my own special bottle of wine," Yardjuma went on. "This is a serious affair being master of ceremonies, and it will take at least a bottle to see me through it. And this bottle here I'm sending over to Lasungo, to encourage the musicians. If they don't play well, people will say it's our fault for not being generous with them."

Fanta, the girl who carried water for us and washed our clothes, was next to arrive. She was dressed in one of the new outfits she had bought with her earnings and had painted blue lines of kohl around her eyes. I was surprised to see her, so shy with us, sprawl across our bench, prop her head on her elbow, and start up a flirtation with Zeeay, one of our neighbor's sons. As more adults arrived Fanta was chased off the bench so the men could sit down. Nonchalantly, she moved into one of our few chairs, which we were saving for important elders, and continued her conversation with Zeeay without a pause. He looked positively charmed.

Soon, the open area in front of our house was filled with people. The men came up to the porch to shake our hands and then drifted off. Many had brought their own stools, so after greeting us, they simply sat down to await the night's events. I tried in vain to distinguish those that I had met during the week. But with a few exceptions, they were a large crowd of complete strangers, oddly dressed, who sat in front of me and stared expectantly.

Tom and I made nervous jokes about being king and queen for a day. We thought of our carved chairs, hewn out of magnificent chunks of swirling red and cream-colored wood, as the most regal thrones possible. These traditional chairs had been made especially for us by Senufo woodcarvers, Tom's larger than mine. They were extremely heavy, but the two pieces could be taken apart and stacked flat against the wall when they weren't being used. On the back of each chair was carved a large spread-eagled lizard. The Senufo found our admiration for these chairs very funny; they preferred our modern desk chairs, made by carpenters in Korhogo.

"Does Yardjuma always wear his pajamas to parties?" I asked Tom.

"I'm so glad you're here," he said grinning. "Before you came, nobody except me thought that there was anything odd about him wearing those pajamas everywhere.

"Look," Tom whispered to me. "The Dyula women have arrived."

A group of women stood uncertainly just inside the row of granaries. Tom pointed out the ones I had met. But now they were dressed differently, some with cloths draped over their heads. The moon was not yet up, and it was very dark. I didn't recognize a single face.

We went out to greet them and then, not knowing what else to do, we returned to our carved chairs. The women sat down on the porch of our neighbor Beh's house, and it was clear they were not coming any closer.

The next time Yardjuma ran by, Tom grabbed him. "Shouldn't we start serving the drinks now?"

"Not yet," he answered and disappeared again into the "shower," where he seemed to be spending a lot of time.

A half hour later, Tom cornered him again. "These people have been waiting a long time. Isn't it time yet?"

"Not all the important people are here yet," he replied. "And besides, *they're* not impatient. They know you have called them here because you have something in mind. So they'll wait to find out what it is."

Tom and I tried not to fidget. At home, a wait like this would have resulted in a small insurrection, but in Kalikaha, efficiency, for its own sake, was not much valued. What mattered was how everyone was served and in what order. The village hierarchy, based on age, must be strictly observed. No middle-aged person must eat before all the elders had been served, no young person before the middle-aged.

Finally, Yardjuma said that it was time for Tom to make a speech. We stood facing the crowd, with Yardjuma between us. Yardjuma reached into his pocket and blew a shrill blast on a silver whistle only inches from my ear.

Tom made a very brief speech in French welcoming the guests and thanking them for coming. He thanked them again for cooperating with the work he was trying to do. "I have asked everyone to come here in order to meet my wife, who has just arrived, and to welcome her. We intend to stay in Kalikaha for the year and we hope that our stay will be a harmonious one," he ended.

I reached around Yardjuma and nudged Tom. "Say my name," I whispered. Everyone but Donnisongui called me Madame.

"And her name," he added loudly, "is Carol!"

Yardjuma translated the speech into Senufo. I wondered if it took more words in Senufo to say the same thing. But we knew when he reached the end because we heard, "Carrrol!"

"What? What?" yelled the crowd in Senufo.

"Ca-rrrol," he repeated emphatically, rolling the *r* and accenting the last syllable like the French.

"Ca . . . Caa? Ca-what?"

"Ca-rrrrrol!" Yardjuma yelled again and blew his whistle several times to quiet everyone down.

The Dyula representative to the one political party in Ivory Coast got up and very slowly translated Tom's speech into Dyula. This time it was very long. He obviously took great pleasure in hearing himself speak before such a large audience, and I suspected that Tom's words were being considerably embellished. Finally, he reached the end, and in a different accent this time, we heard my name.

"Ca-ro!" The *l* had been lost.

"What's her name?" they yelled. "What?"

The party secretary turned to Yardjuma unsurely. "Caa-rrrol!" Yardjuma yelled again. All through the crowd, I could hear people repeating, "Ca, Ca, Ca-ro. Ca, Ca, Ca-ro."

Then one of the Fulani men rose and, turning to the small huddled group at the back of the crowd, translated the speech yet a third time. The Senufo translation had been guttural, the Dyula melodic. The Fulani was very different from either. The young man's voice was high pitched and sounded almost like a woman's. We waited for my name. This time, it was the young Fulani men whose turbanned heads bent forward in perplexity. "Caro?" They laughed among themselves, as if it were a joke. "Caro?"

Yardjuma's whistle drowned out their murmurings. He blew it over and over, out of sheer drunken exuberance. In front of us, the young people and children swirled around the seated elders, and the sound of talk and laughter in three strange languages drifted up to me. Yardjuma and his Dyula assistant ran in and out of the house, frantically serving plates of food, beer, wine, orange soda, and *chapalo,* all, I hoped, to the right people in the right order.

As people came up to greet us and shake our hands Tom introduced them to me. "This is Songolofolo, who lives in Toziadala. This is Piayzeeay from Sediunkaha. This is Bazoumana Traore from Traorera." These quarters were still indefinite places with unpronounceable names. And, although a good many of these people had already been introduced to me, I felt hopelessly confused.

The full moon rose, lighting up the quarter, and finally, we heard the sound of *balafons* making their way across the village toward us. Everyone listened to the sound, faint at first, grow gradually louder and louder until the six musicians reached the edge of the quarter and passed through the two granaries as if through the towers guarding the entranceway to a castle yard. Playing the large *balafons* suspended from ropes around their necks as they marched, they made their way to us.

It was a moment of real drama and grandeur. I felt grand as the queen of the ball. The young men carried themselves proudly, full of their music and aware of the excitement they were creating. Their long white robes of handspun cotton gleamed in the moonlight. The tune was fast and lively. Lasungo's muscular arms moved at lightning speed, and the rubber mallets danced over the wooden bars. His friend Zana and another young man plucked the strings of large instruments like cellos, made from gourds, which kept the rhythm while the *balafons* played the melody. Attached to the necks of the gourd instruments were bits of tin cans and bottle caps that jingled with every movement.

53

Ignoring the crowd behind them, they directed all their attention toward the two of us. Their muscles strained with the physical effort, not only of making the music, but also of sending it across the small space to us. I felt clearly that this, like *Dan-si!,* was a moment of welcome. I forgot my difficulties with learning the Senufo names, my queasy stomach, my confusion. I forgot everything but Lasungo and the music. As long as the song lasted, the party became everything that Tom and I had wanted it to be. The thumping rhythm that never faltered and the lilting staccato notes of the *balafon* needed no translation. For once, I knew that I understood.

When the song ended, the musicians walked in a procession once around the crowd. They stopped in front of Sibatia's house and began to play again. Immediately, women and girls jumped up, kicked off their rubber thongs, and held them in their hands while they danced in front of the musicians. But there was very little space, and so after several songs, they moved behind our house, where there was a larger open area.

Our house was the center of a circle of movement. Behind, there was music and dancing. In front, the crowd talked and circulated, and Yardjuma and Fanta and the young Dyula man ran in and out, carrying drinks and food. The Dyula elders, seated in a line in their long robes, stared soberly at the line of older Senufo men across from them, who got louder and louder as they drank more and more.

Now that there were fewer Senufo, the Fulani men left the back of the crowd and came in a group to greet us. They walked into our house and looked curiously at our belongings.

"Didn't I say no one should come inside?" Yardjuma began as he stepped out of the "shower." But when he saw that it was the Fulani, he walked out the door without another word.

The Fulani live in grass shelters and move their camps periodically to find grass and water for their cattle. They could load everything they owned onto the women's heads and the backs of the men's mopeds and move camp in a day. Ironically, they were the wealthiest group in Kalikaha, and some of the families owned large herds. They knew the name of every cow, how many calves she had borne, the names of each of her calves and what had become of each of them. Of all our possessions, they were most interested in some photographs Tom had hung on the wall in a plastic frame.

"What is this person wearing? Is it a hat?" they asked. "Or a piece of cloth?"

"That's Carol," said Tom. "That was her hair."

They looked at me and then at the photograph and made gestures with their hands, as if they were pulling a thick hank of hair through their long fingers. Never had I seen anyone use their hands as expressively as the Fulani. They gestured with the grace of dancers or professional mimes.

"She cut it off," explained Tom, giving me a haircut with finger scissors.

Their eyes grew sad, and they shook their heads in disappointment. They turned to go, but before they left, each man put his long graceful hand in mine with a delicate touch. In their boubous, they sailed out into the night like large black birds.

"Let's go watch the dancing," I suggested.

"Later," said Yardjuma.

"Why not now? I want to see it."

"It isn't the right time yet," Yardjuma replied.

"Why not?" I asked. "They're dancing, aren't they?"

"It just isn't," said Yardjuma. "We'll go later. I'll tell you when."

"I'm going now," I said firmly. "I don't want to miss seeing it."

Yardjuma shrugged his shoulders and followed us. Behind our house, several young boys were dancing inside a circle of spectators.

"Do you feel up to dancing?" Tom asked me. "It would please everyone."

I hadn't thought of dancing myself, but I nodded. Yardjuma blew his whistle a few times to clear the circle, and the next thing I knew, Yardjuma and Tom had each grabbed one of my wrists and raised my arms like a fighter who has just won a fight. They dragged me out into the center of the circle, and both began to dance. The circle suddenly closed in around us as the crowd pressed closer to watch. Yardjuma, holding one hand, jogged me up and down one way while Tom, holding tight to the other, was going up and down at another rhythm altogether. What an awkward way for three people to dance, I thought, and wrenched myself free.

"We're going to dance our way," I heard Tom say to Yardjuma. To raise my arm and dance with me was a sign of honor in Kalikaha, but no one had thought to tell me this.

Yardjuma blew his whistle in time to the *balafons,* and even more people came over to watch. I love to dance and don't usually feel inhibited in front of people. But at that moment, I felt very awkward. The *balafon* music was unlike anything I had ever danced to, with a fast, syncopated rhythm. I wasn't used to dancing on bumpy, uneven ground, and I was wearing a long sundress that wrapped around my ankles and tripped me up. As I whirled, the circle of people pressed so close behind me that I bumped into them and nearly fell. Yardjuma blew his whistle frantically and forced them back.

But not knowing what else to do until the music ended, I continued to dance hesitantly. I focused on the rhythmic beat of the gourd instruments and tried to follow it. Then I connected with Tom, and we began to do disco twirls. It was the showiest thing we had in our repertoire, and we were both aware that practically the whole village was watching. I forgot my irritation with Yardjuma and his whistle and my nervousness about the crowd around us.

We danced into each other and then separated, together, apart, together, apart, around and around the circle. Our dance had become effortless. We were alone, the two of us in the center of the circle, just as we were alone together in Kalikaha.

Suddenly, Yardjuma's whistle blasted, and abruptly, the music stopped. I stood there for a moment, dazed. Our solo was over, just when I had been starting to enjoy it.

Now the young Senufo men came out to dance, one after another, in a kind of competition. The *balafons* played slowly, and one man entered the circle and faced the musicians. Some of these men had the kind of control and timing that I would have attributed only to a professional dancer. Fast fancy footwork was their specialty. They hardly moved their arms at all. Their bodies remained tense and controlled while their feet kept up with every beat of the music.

The musicians speeded up the rhythm, and the

dancer's feet moved faster and faster. Yardjuma blew his whistle in time to the music, faster and faster, in crazed accompaniment. The dancer went into his finale. He squatted with his hands on his hips and kicked out to the side like a Russian folk dancer, first to one side and then to the other. It was an impressive finish. On an offbeat, he suddenly froze, squatting motionless, one leg extended in perfect balance.

"Now you're really going to see dancing!" said Yardjuma over his shoulder as he kicked off his leather shoes and proudly entered the circle. But his pot belly got in the way and he was out of shape compared to the peasants. He was also quite drunk. His steps were slow, and they lacked that quick precision. In the middle of Yardjuma's turn, one of the best dancers moved out into the circle, placed his hands on Yardjuma's hips, and danced him aside, as if this were a well-choreographed stage exit. Then he took over the arena. In his ragged clothes, his muscular body moved surely, full of grace, and always in perfect time with the music.

The women did not dance in this competition. They formed their own circle and danced together, their babies on their backs, each woman performing the same steps at the same moment. Sibatia, our neighbor, was in the circle, her little boy tied tightly on her back. As the music picked up, the circle moved faster and faster, her feet flew, her little boy jogged up and down harder and harder, and I could hear her laughing, flushed and out of breath.

Back on our porch, Fanta, proud of her familiarity with our house, was serving water to all her friends. Tom, seeing that Yardjuma was serving only the men, decided to serve the Senufo women in his study group himself.

"Hey, Tom! Well done!" cheered the old women each time he brought them another gourdful of corn beer.

One of the schoolteachers cornered Yardjuma drunkenly. "When are you going to bring out the rest of the *chapalo,* Yardjuma?"

"Don't worry. You'll get plenty," Yardjuma replied.

"Come on, Yardjuma," he badgered. "Bring it out so that we can have a real party!"

"We'll serve it out soon," replied Yardjuma. "But not all at once."

"Why are you hiding that *chapalo* in the shower, Yardjuma? Are you keeping it for yourself?"

Confronted in this way, Yardjuma had no choice. If he left the *chapalo* in the back, he would be judged stingy and inhospitable, near crimes in Senufo country. People would talk. Reluctantly, he passed the pot over the wall.

All the men crowded around drunkenly, dipping their glasses and gourd bowls at the same time.

Beh Tuo stood up. "Bring that pot and put it here!" he thundered in his raspy voice, pointing to the ground in front of his chair. Someone quickly did as he ordered. "I am the oldest Senufo here," he said with great dignity, "and I am the one who will serve this *chapalo.*"

Everyone was quiet and looked ashamed of their momentary bad manners. The *chapalo* was served, and the drinking party continued.

At two in the morning, we chased the children out of the house. They were going through the stack of plates, eating any leftovers they found. We closed the door and fell exhausted into bed. The *balafons* were still playing behind the house, and I could hear the reverberation of the women's feet as they stamped and turned.

 FIELDWORK

WHEN I SAID THAT I WOULD GO WITH TOM TO "DO FIELD-work," I wasn't at all sure what that meant. Although we talked to a lot of people who had "done fieldwork" before we left, they were all remarkably vague about exactly what they had done while they were in Africa. Somehow, in some mysterious alchemical transformation, a real experience of living in another culture had been transformed into a set of conclusions, always stated in the same language, the specific jargon of their particular discipline, whether it was anthropology, rural sociology, or cultural geography. "I did a labor allocation study," they would say, or "I looked at women's roles in the marketing systems." Some of these people gave bits of floating advice such as "don't hire an assistant from the village you live in" or "never say that you're connected to the government, because the peasants won't trust you," but they would not state more exactly what in their own experience had led them to these conclusions.

This is all part of the fieldwork mystique, of course, which is maintained by those who have already been initiated. Fieldwork is supposed to be character building, and somehow, the less you know the more your character will grow. More truthfully, I suspect that the old guard, having blundered and suffered their way through, now wants the new recruits to suffer and blunder in equal measure. Before I went to Kalikaha, I didn't think that all this had very much to do with me because I planned to spend the year writing, learning Dyula, and experiencing African village life. I wasn't adverse to helping Tom with his research, but I didn't realize the extent to which the demands of that research would determine every single decision in our lives, mine as well as his.

Before I got to Kalikaha, I assumed that fieldworkers sat around, watched the local people, learned the language, and waited for something like a ritual to happen. Wasn't this what "participant observation" was all about? But the books I read had all been written before quantitative studies had hit the social sciences. Tom's fieldwork, I discovered when I got there, was a structured activity carried out according to a weekly timetable. The first step had been the Great Census, which had provoked a strong negative reaction among the villagers. Although all of Tom's books on statistical methods stressed the need for a census if one was to use random sampling methods correctly, none of these books had pointed out that a census of an African village by a white man might have unpleasant historical antecedents. In the case of Kalikaha, a census had always preceded the call-up of men for forced labor on the roads and in the forests. Since forced labor did not end until 1946, many residents remembered this and were understandably reluctant to answer Tom's questions about how many able-bodied workers were present in their households. "Who is this man and what does he want?" they demanded to know. "Tell them that I have no association with the government, I'm a student who has come from the United States to study their way of farming," Tom told Yardjuma. Yardjuma knew that this would go over like a lead balloon. If a white man was going to appear out of the blue and move into their village, they wanted him to be someone important and powerful, someone who would generate miracles like running water, electricity, and health clinics in his wake. If he really was just a student (which sounded suspicious), why should they bother to answer his many questions? As for his connection to the government, in this particular area, the government extension agents were popular people who gave out free seeds, free advice, and free fertilizers if you grew cotton. If he wasn't from the government, he was doubly suspect.

Yardjuma, in order to gain the villagers' cooperation, turned Tom into someone more like the person the villagers desired and fed their hopes for what was to come. Yardjuma told them that after the census, some farmers would be chosen to participate in a contest, at the end of which there would be substantial rewards for everyone and prizes for the best farmer. These fabrications served Yardjuma well since he didn't want to be the *assistant de récherche* for a mere student. His status rose in direct proportion to Tom's. By the time Yardjuma got through with them, the two of them were carrying out Tom's study at the express wish of the Father of the Nation, President Houphouët-Boigny. Tom was happy that Yardjuma was able to convince the villagers to cooperate.

Only later, when he questioned Yardjuma directly about his specific explanations, did he find out that Yardjuma had made promises that he had no intention of fulfilling and that, if Tom wasn't careful, could compromise his data.

When the census was finally complete and the households had been divided into lower-income or middle- and upper-income brackets, Tom got out his table of random numbers, and this mysterious instrument was used to select which families would be asked to participate in his study. Yardjuma and I marveled at the fact that by pointing to a number on the page, we could choose a family that would constitute a valid and properly "random" sample.

There was one family for each income bracket from the Senufo and one from the Dyula, although one family later turned out to be two separate economic units, so Tom ended up with seven families. Each family was visited once a week, and every member of the family old enough to work in the fields was interviewed. The week was gone over day by day. "What did you do yesterday? You weeded cotton? In which field? What time did you start and what time did you finish?" The villagers would point to the sky in response to this question. "I started when the sun was here and I finished when it was there." How much time the women of the family spent preparing food, gathering wood, and washing clothes was also recorded.

Tom had already made up forms for each member of the family with spaces for each day of the week. There were numbered codes for each agricultural activity and for each field so that all the data could be entered into a computer upon his return. In addition, the household budget was accounted for. Every basket of rice sold, every handful of cayenne pepper purchased at the market, was noted.

Most of the members of Tom's study were remarkably patient with this intrusion into their lives. Week after week they recounted the details of their lives to us. In return, we did them favors, such as going to the local prefect's office with them to obtain birth certificates when their children were born. The educated civil servants at the prefect's office were contemptuous of the farmers and made it difficult for them to obtain papers that were required by law and supposed to be free of charge. If we were present, the papers were filled out and quickly handed over, exactly as per the regulations.

Lonala was a Dyula elder in the study group, a pious old man who formerly had been a slave and who was entrusted with circumcising male Dyula children. His fields were a long way from the village, on the other side of the river, and to reach them we had to cross a bridge made of sticks and vines and suspended from the treetops. For most of the way, I held on to the tree trunks, but when we reached the middle of the river, there were no more handholds and I simply had to hold my breath and walk across the slippery round logs. It was a long way down to the river, and there were crocodiles.

Lonala had two wives, Nasiata, who was quite old, a tiny birdlike woman with a high quavery voice, and Mariam, whom we came to know well. Mariam had a husky laugh and a warm smile that immediately drew me to her. I began to watch for her in the village and to exchange greetings with her. "Carol is interested in all my doings," she observed to Yardjuma during one of my first weeks in the village, and she was right.

The most difficult member of the study group was Bazoumana, a Dyula weaver who was probably in his midfifties. Always cantankerous, during the government's mandatory cotton growing program in the sixties Bazoumana had refused to grow cotton, and as a punishment, he was taken to the prefect headquarters and forced to work as a gardener for the prefect. He was a large man, broad-shouldered, and he had a strong, gruff voice. Although he stooped, he towered over the other villagers. When he saw us from across the village, he had a habit of planting his feet, raising one arm, and yelling a single gruff "Hey!" as if that should have been enough to bring us running to him. A long peg tooth protruded from one side of his mouth and waggled wildly as he talked. Had the tooth been pointed, he would have looked like a village Dracula, but it was square at the end, which ruined the effect so that he looked more like a clumsy cartoon monster.

Although Bazoumana was not a good farmer, he was sought out for his weaving, and he managed to sell whatever he wove, despite the fact that he charged more than the other weavers. His two wives both looked beaten down and exhausted most of the time. One was not in good health and had produced a string of children who also were not healthy, including one crippled son who was carried everywhere by the other children. His wives were patient and welcoming with us and appreciative of whatever help we gave them, but Bazoumana himself hindered the study in every way possible. Each time we went to interview him, we wondered if he would once more agree to answer the questions. Often we had to buy his time with gifts of Nescafé and sugar. Late at night, when we were tired, Bazoumana would show up at our door, trying to badger us into buying some fabric he had woven, always at three times the normal price. Tom worried that Bazoumana lied about his farm in order to hide the fact that he was such a poor farmer. "Don't worry," I consoled Tom. "If nothing else, Bazoumana proves that your sample was random. No one would ever choose to work with him."

The other Dyula farmer in the study was named Bayma. Bayma was relatively wealthy by village standards because he had inherited a small herd of cattle. But Bayma was an ineffectual man whose affairs never seemed to go well, despite his inheritance. Many of the animals were lost or died of disease, and his fields always seemed to be trampled by Fulani cattle or ravaged by birds and monkeys. Worst of all for poor Bayma, he was followed everywhere by an older relative of his, a very religious man who muttered prayers to himself constantly, and to whom Bayma always deferred. His wives were anything but deferential, so his compound was always a noisy place full of laughing women and children. Natagari, the senior wife, had come to Bayma when her husband, who was a relative of his, had died. Natagari was tall and thin and carried herself with style, wrapping her headscarf and her clothes with a flair for the dramatic. She was no longer young and complained to us that since she had come to Bayma she no longer had her periods and thus could not give him a child. She was hoping that we had some medicine that could help. Her younger wife, Jeneba, was round and robust, hard working and friendly. She rarely stopped to sit down, but when she did she was always surrounded by small children. The two got along well, which made their courtyard a pleasant place to visit.

Of the Senufo farmers, the oldest was Menergay, an important Senufo elder and member of *poro* who stuck to traditional Senufo ways. He was said to know a great deal about medicinal herbs and potions, although he refused to talk to us about his knowledge. He had two wives. Nofigay, the elder, was light, almost freckled, and had a reputation for stubbornness. When Tom and Yardjuma came to interview her, if she wasn't in the mood, she would chase them away, pestle in hand. The first day that I met Nofigay she gave me a handful of hot red peppers, and I always thought of her as being like the peppers she grew—to be handled carefully, explosive, but full of rich color and juice. She and I always got along by laughing together. My very presence in her courtyard seemed to her uproariously funny. Her cowife, Wahdonan, was pretty, with the delicate, heart-shaped face that one sees on the finest Senufo statuettes of women. Her son, a beautiful child, had his mother's heart-shaped face and big eyes. Wahdonan was shy, and we never came to know her well.

Kolo and N'golo were two Senufo brothers who farmed together along with their mother and N'golo's young wife. Physically, they couldn't have been more opposite. N'golo, the elder, never looked healthy. It was as if something in his thin body was twisted slightly askew and could not be righted. Kolo, on the other hand, was short and compact, very muscular and extremely hard working. He looked like a young wrestler or a weight lifter. Both brothers were friendly and open with us and obviously revered their mother, a tiny woman with a lively, mobile face. She was a diviner and still walked to her fields every day with the help of a staff. Thanks to Kolo's strength, their fields were always in excellent shape and their harvests were plentiful.

The other two Senufo brothers in the sample had followed less traditional paths. Tenena had gone south to work on the palm oil plantations, came back, and married, but his wife had died. He now farmed with his mother, an old woman who despite her age cultivated an enormous swamp rice field. Either Tenena had always been a loner or his experiences away from the village had made him one, for he remained outside the social life of the village. His brother, Tugawo, had established the only store in Kalikaha, a tiny adobe house filled with flashlight batteries, bouillon cubes, cans of tomato paste, wicks for kerosene lanterns, and spare bicycle parts. His wife, Bara, hardly had to farm at all, for they were quite affluent and had the air of young entrepreneurs. She always wore her headscarf wrapped very high, and this, together with her long chin and her proud manner, made her look to me like a blue-black Nefertiti. Tugawo and Bara doted on their small son, who was always dressed in new clothes from the Korhogo market. This family had been counted in the census as one household, but it turned out that the two brothers farmed separate fields and kept their affairs separate, so that they could not be counted as a single economic unit.

After Tom had followed these seven families for some time, he composed another questionnaire and administered it to a different sample of thirty-eight households. In addition, he interviewed Fulani herders about their cattle-raising practices, noting on maps how often they moved their herds and why. The Fulani had an amazing grasp of topography and landscape, even though most of them had been in this area only a few years. Several of them even came to understand Tom's topographic maps and could, with some help, locate where their camps were in relation to hills and streams.

Tom also conducted historical interviews with Senufo and Dyula elders about how farm work had been conducted in the past and about the history of the village. Beh Tuo, one of Tom's best informants, used the six-and-one-half-year *poro* initiate class to establish dates. "That happened when Menergay was the head of the *poro* group," he would say. Through patient questioning and Beh's remarkable memory, Tom was able to piece together a timeline for Kalikaha going back to the 1890s. He correlated well-known events in the area—such as the end of forced labor—with *poro* initiation classes, so that eventually he could ask Beh Tuo who was in the *poro* class when a certain event happened and by consulting his timeline, pinpoint the year in question.

This historical research was the most interesting part of Tom's fieldwork to me, since it involved something very much like detective work, putting pieces together, trying to unravel clues, or searching to find the one person who would know and remember what Tom wanted to find out. When we weren't being detectives, fieldwork was often like being in public relations. The goal was to maintain good relationships with as many of the sixteen hundred villagers as possible. In a smaller village, this might have been easier and less time consuming, but in Kalikaha, it was nearly a full-time job. The chief came to the house asking for money to buy gasoline, someone else needed medicine that we didn't have, a woman was offended because I had never given her any of my empty oil bottles, someone else upbraided me because I had passed through her part of the village without stopping to greet her. All these requests had to be responded to tactfully, and Tom was always anxious about not alienating or insulting people. After all, if the villagers withdrew their cooperation, his study would be a failure and his career as a geographer would be finished. Yardjuma fueled Tom's fears by constantly asserting that the peasants were greedy, that they expected us to solve all their problems for them, and that no matter what we gave them, they would never be satisfied. At first, I let Tom's anxieties rule my relationships with the villagers, and I tried to get along with everyone, a heavy strain and an impossible task. Eventually, as I came to know the villagers as individuals and as I saw that Tom's work was progressing well despite his fears, I relaxed my stance as public relations agent for him and began to avoid people that I didn't care for and seek out those whose company I enjoyed. As soon as I quit trying to pretend that I liked everyone equally well, my life in the village became much easier, and I felt much more comfortable.

In getting to know people, I had to reconcile myself to a large measure of frustration. My early conversations were painfully short because I had hardly settled myself on my stool when I came to the end of my vocabulary. The only alternative was to speak through an interpreter, but hearing what everyone had to say in Yardjuma's words made me very aware that I was missing the unique qualities of each voice. Some people, like Nofigay or Beh Tuo or Mariam, had such strong personalities that they came across clearly, even in translation. More subtle voices blurred, the distinctions lost in Yardjuma's idiomatic French.

The one person we came to know best was Donnisongui. He took his role as *jatigi* seriously and came to greet us every morning and every evening. Visits with Donnisongui were companionable, and since we rarely saw his wife, he seemed like a bachelor friend who attaches himself to a couple. He recounted what he had done in his fields that day, and since his Dyula vocabulary was not

much larger than ours, his accounts were always easy to
follow. The interviews and questionnaires yielded lots of
facts, but it was through our daily talks with Donnisongui that we came closest to understanding peasant life.
When the cotton money arrived in the village, Donni
came straight to us with his receipt and his handful of
cash. "Is it correct?" he wanted to know. "Does the
amount on the paper match what I have?" It did, but
who knew if the amount of cotton he had brought in to
the scales several weeks earlier was the same as the
weight written on the receipt. There were so many easy
ways to shortchange the farmers.

The cotton money had to buy everything for Donni's
family for the coming year: clothes, shoes, gas for his
moped, bicycle parts, salt, batteries, and food if theirs
ran out. Donni's oldest daughter, Dofunyoh, went to the
village school. When school started, Donni gave me the
list of supplies she needed, and I bought them in Korhogo—workbooks, ruler, pencils, compass. I hesitated a
long time over the regulation gingham-check dress lest I
get one so small that she would outgrow it quickly or one
so large that it would dwarf her delicate frame. When I
handed the books to him, Donnisongui turned them over
and over, holding them as delicately in his rough hands
as he would have held something alive and breathing.
Then he looked up, embarrassed, and laughed at his own
wonderment.

One dark, quiet night, when everyone in the quarter
had gone to bed, only the three of us sat outside on the
porch. "I am leaving," Donni said, almost in a whisper.
"I am going south to work on the coffee plantations. I
am not making anything here growing cotton, and I have
to feed my family."

We were shocked. Donnisongui leave to do manual labor for a pittance and to live alone on a plantation among other displaced laborers?

"I haven't told anyone," Donni continued. "Not even my mother. When I am ready, I will simply tell them that I am leaving, and I will go. If I stay there five years and work hard, I can have a small plantation of my own."

"It's not worth it. The coffee prices are too low now." Tom named men who had tried this, most with disastrous results. They had come back with nothing to show for their years of work. "You can make more by expanding your cotton acreage," Tom told him.

"Yes, but there is only me working the fields," Donni replied. "I am alone. If I fell ill, we would have nothing. We would go hungry."

Tom used all the knowledge he had gained studying agriculture in Kalikaha to convince Donni not to go and to help him come up with other solutions. Donni decided to stay on.

When Tom began to research *poro* history, we finally got a clue to a question I had had from the beginning: Why had Donni offered to take us in and given us his house? Donnisongui, it turned out, was a rebel. His group of *poro* initiates had rebelled against a cruel chief who was abusing their services. The dispute had been appealed all the way to the head of the *poro* in Korhogo, and surprisingly, he had ruled in favor of the young men. Now the *poro* initiates no longer worked in the fields of the elders during their six-and-one-half-year initiation. Donnisongui went to his fields during *poro* celebrations instead of drinking corn beer in the sacred grove with the elders.

Despite Yardjuma's dire predictions about the villagers, Tom's main fieldwork problem was maintaining Yardjuma's cooperation, for without his interpretation, Tom could not continue the research. Yardjuma, with his round belly and round face, reminded me of a cat who likes to lie in the sun. On his plump cheeks, the three Senufo scars that radiated from each side of the mouth looked like whiskers. When he wasn't working, he could usually be found stretched out in the hammock in front of his house, a liter of spicy corn beer at his side. Often, a group of youths was seated on the ground beside him, listening intently to his stories of his jobs in the forest region, stories in which Yardjuma got the better of cruel French bosses. In other tales, traditional Senufo values like hospitality and generosity were glorified. In one story, Yardjuma defended his mother from a policeman who tried to beat her for dressing without a blouse, which was the traditional Senufo way.

Yardjuma loved to entertain and to play the generous host, particularly to those who were in a position to do him favors. When his guests—the extension agents, *gendarmes,* and schoolteachers who worked in nearby villages—left after a Saturday night of drinking, Yardjuma would be deep in debt at Chez Mariam, and he had often given away everything he owned. Once he even gave away his beloved black leather shoes.

He disliked Frenchmen and demonstrated the difference between them and Americans. "Frenchmen walk like this," he would say, walking hurriedly in a straight line and staring straight ahead at the ground. "But Americans walk like this," and here he would amble casually along, looking around to all sides with curious glances.

"But Americans work too hard," he would continue, with a meaningful look toward Tom. He claimed that

73

when American missionaries had opened a hospital in the region, the entire staff had quit three times before they found people willing to work the long hours they expected. "They wanted you to work eight hours without stopping," he would say, shaking his head, "and if you were late, even if your moped broke down or you overslept, they fired you. Can you imagine?"

Yardjuma practiced his own brand of public relations with the Senufo elders who passed by Chez Mariam. "Since Beh Tuo is here, we have to stop and buy him a bottle of wine," he would say conspiratorially to Tom. "It's very important for our work. Yes, I know we're on our way to Bayma's field, but just to walk through here without stopping to drink with him would be very rude, a very un-Senufo thing to do. It would practically be an insult."

Tom could accept the fact that he had to "encourage" Yardjuma all week with the promise of a bottle of wine on Saturday if the work went well. What really upset Tom were Yardjuma's unannounced and unforeseen disappearances. Once he borrowed Donni's moped to go to a party in another village and then vanished for a week, coming back on Saturday, his payday, to ask politely for his week's salary. When Tom protested that he hadn't worked all week, he explained to Tom that his absence was all Tom's fault because Tom had refused to help him with his nephew's school expenses. Yardjuma boasted so much to his family and friends about the importance of his position with Tom and his large salary that all his relatives came to him, expecting him to pay for all sorts of things. Tom's greatest fear was that Yardjuma's elderly mother would die while we were there. If she did, we knew that Yardjuma would demand that Tom finance a grandiose funeral that would finish

off Tom's grant money and leave us stranded in
Kalikaha, destitute. So it was not for nothing that Tom
asked Yardjuma about his mother's health each time
Yardjuma made a visit home.

Between Yardjuma and me, an uneasy truce existed.
It was obvious that Yardjuma had not expected me to
accompany them miles into the bush to visit Fulani
camps, but this was something he could accept. He was
more surprised that I wandered around the village repeating and writing down Dyula phrases constantly.
Yardjuma was an astute observer of people and saw that
I was quick at languages and would soon be able to talk
to the villagers on my own. Most disconcerting of all to
Yardjuma was the way Tom solicited and listened to my
opinions. Before my arrival, Yardjuma had been Tom's
sole advisor and confidant. He had not expected to be displaced by the arrival of Tom's wife, and he did not intend
to give up the position without a fight.

In Senufo terms, a wife was someone who bore one's
children and cooked one's meals, not an intimate friend.
From Yardjuma's point of view, he was the one who had
taken Tom to his own village to be initiated into his own
poro group and he was the one who day after day helped
Tom carry out his many far-fetched and demanding requests. Yardjuma felt that he was destined for greater
things than peasant life. He wanted to drink imported
gin rather than corn beer, be a "big man"—preferably
without working very hard—and have lots of women
trailing after him. He hoped that Tom would be his ticket
into the middle class and that after a year and a half of
service, Tom would secure him some sort of permanent
position before leaving the country. In the best of all possible worlds, this position would provide an opportunity
to demand a little something from his clients that he

could put aside, as the *gendarmes* demanded a little "gift" in order to let you pass on the roads. He shared none of Tom's enthusiasm for the work and often slowed it down to a speed more to his liking. But Tom needed someone and Yardjuma had presented himself. So there we were, an unlikely trio: the determined fieldworker, his ambitious interpreter, and unsure exactly what her role was in this undertaking, the fieldworker's restless wife.

THE MAT,
THE CLOTH
& THE AFRICAN SKY

I AWOKE ON THE TUESDAY OF MY SECOND WEEK THINKING how, already, I liked mornings in the village. Already it seemed normal to wake to the wild crowing of roosters and the thunk of pestles in mortars, the click-clack of goats' hooves across our cement porch and footsteps passing just outside the house, several feet, no more, from the bed where I lay. I listened to the sounds of water: streams of water hitting mud as people urinated, the splash of water as they bathed, the thick sheet of water being poured from on top of a woman's head into a large ceramic jar to cool for that day's drinking.

We crawled out from under the mosquito net and put a pan of water on the stove. When the water was warm, we bathed in the courtyard from the enamel basin, joking and prancing in the half-light. At this moment, the house was still our own, the door still closed. I put on more water, this time for tea, and Tom shaved. When we were dressed, we gave each other one long look and resolutely opened the door.

We were waiting for Yardjuma when we heard drums—a slow, muffled thump, hollow in the gray air, the same rhythm over and over.

"Those are funeral drums," Tom said quietly. "Someone has died. The *poro* is in the sacred grove announcing the death."

The sound of clapping warned of someone's arrival, and Lasungo, the *balafon* player, and his friend Zana entered, wearing nothing but loincloths, a sign that they were on *poro* business. Over their shoulders, they carried small cloth bags and knives in decorated sheaths, part of their *poro* paraphernalia. Their young muscular bodies were models of how the perfect initiate should look and their demeanor was serious. Zana and Lasungo were in the final stage of initiation, and much of the responsibility for carrying out funeral duties fell on their shoulders.

The funeral, they told us, was in Bohdanon, a very small village about four kilometers from Kalikaha. A man had been bitten by a poisonous snake; he had not made it back to the village; they had found his body in the fields. A bad way to die, they said quietly. Tom gave me a meaningful look. He kept a syringe and serum in our refrigerator, but the serum was labeled vaguely FOR CENTRAL AFRICA and we were definitely in West Africa. Zana and Lasungo had come to say good-bye. They were leaving that afternoon for the funeral and would be gone all week.

The morning passed very slowly, punctuated by the slow thump of the drums and the sound of the funeral trumpet, a deep-throated, muted bellow that resonated in the air, as if someone were blowing over a giant bottle. A gray sky hung low over the village.

Yardjuma still hadn't turned up, and without him, we couldn't do interviews. Tom typed field notes and I finally opened a book by an American scholar on Senufo art and its most dramatic event, the multimedia Senufo funeral. I had ordered this book months before, but in Berkeley and Abidjan the long Senufo names had been incomprehensible, and I had given up trying to sort out the different masks. Now, the sound of drums from the sacred grove provided a background rhythm for my reading. This scholar, Anita Glaze, calls her book *Art and Death in a Senufo Village.* Art I was anxious to see; death was something I rarely thought about. The Bohdanon farmer's funeral reminded me that it was nearer than I might like to admit. This man was neither old nor ill. The powerful serums and the hospital in Korhogo were useless against a death as sudden as this.

From time to time, Tom and I speculated on where Yardjuma could be and when he would turn up. Lasungo had told us that Yardjuma had gone on Saturday to Siata's maternal village to give chickens and cowries to the head of Siata's lineage, the eldest person in her mother's family. Lasungo had been surprised that Yardjuma wasn't back for work. He might be held up in the village haggling over the number of chickens or else broken down somewhere between Korhogo and Kalikaha, pushing his moped along the road.

"He's probably broken down somewhere," Tom said to me. "It doesn't take long to settle a Senufo marriage." Tom had attended when Donnisongui negotiated the final settlement for his second wife, Fatouma, who had not yet come to live near him.

"They agreed on how many chickens should be sacrificed and then Donnisongui had to pay a fine for every time he had ever insulted her family. The whole thing only lasted a couple of hours. What took a long time were the years of work in her family's fields."

In Yardjuma's case, Siata was a gift; he hadn't had to work for her. Yardjuma liked to remind us that there was a precedent for this kind of marriage in Senufo tradition, when a bride was given as a reward for a favor rendered. The marriage "payments" he had gone to make were only a gesture of courtesy.

Donnisongui and Yardjuma, we both agreed, were very different people. Yardjuma would try to talk his way out of paying any chickens at all, even if it took weeks. This thought depressed Tom, who was worried about his interviews.

About three o'clock that afternoon, we heard a moped pull up.

"Koko," said a tired flat voice.

Yardjuma was wearing his blue pajamas, which were very dusty and looked as if he had indeed slept in them for several days. His whole body drooped like the baggy blue cotton.

"I'm sorry to be so late for work," he began, "but I had some *petits problèmes.*" In a vague, meandering explanation, it finally came out that Siata's family had asked for a lot more money than he had anticipated and that he had been unable to raise it, although he had gone all over Korhogo asking his friends for loans. Finally, desperate, he had sold his moped, paid the family, and borrowed the moped of a friend to get back to Kalikaha. The negotiations had gone on until one that morning.

Yardjuma looked absolutely exhausted and even more than that, somehow beaten. Nothing we had read in the ethnographies about Senufo marriage had prepared us for this. Never, in all our speculations, had it occurred to us that such large sums of money would be required, nor had we ever thought that Yardjuma might sell the moped.

"I had this problem and I had to find a solution," Yardjuma said slowly. "So I found a solution. Now, if you'll advance me the money from my salary to buy another used moped, the whole affair will be settled and we can get on with our work."

"That's not even a possibility," Tom said firmly. Yardjuma's salary, which had originally been a good one, was being spent before it was ever earned, and his take-home pay was being reduced to nothing. And yet, Yardjuma assured Tom, this was how it was always done in Ivory Coast.

This stalemate was interrupted by clapping, and Beh Tuo entered. He had come, he announced, settling himself on the bench next to Yardjuma, to thank us for the party we had given and to wish me once more a warm welcome and good health. And, most important of all, he hoped that I would soon have a child.

I was taken aback by this last, but I tried not to show it. I didn't want to offend Tom's best informant. Beh Tuo suggested that we attend the funeral in Bohdanon on Friday for the dancing on the last day, a kind of grand finale. Then he rose to go, as if he found the tense atmosphere in the house uncomfortable. Pulling his robe about him and gathering up his cane, he shook both our hands, his eyes serious but full of twinkling, darting life as always.

Yardjuma often said that Beh Tuo was a schemer who wanted to discredit him so that Tom would hire Beh's son instead. The son lived in Korhogo and spoke

French. I had no way of knowing whether this was true, but I did have a sense that Beh Tuo's arrival just after Yardjuma's was no coincidence. I wondered whether those piercing eyes of his had been checking up on Yardjuma. From the sacred grove, the funeral drums beat on.

"What is most important to me," Tom told Yardjuma, "is that you must have a moped this week so that we can get our work done. We have fields to measure and we have herders to interview."

"Don't worry about that," Yardjuma said proudly. "I will have a moped to do my work. My work will not suffer." Then he left, still looking miserable but holding his head up proudly. Having to defend himself against Tom's anger had perked him up considerably. I felt irritated with him and sorry for him at the same time.

"I don't feel sorry for him at all," Tom said to me after he was gone. "I'm angry. He had no right to sell that moped. He hasn't worked the hours to pay for it yet."

"What are you going to do?" I asked him.

"I don't know what I can do," said Tom angrily. "I need him to do the research. And he's got to have a moped to go around with me." Tom slammed his account books closed. "Let's go visit Donnisongui in his fields," he said. "That's the only thing that will cheer me up."

The gray afternoon had given way to a beautiful evening sky with clouds piled up in masses and colors of blue that ranged from palest azure to deep indigo and purple.

"Donnisong!" Tom called out as we rode up. Donnisongui looked up from patching his patchwork bike tube one more time so that he could ride back to the village, and his face broke into a wide smile. He was wearing ragged shorts, a ragged shirt, and a blue woolen knitted cap. He had been sweating so hard that I could see small towers of salt crystals encrusted on his eyelids.

Grabbing his machete, he led us proudly on a tour of his fields. There was cotton, corn, millet, and a small field of "green leaves" that his wife, Nyon, was growing for sauce. His son, Tenena, and his niece, Kali, trailed behind us.

"Look at all the work you've done-*dé*!" Tom exclaimed in Dyula, adding the emphatic suffix *dé* to show he really meant it. "You have really worked hard-*dé*!" He thumped Donnisongui on the back.

Donnisongui grabbed him and they pounded each other and wrestled. *"Fort garçon!"* Donnisongui called Tom, measuring Tom's biceps admiringly, although they were no match for Donnisongui's own.

"A real farmer!" Tom replied, gesturing with a grand sweep to the fields all around us. "A champion cultivator!"

The Senufo in Kalikaha no longer had carved staffs that were awarded to the champion cultivator after competitions in the fields to the music of *balafons*. These traditions had died out. But even so, Donnisongui appreciated the compliment. The Senufo are proud of their reputation as good farmers. Only much later, when Tom asked questions for his research, did Donni admit to us that he had been the last champion to be awarded the carved staff.

That night, Yardjuma barely greeted us when it was time to interview the farmers who had been in their fields all day. He asked questions in a monotone and barely looked up from his clipboard. As soon as the work was finished he shook our hands coldly and walked away. He didn't even mention the funeral in Bohdanon, which must have interested him.

Sadly, we went home to our house and sat on the porch, reading. The stars were very bright and the Milky Way clearly visible, as if someone had taken a broom and brushed a stream of liquid stars across the sky. Our neighbor Zeeay, a boy of about thirteen, came by in his *poro* loincloth and gave me his usual smart handshake, snapping his bare heels together and saluting as he extended his arm stiffly, military-style.

"What's happening?" I asked him in French.

"Bien!" thundered Zeeay in reply. "Well!"

I suppose he meant *rien,* nothing, but I didn't correct him. He had come to tell us that he was leaving with the other musicians to spend the night at Bohdanon. Zeeay was younger than Lasungo, but he was already known as an up-and-coming *balafon* player. His father, Doh, was said to have been one of the best. I had never yet seen Zeeay in a bad mood, even after his skinny body was exhausted from a long day in the fields.

The next morning, the interviews were again completed without so much as an extra syllable from Yardjuma. But afterward, he walked back to our house with us. He said that he felt unhappy and wanted to talk about the problems between Tom and him.

"I understand you," he said to Tom, when he was seated on the bench. "But you don't understand me. I have left my family to work for you and you are much more than just my boss. At this time, you are my father and my mother. In Africa, other bosses come to the aid of their employees at these times."

"I'll explain why I'm angry," began Tom. "You sold a moped that is not really yours yet because you are still working the hours to pay for it. You sold something that we need to do the research." It was clear from Tom's voice that research tools were sacred articles and not to be disposed of lightly.

Yardjuma knew Tom too well to argue that point. He explained once more about the costs of the marriage, and it turned out that when they had calculated all the marriage expenses—chickens, taxis for the entire family to this village, cowries, and fines for grievances—that Yardjuma had spent about one hundred and fifty dollars for the marriage and had thirty dollars remaining from the sale of the moped.

"Why didn't you ask Baba for the money?" Tom asked Yardjuma.

"I've gone to him too many times. I would be ashamed to go to him again," said Yardjuma. Baba, who had befriended Yardjuma when he was a boy, was a member of one of Korhogo's most powerful families. Baba had come to Yardjuma's village on an official tour, and Yardjuma had been one of the musicians in the *balafon* group that played to welcome him. Yardjuma told us that as he played the gourd lute he danced in front of Baba again and again, using every ounce of his strength to impress him. Afterward, Baba called for Yardjuma's mother and gave her a large bill as a gift. "Until the day I die," Baba told her, "your son will be my friend." Although we doubted Baba's existence, the tales of all the things that he had done for Yardjuma entertained us many a night. Like a genie, he pulled up in his black limousine to rescue Yardjuma at the most opportune moments. Once, after Yardjuma got into a fight in a bar over a woman and, unluckily, his adversary turned out to be the chief of police, only Baba's arrival in his black limousine had saved Yardjuma from a week in jail.

"There's only one solution," Yardjuma maintained,

"and that is for you to advance me the cost of a second-hand moped. After all, it's my salary." Tom said that he had to think it over.

"I hope that you will come to understand our way of doing things," Yardjuma said gravely.

This was too much for Tom. "I do understand," he said quickly, the irritation showing in his voice. "But I don't agree. I understand your way of doing things, but I don't agree with it." Then, seeing Yardjuma looking glum again, Tom added, "I'm glad you came and talked this over. I don't want bad feelings between us."

After Yardjuma left, Tom sat down with paper and pen. He figured that he could advance Yardjuma enough for a used moped by subtracting about three dollars more from Yardjuma's salary each week from now until the end of the research the following June. Tom was clearly relieved to have found a solution.

"This time, put conditions on the loan," I called out from under the mosquito net. "No more money to that friend in Korhogo who wastes it all."

The crisis in the fieldwork momentarily resolved, I turned back to *Art and Death*. No longer abstract, the scholarly study had come alive, and the rituals it described were being enacted in front of me. I read it at every spare moment, searching every page for the information that would help me to understand the events I was witnessing.

This funeral, I learned, fit into a specific category, the funeral of someone who "suffers sudden death by violence or accident outside the microcosm of the village precincts. . . . Because the welfare of the entire village is endangered by such a death, the village chief, traditional trustee of the land, becomes responsible for setting into motion an elaborate series of precautions, sacrifices, and medicines which will purify the land and protect the villagers from further calamity. Every man, woman and child in the 'infected' village must taste of the medicine. . . . Only men and women of great age and authority have sufficient supernatural protection to risk exposure to the body and supervision of the burial."

Friday afternoon, we took the road to Bohdanon. The road was filled with men on mopeds and bicycles, boys standing up to pedal bicycles too large for them, women and girls on foot, dressed in their best. Everyone waved gaily as we passed, as if we were all going to a county fair.

The village of Bohdanon is tiny, no larger than the quarter where we lived, and all its paths were filled with people. *Balafon* music vibrated against the adobe mud houses. Tom, Yardjuma, and I climbed on top of a large pile of wood near the funeral grounds so that we could see. We recognized Zeeay and Lasungo among the musicians, dressed in their robes of hand-spun cotton. The *poro* of Bohdanon was a daughter group to the *poro* of Kalikaha, and strong ties remained between them.

The men formed a circle on the funeral grounds, their long cylindrical funeral drums hanging at their sides, special curved sticks ready in their hands. Inside the circle of drummers was a reed mat on which lay a folded cloth. This handwoven cloth represented the body, which had already been buried. As we watched, a circle of older women took hold of this mat and, in rhythm to the drums, bent down and raised the mat over their heads, their arms upstretched. Then, as the drums thumped, they laid it down again. Again and again, they offered the "body" on its reed mat to the sky—in rhythm to the drums, a slow rhythm that kept me hanging, holding my breath, waiting for the long pause to end and the beat to come again.

These were the women initiates of Kalikaha. Unlike the other women, who were dressed in their best clothes, the initiates wore only indigo blue cloths knotted around their waists. I searched the circle carefully to determine their ages, but to my disappointment, every one of them was old, their muscles stringy as they raised the mat skyward; on their thin arms I saw the hanging skin of old age. There were no women initiates my age.

I did not understand the exact meaning of these gestures, nor did I ever see this done again in the same way. I simply watched intently. Nearby, an old man carried a large bunch of green grass dripping with some liquid. This was the medicine against snakebite. One at a time, men, women, and children stood before this man, and he shook the medicine grass over their heads and shoulders, so that drops of the special liquid fell upon them.

In another courtyard, a *balafon* group from a neighboring village was playing. A circle danced continuously, and those who were related to the deceased farmer carried black cowhair fly whisks. Often, people went up to the family members and, taking them by one wrist, held their arms aloft as they danced to honor them.

"The masks are coming," Tom whispered. I turned, looking for carved wooden face masks like those I had seen in pictures but, instead, saw masqueraders dressed in cloth suits who strolled through the crowd. The cloth costume covered the young man's head, except for eyeholes, and was drawn tight at the neck. The baggy costumes were made of homespun painted with ochre-colored geometric designs. Around the wrists, ankles, and neck were cuffs of fringed raffia dyed bright red and green. Some of the masks wore headdresses of tall black feathers. The masqueraders talked through a mouthpiece built into the costume, so that they sounded as if they were talking through kazoos. Knowing that their voices were unrecognizable, they talked freely with *poro* graduates who understood the secret *poro* language, and they laughed loudly—unearthly laughter that echoed through the small village. They were supposed to be great punners, if you understood the secret language. The masks carried large cowhide bags over their shoulders, and many people gave them coins or cowries. Tom had carefully assembled a pocketful of change just for this purpose before we left the village. When the initiated gave money, they took off their hats, saying something in the *poro* language, put the money in the bag, and then thumped the bag in a particular way. Tom, too, tipped his wide straw hat to the mask as he gave him a coin, and I watched, surprised and a little envious, as he whispered to the mask and the mask replied in its odd kazoo voice.

One mask suddenly reached into his bag and threw a wooden figurine of a woman at the feet of a young man dressed in brand-new jeans and a Western shirt. There was bawdy laughter at the expense of the embarrassed young man, who had left the village to work and did not know the secret *poro* language. For once, the boys who had stayed behind had the upper hand and, hidden by the costumes, they were getting their revenge on their successful comrade. To save himself, he gave them money.

The actual ceremony seemed to be over, and the different *balafon* groups came together for a parade around the village. People danced behind the musicians, greeting each other tipsily. We followed behind with Yardjuma, Donnisongui, and Donni's good friend, N'golofaga, the drunkest of all, shaking hands with everyone from Kalikaha.

Yardjuma was in a wonderful mood, so he listened to my questions willingly, but the actual answers were scanty. "That has to do with *poro*," he said about almost everything connected to the funeral, and I knew that I couldn't go any further until I had been initiated.

As we promenaded around Bohdanon, Donnisongui told everyone how we had cured his stomachache and enabled him to attend the funeral. He pantomimed dropping two Alka-Seltzer tablets into a glass of water and made the sound of them fizzing. *"Pshshh-shhh-pshhshsh-shhh!"*

His audience listened raptly. "And now, I'm all cured," he declared, rubbing his stomach contentedly because it was presently full of fried goat meat and *chapalo*. His testimonial would make a great commercial for Alka-Seltzer, I thought to myself. Donnisongui would make a fortune, and all his money problems would be solved. Lasungo could make his American debut playing the *balafon*, and Yardjuma, I was sure, would find a place in Hollywood as their agent.

All the way back to Kalikaha, I smiled to myself, imagining the evening news being interrupted for a few moments by the dusty carnival of a Senufo funeral. We rode straight into a magnificent purple sunset that filled the enormous sky and spilled over onto the red dirt road.

The next Saturday when we went to the market, we heard the news that an old woman had died. We didn't know her well, but Tom remembered interviewing her when he did a census of the village. The Poro Boys were already exhausted from the long funeral in Bohdanon. They had been up four nights in a row without sleep, and I wondered if the body would be buried quietly and the funeral held later. If the death comes at a difficult time of year like this one, the family can decide to put off the funeral celebration until after the harvest, when the granaries are full and the work in the fields is finished.

"They will wait," we heard.

Then, "No, they have bought eight sacks of rice."

"Eight sacks? How can they afford it?" Rumors flew around the village.

The woman's body was moved into an empty house in the compound of her lineage. In the early evening, as I sat on the porch, I heard the funeral drums coming from there. Zeeay and Lasungo came by, still dressed in their *poro* loincloths. Neither Zeeay's thin body nor Lasungo's muscular one hid their exhaustion. Zeeay looked utterly worn out, but he pulled himself together and gave me his usual smart handshake, snapping his bare heels together in the dust.

"What's happening?" I asked him in French, hoping for news.

"Very well," he replied as usual.

Zeeay and Lasungo still weren't sure if the funeral would start that night or wait until the next day so that they could all get some sleep. The family must have made a decision shortly after that because about dark, the Poro Boys, all in their loincloths, arrived on the funeral grounds, the open area just behind our house. Young boys cleared the field of weeds, supervised by older boys with thatch torches. They were using short-handled hoes called *dabas,* and they worked hard, crouched over, scraping off a thin layer of earth. They didn't pause or straighten up once until the entire area was cleared.

Now that the weeds were cleared and the funeral drums stacked nearby, the ground had become sacred and we could no longer walk across it wearing our shoes or ride the motorcycle across it, as we normally did. Directly behind our latrine was a small round house with two doors that was usually empty. This was where the *poro* stored their drums and masks during funerals.

Later that night, hearing the slow thump of the drums and the low, vibrating sound of the funeral trumpet, I went outside and stood in our back courtyard, watching the figures move past the gap between the *poro* house and the granaries. A light rain was falling. As they circled, each of the figures crossed the opening between the two buildings and was lit up by the fire in the center of the circle. First, several young men passed by, wearing the long cylindrical funeral drums around their chests on ropes, so that they hung down at one side. All at the same moment, they tapped the drums softly with their curved sticks, creating an ominous rhythm that held me in a state of tension, counting off the slow seconds until the patter came again. A boy passed in front of me with a blazing thatch torch and then another holding the funeral trumpet. This was the first time I had actually seen the trumpet. It was a wooden cylinder about three feet long, but not perfectly cylindrical. It tapered softly, like a zucchini, and its wooden surface was worn by many hands to a shiny patina. The boy held it in front of him vertically and blew into an opening near the bottom. The tall silhouette of a mask passed by, larger than human size in the bulky costume. The mask was not entertaining that night but simply standing guard, the long black feathers on its head pointing up to the night sky. Three old women walked quietly behind the mask.

Before going to bed, I was drawn once more to the

edge of the quarter to watch the circle of figures around the bonfire. In unison, the drums thumped softly and the night air vibrated as the funeral trumpet resounded. The drums, dark night, blazing torches, and light rain made me shiver. Death is all around us, I thought. The farmer in Bohdanon found it in his fields in the form of a snake, and this woman died of old age after a lifetime of hard work. Despite the rain, the boys and young men would spend the night circling and drumming on the funeral grounds to honor the work she did and to protect the village so that life could go on.

In the past, the *poro* initiates would have been men in their late twenties or early thirties. Now many of the young men had gone south to labor for a pittance on the coffee plantations or to high school or jobs in Korhogo. Only the boys who were left in the village and hadn't been sent to school carried on the tradition of *poro.* Since there were so few, the *poro* had to take younger and younger boys in order to have an entering group every six and one-half years. Now, most of the initiates were not mature young men like Lasungo and Zana but gangly, skinny-legged boys. Seeing me watching him blow the funeral trumpet, the son of our neighbor Zanapay puffed out his thin chest and grinned proudly. He was the benchsitter par excellence, coming every day and staying for hours. Compared to Lasungo and Zana, he looked childish, but he was one of the oldest boys in his *poro* group.

During the four-day funeral, daily life in the Senufo part of the village was disrupted, and with time on their hands, everyone came to visit us. The exception was Fanta, who was afraid of the masks, so our water supply became erratic. When she did come, it was often just after dawn, when the masks were not yet abroad.

93

She opened the house door before we were awake ourselves, and moments later, the entire funeral party crowded onto the porch. I barely had time to pull a sundress over my head. They were dressed in their best clothes and carried black cowhair fly whisks. I felt suffocated by their greetings and their stares and their cowhair fly whisks. Why didn't these people ever wait to be invited? They completely blocked our meager light, and for the first time, I comprehended the old expression "They darkened the door."

From somewhere deep inside me, an American cowboy raised on "Gunsmoke" yelled, Don't let them in! Head 'em off at the pass!

Wait, counseled a softer voice. All they really want is to see you. Reassured by this second inner voice, I took a deep breath and stepped out. We exchanged long greetings. They looked me over very thoroughly and, satisfied, went gaily on their way.

Later that morning, I was washing dishes in the back courtyard when I heard laughter and the strange kazoo noises that the masks make. I looked over the wall, but I didn't see any masks. The noises came again, sounding very close, and mixed in with the kazoo talk was the sound of young boys' laughter. From the latrine, I bent down and looked through a hole in our earthen wall directly into the house where the *poro* stored the drums and masks during the funeral. There, two young boys were putting on the costumes, trying out the mouthpieces that distorted their voices, and teasing each other. The metamorphosis was striking: Their bodies had changed to otherworldly creatures except for their heads, which were those of two young boys laughing. For me, it was a precious moment, something rarely seen by an outsider: the moment of transition from everyday to otherworld—arrested in midpath. The Senufo say that it is not the person inside the costume that is sacred. The costume itself holds the power, but what is sacred is the ensemble created when a willing boy wears the costume and not only impersonates, but for a brief time, *becomes,* a being from the otherworld.

For two days and nights, the circling and drumming continued. I would wake in the night to the sound of drums behind the house, and when I woke again at dawn, it was to the resonating notes of the huge wooden *bala-fons.* It is necessary to pay the dead person the respect of at least one full night, from dark to dawn, of music and dance.

Tom was able to interview many people because the Senufo were in the village all day, visiting friends and drinking *chapalo.* The masks came and went in the village with their odd kazoo talk and laughter, strange creatures that had miraculously come to live among us. I felt grateful for their presence, as if it were a great gift. Dressed in baggy cloth costumes, they entertained like clowns and also guarded the funeral grounds, sometimes chasing children away with their long canes. Every time I saw these cloth and raffia masks, I wondered about the carved wooden masks for which the Senufo were renowned, the ones shown in every book of African art. I imagined them hidden away inside the sacred grove, and I wondered whether I would ever be able to see them.

One morning, we were sitting in the house talking to a young farmer in Tom's study group who had come to greet us. I heard the sound of drums and a bell, a signal that a sacred mask was coming out of the sacred grove.

"You've never seen this mask," the man told Tom. "Come with me." I stood up, too, but he motioned to me to sit down. "Only Tom can come."

As soon as they had left I went out to the latrine and peeped over the wall. Two new masks circled on the funeral grounds, and an initiate walked between them ringing a bell. This was a sign that the mask that followed was particularly powerful. The first mask was a cloth mask and similar to all the others except that he wore a red hat like a Shriner's that was decorated with cowrie shells, and the belly of his costume was stuffed so that he looked pregnant. The second mask was a helmet mask, a mask of carved wood that an initiate wears on top of his head. This one was beautifully carved like a crocodile with a long snout and wooden teeth that stuck out in front. Curving back from the mask were two long carved horns. The young man was dressed only in a loincloth and a leopard skin, and he carried a drum. He circled solemnly. Then he put down the drum, took the bell and began to ring it and, crouching, hit the drum over and over. In unison, the other mask cried out again and again in its strange kazoo voice.

I stared, transfixed by the sight of the two creatures before me—the strange stuffed creature in his red Shriner's hat who cried piteously with the voice of a being from another world and the other—with the body of a muscular youth and the head of a crocodile. He looked as if he had stepped out of an Egyptian frieze and sprung furiously to life.

I suddenly realized that I was staring over the wall and could be seen, so I turned and dove through the low back door into the house. Moments later, Tom and the others came through the front door and found me sitting at the table, book hastily opened, pencil in hand.

"They said it's a good thing you didn't see that mask," Tom said to me when the others had gone. "They say the sight of it could kill you." The lightness in his voice sounded forced.

"I saw the whole thing," I confessed. "I was in the latrine."

"I thought you would be. Then you saw how it drummed?"

Tom and I looked at each other as I nodded. There was nothing more to say.

This particular mask, we learned from our books, has a benevolent power to chase away sorcerers and evil magic, and its cries and drumming help to release the soul and send it on its way. To the Senufo, it is one of the most important masks.

The ethnographic articles that we consulted we kept hidden in the bedroom, lest anyone see the drawings and photographs of sacred *poro* masks they contained. We had heard the story of an anthropologist-priest who had lived in the area for many years and had been writing a book about *poro*. A servant cleaning his room opened the manuscript one day and saw the masks pictured there, masks about which one is forbidden to speak to the uninitiated. The priest had to leave the country abruptly and could never come back.

One Senufo man we knew, who was a government official in Abidjan, had a fine collection of these carved masks in his home in an exclusive suburb of Abidjan.

"How do dealers come by these?" Tom asked him. "I can't imagine a *poro* group selling them when they're still in good condition like this."

"Some are carved for the art market," he replied. "They have never been consecrated and so they are not, in the strictest sense, truly sacred. The rest were stolen out of sacred groves."

Tom, recently initiated himself, was shocked. "Doesn't that bother you?" he asked our friend.

"By the time they reach Abidjan, the deed has been done," our host replied. "Someone else will buy them if I don't. At least, here in my home, they will be appreciated for what they are. And they will remain in Ivory Coast."

When I admired the masks at his house, it was for their fine carving and for the eloquent ways in which the animals that adorned them were stylized. Now, I realized that a well-carved mask on a white wall was a far cry indeed from a mask in use. In a funeral, this mask exits the sacred grove preceded by a bell, replaces the head of one of the community's own members, and drums emphatically to release the soul of someone who has just died.

Masks like the one I had seen are displayed in important museums around the world. But none of these exhibits show the costume with which the mask is worn, none show the drum. Nor do they show the initiate's body, also part of the sculptural whole. The animal mask atop a muscular male body, the essence of youth and strength, creates a striking juxtaposition. No exhibit could show the performance in which the initiate wears the mask and the costume and drums. What a pale shadow the museums have captured and hung on their walls.

The fiber and skin costume is usually considered ethnographic material, not art. These articles are stored in the basements of museums to be shown to visiting anthropologists. The performance is in that great tradition where religion and theater come together. The mask itself is sculpture, of course, a category the Western art market can recognize and sell, can hang on a wall or mount on a stand, can own. In our museums, these masks stand alone as art objects, as we mean the word, and they do more than hold their own; the best of them shine with power; they fascinate, they touch us. Our artists recognized the elegance and strength of their forms before anyone else. But to see the whole is to see something more. To experience the whole is to see all the media—music, dance, performance, fiber art, wood sculpture—united toward one great artistic and religious end. That is what I saw and felt and heard in Kalikaha. Art was called upon to mediate death.

The woman who had died had been a Sando, a diviner. At some point in her life, she had fallen ill and had to become a Sando in order to recover, because the bush spirits wished it. Sandos have miniature houses in the village where clients come to them with a question or a problem. Holding the client's hand in hers, the Sando slaps it against her thigh as she throws out a collection of divining articles on the ground. By reading the seeds, nuts, cowries, and brass miniatures, the Sando is able to give the person a response, which is transmitted through her from the bush spirits. Sometimes, it is the bush spirits themselves that are causing the problem, and they must be appeased with a jar of water or a sacrifice left in the bush.

"Come see," Zeeay called out to us from outside the door. "The Sandos are singing."

A group of women was making its way down the path toward us. They wore only blue loincloths and they carried a large basket between them filled with leaves. As they walked, they sang. I stood, mystified, and watched as the line of women passed me and disappeared into the distance. Whether they went to the sacred grove or to somewhere else in the bush, I don't know. Why they did this I could only guess. When I asked, I was told, "It's the custom."

The next day, Tom and I left for Korhogo. We wanted to pick up our mail and buy a few things. Although I was fascinated by the funeral, the days of drumming and all-night *balafon* music and the constant visitors were wearing, and a trip to Korhogo would give us a breath of peace and privacy.

We returned the following day just about dusk. The air was heavy with the loaded feeling that comes just before a storm. The drummers were still circling the funeral grounds, and I walked up to stand between the granaries and watch. Lightning and a very dark cloud moved across the horizon together, lighting up the landscape and silhouetting the enormous baobab trees, with their stolid trunks and armlike branches. The wind whipped through the village, sending dust into my eyes and binding my skirt around my knees. It swept the heavy humidity away, out through the narrow passageways between houses. It cooled and refreshed every pore of my body.

The wind got even stronger and sparks flew wildly from the fire where the initiates were cooking their dinner. Everyone else ran inside for cover, moved back to the far corners of their houses, and closed their doors against the blinding dust. But the *poro* initiates stood out in the field, preparing even in the face of the storm, to spend the night in the open. The wind tossed the boys' loincloths against their legs and showered them with sparks, as if to test them. The lightning moved closer. I stayed, watching, until the first huge raindrops fell. Then I, too, ran inside the house for shelter.

Early the next morning, hearing gourd rattles, I walked up to the funeral grounds. The Sandos were there again with hoes, and they were digging a path in the dirt. When complete, the muddy path circled the wooden structure that is on the funeral grounds of every village, a structure made of four log poles with forked ends and a roof of stacked logs. Rebuilding this structure every six and one-half years is one of the tasks of each class of *poro* initiates. Underneath the structure was a wooden bed carved out of a single enormous log. During funerals, the body is laid on this bed and often, an old woman watches over it. If the body has already been buried, it is represented by a folded cloth.

At midmorning, the Sandos reappeared, wearing only loincloths, to dance with gourd rattles covered by string nets of cowrie shells, which they clacked against the gourds. One woman sat down on the muddy circular path and scooted around it, using only her bare legs to propel herself and shaking her gourd rattle as she arduously made her way around the muddy circle. Spectators threw down cowries and small change to reward her efforts. The other women chanted and shook their rattles to encourage her. One woman held a stick carved like a musket and decorated with cowries, a red plastic pail, and the lid of a cooking pot as she sang. Several women laboriously made their way around the mud path. Then, without any warning, all the women raised their arms in the air, shook their rattles, yelled a strange battle cry that echoed fiercely, and took off running through the village. I was left staring after them in amazement.

Most of the morning, I stood quietly by the granaries and watched the women dance around and around the wooden structure. Several times, one old woman gestured to me to come and join them. I wanted to go and see how it felt to dance out there, both alone and with them. But I held back. When Tom came looking for me to join him for lunch and a siesta, I went. I thought that for some reason he disapproved of my desire to dance with the elderly women. Later, when we talked about it, he said that what I took to be his disapproval was more truly surprise—surprise that after only two weeks in Kalikaha I would want to go out and dance with the women.

The longer I stayed in Kalikaha, the more clearly I realized how false were my fears of intruding. When I held back out of shyness, the villagers took my hesitation to be aloofness or disapproval. Whenever I did join them, they were delighted and took it as a gesture of my respect for their ways. When they didn't want me to see something, they made that perfectly clear. Sometimes, they made sure that the event had already taken place before I ever heard about it. They had no qualms about telling me what I could and couldn't do, and frequently, they made a point of telling me what I should do as well.

In late afternoon, the drumbeats became more insistent. The entire Senufo village was gathering on the funeral grounds for the finale. We walked around the perimeter of the funeral grounds in our shoes, greeted the elders seated under a mango tree, and then joined Donnisongui. I left my Birkenstock sandals (my own particular native dress, the tribal garb of the Berkeleyans) with everyone else's shoes next to the sacred drum. The drum had been brought out of the sacred grove for the funeral. The base was of black wood, carved in the shape of a woman seated on a stool, her sturdy arms upraised to support the drum itself. Around the drum were carved crocodiles, monkeys, chameleons, and snakes. Beh Tuo's blind son was the drum's caretaker. He stood beside it in a ragged black suit, accepting small gifts of cowries, his head tilted slightly toward the sky and his cloudy eyes fixed on the music.

Inside the circle of onlookers, the masks were performing. One after another, the masqueraders in their cloth suits danced brilliantly in the same style as the young men had danced the night of our party. They crouched, hands on hips, and kicked out their legs as if they were Russian folk dancers, to one side and then the other. As they kicked they wagged their heads rhythmically in the opposite direction. This movement had been striking when the young men did it uncostumed. But now, adorned with enormous feather headdresses that emphasized the gesture, when their legs went one way and their heads another, it was breathtaking.

One mask flounced his way around the circle, wiggling suggestively at the audience, and they were delighted. The mask with the pregnant belly and the Shriner's hat danced even more wildly than all the rest; the crowd roared! The village world is a world of hard work day after day after day, drab color and sameness; the mud houses are the same color as the mud earth; the thatched roofs are the same muted earth tones. The utensils that everyone has are the same, made of the same tin and gourds and clay. In this world, the masks were a feast of color and exuberance. How we all enjoyed their spectacle. The children even enjoyed the terror when the masks chased after them with sticks.

One mask took his stick and pantomimed that he was climbing onto a rickety old moped. Every gesture was perfect. We watched as the old moped sputtered and then started up, and we roared, too, as he roared away on his stick!

How we all needed that lightness. How much every detail of their costumes, every cowrie, every bit of tin sewn on for shiny effect, was appreciated by us. Already, after only two weeks in the village, I was hungry for color and design, for change. No wonder, I thought, I get sated too quickly when I go into an art museum at home. Our world is already too crammed with images. There, I have no room in my eyes for more, no hunger, no longing. In Kalikaha, life was sparer and harder. Every pottery jar decorated with the zigzag line that represents the python and every brass python bracelet were interconnected, were waiting for this moment, when the masks came out of the sacred grove and the sacred drum appeared again. At this moment, the circle of connected images became complete. Here, there was no surfeit. Each image was appreciated. Each had its place in the whole.

An old woman lifted my arm and we danced while the onlookers laughed. And then I lifted her skinny arm and we danced again. The carved woman watched from her stool, black as night, her sturdy arms upraised to honor the drum. I remembered the old women in Bohdanon, their stringy arms holding up the cloth "body" to the blue African sky.

We were talking to Donnisongui when Zele came to say that I should leave, because the *poro* was coming. I looked around, and where, moments before, there had been laughing women and children everywhere, suddenly there were only the old initiates left. I could see women's backs in the alleyways drifting away. I had nearly reached our house when I remembered that the key to our lock was in Tom's pocket. But the drums and bells had already started, so I didn't dare go back.

Disappointed, I sat down on our porch. I had hoped to watch everything from our latrine. And here I was, shut out, just like all the other women. Sibatia went into her house and closed the door tightly. A woman who saw the masks would become sterile.

An old woman came around the house, and seeing me, she gestured furiously at me to go in. "They're coming! They're coming!" she cried. I nodded and went up to the door, pretending to open it. I hoped that she would leave and then I could sit on the porch, where I might catch a glimpse as the masks passed by. But she waited stubbornly to see me go in. Seeing that it was no use, I showed her that the door was locked and told her Tom had the key. She took my hand and led me to her house, deeper in the quarter. She brought me a stool, and we sat down with several other women and two small children.

Now that she had gotten me away from the men, this old woman quickly got down to business. She picked up her long, empty breast and pointed to mine. No, I answered her. No children yet, none on the way. She examined my short hair, exclaiming over the length of it and the straightness, running her fingers through it in a way she never would have done when the men were there. This woman was the same one who had gestured to me to join the dancing. She lived just below us and often came by, checking on us proprietarily. Her name was Bara. Later I learned that she was Donnisongui's mother.

When the drums ended, Tom came to find me. The musicians circled the funeral grounds once more and then left in a procession, playing as they walked to the grave. The crowd dispersed, and we went back to our porch and sat down to talk over the afternoon's events.

We had barely settled into our Senufo chairs when several men appeared, leading a black steer by a rope. Just above the granaries, they forced the steer to the ground. Two of them took a long log and laid it across the animal, pressing down on the ends so that it couldn't move. The Dyula butcher said a Moslem prayer and slit its throat, so that the Dyula would be able to eat any meat they were given. From our porch, I could see its slit windpipe still trying to suck in air. The blood ran down the hill toward us, and as the sun set, we watched the animal die. It was butchered on the spot. The meat was divided up, and each portion set carefully on a plate-sized leaf. An army of children scurried through the village, delivering these portions, their hands cupped in front of them to hold the leaves. If each child had held a ball of string, unrolling it as he or she went, we could have seen next day the hundreds of threads, like spokes in a wheel, that radiated out from the funeral grounds to the houses with which this family had connections. And from each of these houses, meat was portioned out to one or two others. At this time of year, which the Senufo calendar calls "everyone is hungry," the meat was welcome.

The next day, we heard that an elderly Dyula man had died. I was beginning to realize how difficult this period of scarcity was. Most of the deaths that occurred while I was in Kalikaha occurred in these few months before the harvest.

A few weeks later we were in the fields when we heard drums coming from the sacred grove. As soon as I heard that slow beat with the long pauses, the thought of death flowed through me. Who was it this time? Was it someone I knew?

"Funeral!" sang out Yardjuma. "We'll be drinking *chapalo* and dancing! What do you think of Senufo funerals, now that you have attended two, Carol?"

"Amazing. I've never seen anything like it."

"To tell you the truth, since I know," he answered, "these were nothing. Now the funeral we went to before you came—the one at Bahkaha. Wasn't that something, Monsieur Tom? Now that was a real Senufo funeral! Magnificent! They spent a fortune. Singers and dancers came from all over. Too bad you missed it."

Zeeay met us at our house with the news. It was the very old wife of a former chief, not even the chief before this one, but the one before that. "She was very old," said Zeeay as if to reassure us. "She hadn't gone to the fields for three years." When someone as old as that dies, the Senufo funeral becomes a true celebration. The person is ready to become an ancestor.

Her body was placed in a house in our quarter, for we lived in the quarter of the chiefly lineage. We were taken to visit the body, wrapped in white homespun, and we gave our offerings to the women who watched over, throwing our coins across the body, as we were told to do.

That evening, Donnisongui came for us and we walked with him to the compound just behind ours where the old woman had lived. It was just dusk and bluish-gray light filled the courtyard like smoke. The *balafons* played hauntingly, and people danced with slow movements, waving their arms like gentle trees. In the middle of the courtyard, on a reed mat, they wrapped her body in shroud after shroud. People close to the family of the deceased give the shrouds as gifts. They are counted publicly, and each donor's name is called out. The more cloths, the greater the honor. There are often fifty or more wrapped around the body. The last one was very large, of white homespun. While people danced all around and the *balafons* played softly, one of the men in her family sewed up this shroud.

I stood with my shoulder against Donnisongui's, comforted by his nearness. How very solid his shoulders were, and how rooted he was in this particular piece of earth. He would be wrapped in shrouds one day in exactly this way, not in this courtyard but in the next one over, just a few feet away. I wondered how it felt to know that. I wished that I belonged to a place the way Donnisongui belonged to Kalikaha.

THE TALE OF YARDJUMA'S MARRIAGE

Yardjuma GREW UP IN A VERY SMALL VILLAGE IN AN AREA south of Kalikaha, in a region known for its persistence in holding on to traditional Senufo values. Yardjuma, however, was determined not to live the traditional life of a Senufo peasant. Against the wishes of his uncle, who wanted him to work in the fields, Yardjuma went to school and received a sixth-grade education. Schoolboys cannot participate in *poro* activities because the *poro* requires large contributions of time and labor. Nor can they earn a wife in the traditional Senufo manner—working one day a year with twenty of their friends in the field of an older man. When a Senufo youth begins this work, at the age of fifteen or thereabouts, the man for whom he works may not even have a daughter. But fifteen years later, the young man, who has also helped each of these friends work for a wife one day a year, has put in enough labor, and the older man will give him a daughter or a niece as his wife. By this time, the young man is in his early thirties, has completed his *poro* initiation, and is therefore eligible to marry. Someone like Yardjuma, who spent these years in school and subsequently left his native village, had to fend for himself when it came to acquiring a wife. In Yardjuma's case, it happened like this:

Yardjuma's "brother" (meaning, in this case, someone from the same village) Soro was renting a house in Korhogo from Siata's mother, who had a reputation as a shrewd businesswoman. Soro, it was generally accepted, even by his friends, was lazy and shiftless, and he had not paid his rent for several months. When Yardjuma, recently employed by Tom and proud of his new status, went to visit Soro, he pulled out a large amount of money and gave it to Siata's mother, generously paying his friend's back rent. Several months later, Siata's mother called for Yardjuma and told him that she would like to give him her fourteen-year-old daughter, Siata, in marriage. She obviously thought that Yardjuma was the wealthy son-in-law she had been seeking.

Yardjuma told us that he had reservations about Siata because he suspected that, having grown up in Korhogo rather than in a village, she was spoiled and lazy. But he had no other prospects in sight and so, after protracted consultations with his friends, he decided to accept the offer. He turned up with her one weekend at the house in Korhogo where Tom was staying, and while Tom wrote me a letter in the living room Yardjuma and Siata's marriage was consummated in the bedroom.

Before Siata's arrival in Kalikaha, Yardjuma fantasized happily to Tom about the joys of married life. These consisted of having someone to bring him water, cook his meals, and wash his clothes and sheets. He especially looked forward to coming home to a hot lunch.

"What about love?" Tom asked him.

Yardjuma took this to mean sex.

"You can get that anywhere," he replied.

"No, I mean something more than that. Warmth, companionship, trust."

Yardjuma looked at Tom blankly.

"I'm talking about friendship between husband and wife," Tom went on. "In a good marriage, the husband and wife are good friends. They enjoy each other's company."

Yardjuma's face was blank. "A good wife," he said finally, "is one who takes care of her husband. I'm African," he reminded Tom, and the conversation ended.

In June, Siata moved to Kalikaha and, unlike a traditional Senufo wife, shared Yardjuma's tumbledown house across from Chez Mariam. Their married life was stormy. Siata often refused to cook for Yardjuma or to sleep with him. And once, she ran away, getting four kilometers outside the village before Yardjuma caught up with her and convinced her to return.

When I arrived in August and met Siata, I looked hopefully for visible signs of this stubborn streak, but I couldn't detect any. She looked more like a shy, skinny-legged girl than a woman, with the exception of her breasts, which were so large and full that they looked out of proportion to the rest of her thin body.

One night we heard that a guest had arrived at Yardjuma's, a friend from his native village. Since Tom had been initiated into Yardjuma's *poro,* this man was one of his "brothers," so that night after dinner we walked across the village to greet him. He had come to deliver a message from Yardjuma's uncle. The uncle was angry and upset that Yardjuma had married Siata on his own, and the family planned to send him a new wife from his own village.

This proposal seemed rather late to me, since Yardjuma had paid so much money and Siata was already pregnant. "They're angry because all my money will leave the village and go to Siata's family," Yardjuma told me. Knowing the way he ran his financial affairs and how little he gave Siata, I thought their concerns were considerably exaggerated.

"What if you took Siata to meet your mother?" I asked Yardjuma. "Maybe if she got to know Siata, she would change her mind."

Yardjuma laughed and rolled his eyes. "Oh, no, I couldn't do that. It would be a disaster. She would be very badly received. What kind of wife is she anyway?" Yardjuma went on. "She doesn't act as a hostess when guests come. She doesn't even offer my guests a drink of water. A good wife should sit a short distance away in case her husband or his guests need anything. But look where my wife is!" he said disgustedly, waving toward Mariam's porch, where Siata was playing cards with a group of children.

"She's only fourteen years old," I temporized.

"How old are American girls when they are married?" he asked me.

"Oh, eighteen at the youngest, usually they're at least twenty," I replied. I didn't say that I was twenty-seven and still not exactly married to Tom.

"A girl couldn't wait that long here," he replied. "But fourteen *is* young," he agreed. "Even here, girls don't marry until sixteen. She is just too young to be a good wife. She was born in a hospital!" He put an odd emphasis on the last word. "She's not like us," he repeated. "She was born in the hospital."

We come into the world in the hands of others and we leave carried in the hands of others, said one of the proverbs in our Dyula grammar book. In a hospital, the first hands would be those of a stranger. I didn't tell Yardjuma that in America, most people also die in a hospital and their bodies are washed and dressed by hands they have never known.

One Saturday, after a half-day of interviews, we were sitting at Yardjuma's around a bottle of Le Roi Valpierre, the red wine that is found everywhere in Ivory Coast, even at the bar in Kalikaha. The bottle has no cork, just a pop top, and rumor has it that it is shipped out of France as a powder and reconstituted on arrival in the former colonies. A bottle cost about a dollar and was considered quite a luxury in Kalikaha by everyone but Yardjuma, who viewed it as a necessity for survival.

"Think what you'd get in the States for a dollar," said Tom. "For the price it's not a bad table wine." Tom was painfully aware that we had a year of fieldwork ahead of us and wanted more than anything to somehow get through it, which swayed his judgment on the matter. I wasn't used to seeing Tom drink so much, and it made me uneasy.

"I need to drink wine because then I eat well," Yardjuma always told me. "It isn't good to be thin." Yardjuma was the proud owner of the only pot belly in Kalikaha.

"Why do whites always want to be thin?" Yardjuma once asked a French friend of ours, a tall, skinny veterinarian who lived in Korhogo.

113

"Because we're afraid to get old," he replied. "We think that being thin makes us look young."

As we sat in a circle drinking the wine, Tom leaned over to me and whispered that it would be a good time for me to present a small gift to Siata. Tom spoke for me, in the traditional Senufo way, saying that I was concerned about Siata's welfare and wanted to give her a gift of money so that she could buy something for herself at the market. He handed the money to the next man.

Carol, said the next man, had given this money to Siata so that she could go to the market and buy condiments to make flavorful sauces for her husband.

I groaned. By the time the speeches had gone all the way around the circle and the money had reached Siata, the men had turned my gift into a lecture. I had given the money, they said, to help Siata become a true wife, so that she would always respect Yardjuma and fulfill all her responsibilities to him. It was that old game we used to play when we were children—Gossip. One of us would start a phrase and at the end of the line we would laugh about just how distorted it had become. I wouldn't have blamed Siata if she had thrown the money into a well. All I had meant was for her to go to the market and buy herself a treat. But without an interpreter, I could not even tell her so.

The decline of Yardjuma's marriage was speeded up by an unexpected visit Siata's mother paid to Kalikaha one Saturday. She turned up unannounced with a determined tilt to her head and a defiant glint in her eye. She was a tall woman, ramrod straight, swathed head-to-

toe in expensive fabrics that were not the least bit faded.

After she left, Yardjuma was furious. "It was wrong of her to come here," he said.

"I thought it was nice of her to come," I replied. "She hadn't seen her daughter in four months."

"Exactly!" said Yardjuma, pouncing on my words. "It was too soon. She should have waited a year. That's the custom here." I never heard anyone else mention the year-long wait custom, but the men criticized Siata constantly after this visit because Siata's mother had "found out things." Even some of the older women upbraided Siata. What Siata's mother "found out" was that Yardjuma had twice left the village, for days each time, leaving Siata without food or money. Despite all the harping at Siata, Yardjuma's behavior was unjustifiable by everyone's standards.

Siata went home to her mother's to have her baby. Yardjuma said it was all for the best, since she was too lazy to do any work anyway, but it was clear that he had been bested by his fierce mother-in-law, and was just trying to save face. Everyone claimed that Siata would soon have the baby. This seemed odd to me. When I counted up the months since the day Tom had written me the letter while Yardjuma and Siata consummated their marriage on a borrowed bed, I came up with four. Siata was stick thin, except for her breasts, and barely showed.

About the same time, Lasungo was kicked out by his mother, Zele, for continuing to have an affair with a young married woman. Though Lasungo had lived in his own house for years, this meant that Zele would no longer cook for him. Lasungo and Yardjuma decided that they would cook and eat together in their own bachelor camp. Yardjuma was the only African man I ever knew that not only cooked but boasted publicly that he was good at it. The two friends put on a good face and declared good riddance to women.

What Yardjuma wanted to do, he told us one night when we were bored and went over to his house after dinner to be entertained by his monologues, was to find a girl who was free and with whom he had a mutual attraction. *"Le mariage américain, n'est-ce pas?"* Then he would go to her parents and ask permission to marry her. "They'll agree," he said confidently. "Then I'll tell Siata's mother that I've arranged a second marriage. She wants her daughter to be an only wife, and so she'll never stand for that. She'll ask for her back."

The whole thing would be over, except for the child, which was his main interest in the affair. He carefully sent small amounts of money to Korhogo each month so that if there was a custody dispute, he could claim that he had supported Siata during her pregnancy. This would give him an unquestioned right to the child, even if they were later divorced. "When the child is about two years old, Whoosh! I'll swoop down, take it, and give it to my mother to raise," he said. He didn't really care what happened to Siata. He would just as soon not be saddled with her.

"My mother was very unhappy when she heard about my marriage," he told us. "Even though I have a wife, I still suffer. She isn't a good wife, and my mother says that is the worst possible thing of all. If you were still alone and you suffered, that would be one thing. But to have a wife who doesn't provide well for you, doesn't cook meals on time, doesn't take care of you . . . that is terrible!" His mother thought he should leave Siata right away and marry a nice girl from their own village.

Yardjuma had other plans as well. His favorite involved Tom buying a tractor so that the two of them could go into business. Yardjuma had once worked as a tractor driver. They would charge the peasants high rates to plow their fields for them, and in a few years, they would both be millionaires. In fact, someone had come through Kalikaha with a tractor the previous spring and done exactly that. But the fields that had been mechanically plowed had all yielded badly, and those farmers who had borrowed money to rent the tractor's services were now deeply in debt. This didn't interfere with Yardjuma's fondness for this plan. Nor did he believe Tom for a minute when Tom assured him that he could no more afford a tractor than he could fly to the moon.

Another plan was that he would come to America with us and train to be a mechanic. "You'll have to learn English," I reminded him.

"That's no problem for me. When I had to work in Baule country, I learned Baule. There's no need to start now. It won't take me more than a month."

Once, after one of these discussions, he asked me, "Are there really black people in America?"

"Yes."

"How did they get there?" he wanted to know.

I told him about the slave trade.

"Do they speak Dyula?" he asked me.

I shook my head.

"Senufo?"

"No."

"Then they must have come from Ghana," he continued. "Do they speak Ghanaian languages?"

"They speak English like Tom and me. They're American."

"They don't speak any African languages?" he asked me incredulously.

"It's been too long since they were taken there," I answered, counting up the generations on my fingers.

He found this concept—of blacks who were American and spoke English—very hard to believe. Then another idea dawned on him, and he asked me, his voice rising excitedly, "Then you mean there are black women in America?"

"Lots of them," I said, laughing out loud.

"Would their parents agree to let me marry them if I asked?"

"If you want to marry an American woman, you'll have to convince her, not her parents," I told him.

Yardjuma was relieved. "Good," he said. "Then it won't be a problem."

"You don't know American women," I warned him gleefully. "It's not like here."

After this, Yardjuma was more interested than ever in coming to visit us in America, and would often talk about it. When I was irritated at him (I usually was), I would imagine this visit as a kind of revenge when Yardjuma would be entirely at my mercy, the way I was so often at his. What made me really mad was that although I adapted constantly, Yardjuma refused to even try our ways of doing things. If I offered him American food, he said in an insulted voice, as if I were trying to poison him, "Oh, no, I can't eat that. I'm not used to it. It would ruin my digestion." And to keep the peace and for the sake of Tom's work, I would fix him what he wanted, which usually involved more meat and more wine than what we were having. "It's important for my health to drink wine," Yardjuma always told me. "If I don't drink enough, I don't eat well. It isn't good to be thin."

But in America, at my house, he would have to adapt. Therein lay my pleasure in this fantasy. No,

Yardjuma, I imagined myself saying sweetly, there's no beer for breakfast. Would you like tea or coffee? And how about some scrambled eggs? They're very typically American.

One day, Yardjuma showed up for work late in the afternoon, dressed in his most resplendent outfit, a black pin-striped suit that had been one of the items in a large box of clothes given to us by American friends in Abidjan to distribute in the village. *"Voilà!"* Yardjuma had exclaimed when he put on this coat for the first time. "You see before you a minister of the cabinet!" For Donnisongui, there had been a navy blazer with gold buttons, which he wore proudly to every funeral in the region, looking like a handsome young football player because of his bulging shoulders. Yardjuma was very apologetic about being late for work. He had been to Korhogo to see Siata's family and was now officially divorced.

A short time later, Yardjuma heard that Siata had gone to the hospital to have the baby. He no longer cared about the child because Siata's mother had thwarted his claim by making it public that Siata was already pregnant when she married Yardjuma. This was what Yardjuma had never told us, and why the number of months never added up to nine when I counted them. This also explained why Siata's mother had been so anxious to marry her off. Ownership of the child was a moot point, for the baby did not live. Siata was fine, and her mother already had plans to marry her off to someone else, someone who more truly filled the description she had had in mind when she chose Yardjuma.

119

A SACK OF RICE

We HAD FINISHED DINNER, AND TOM AND I WERE SITTING on the porch talking to Donnisongui, as we did almost every night. "Saturday I won't go to my fields," he told us. "I'm going to the market to buy a sack of rice. There's nothing left in my granaries."

We were shocked. It was the end of August, and although the upland rice harvest was only a month away, Donnisongui's lush bottomland rice would not be harvested until December. They were just now transplanting the young seedlings into the swamp rice fields. Donni's family ate rice three times a day, and it would cost a great deal to feed them until the harvest was in.

When he had gone, Tom turned to me. "This is what we can do for Donnisongui. He needs our help now." Donnisongui had refused to accept any rent for his house, in part to outwit the chief, who insisted that he be paid one half of any rent Donni received. Therefore, we paid no rent and half of nothing being nothing, the chief never got a franc. Instead, we gave Donnisongui gifts from time to time. On Friday, we bought a fifty-kilogram sack of rice.

"When is the best time to present a gift?" we asked Yardjuma.

"When there are a lot of people around," he replied. "So that everyone will see what good people you are and so that you can receive a lot of thanks."

That night, when Donnisongui came in to greet us, we presented him with the sack of rice. He shook our hands over and over, called loudly for Little Beh to come and help him lift the sack to his shoulder, and carried it off to his family. Yardjuma needn't have worried about witnesses because Donnisongui announced to everyone within yelling range just where he had gotten the big sack of rice.

When he came back, Lasungo and Zana were finishing the thatch roof we had hired them to construct over part of our courtyard. This gave us an additional private space, shaded from the sun and protected from the rain. Tom made a trip to Chez Mariam, and we all sat under the new roof to celebrate its completion, sipping warm beers.

The kerosene light reflected softly off the walls, and the new space felt cozy and protected. Donnisongui and Tom sat on the bench, leaning comfortably against the wall. Lasungo and Zana squatted on their haunches because they were at the stage of *poro* where they weren't allowed to sit on chairs or even stools. Zeeay was at the same stage, but he was seated comfortably on a log, which he said didn't count, with a leftover vine from the construction wrapped rakishly around his head like a bandana.

121

"Do you go to America on an airplane?" Zeeay asked me in Dyula.

I nodded.

"Well, I'm going," he declared. "I'll earn lots of money and then"—his hand took off into the sky—"I'm going!"

"Tom's going to be a professor when he goes back," Donni said to Lasungo, his eyes gleaming proudly. "He'll make lots of money!"

"I won't really make a lot of money," Tom said to Donni.

Donni thought Tom was being modest. "Yes, you will. You'll be rich."

"Look at the schoolteachers here in the village," Tom replied. "They live comfortably, but they're not rich men."

Everyone agreed to this. "I want to be a professor because I can do what I like," Tom told them. "I can read, write, teach, I can study the things that interest me . . . and I can have long vacations in the summer."

"You are going to speak good Dyula when you leave here," Zeeay predicted. *Fort! Beaucoup!* But who will you speak Dyula with over there?"

"Carol, of course!" This reply made us all laugh. "There are some students from Ivory Coast where we live," Tom added. "At the university. I'll be able to speak Dyula with them."

This visibly surprised them. "That's the way to go to America," I said to Zeeay. "Study hard and go to the university. That's how those Ivorians got there."

Zeeay took this in quietly. His father, Doh, was not even sending him to grammar school, I realized after I had spoken. It wasn't his choice to make.

Donnisongui said something to Lasungo in Senufo

about Tom, obviously with pride. "Donnisongui says you are intelligent," Lasungo repeated in his broken French. "The whites are more intelligent than the blacks."

"It's not because he's white that he's intelligent," I said. "He's had lots of education. He studied hard for years and years."

"It's not the color of my skin," began Tom.

"We didn't mean just you," broke in Lasungo. "The whites—all of them—are more intelligent than the blacks."

"It's a matter of history and education," Tom began again. "Our cultural history is different from yours." But this was too complicated for them to understand in French and he didn't know how to say it in Dyula.

"Look," I said in Dyula. "There are Africans like Tom. Intelligent, educated ones. They come to America. They're professors at his university. They were his teachers."

This surprised them, and we all sat thinking in the half-light.

"Well, I'm going," Zeeay said again, zooming his hand into the sky and knocking his vine headdress askance. "Then I'll know everything. EVERYTHING. Evv-RY-thing!"

This certainty of Zeeay's made all of us burst out laughing, and the night ended on a comic note. But when I thought over the conversation, it didn't seem at all funny. It was the first of hundreds of these conversations, which made it impossible for me to forget the unequal relationship that exists between Africa and the West.

When the villagers called us intelligent, they credited us with knowledge and ingenuity that we did not possess, for they assumed that we understood the work-

123

ings of the marvelous mechanical trinkets we owned, as if we had invented them ourselves. Yardjuma's nephew, who was a high school student in Korhogo, told us that there had once been an American teacher at his school. "He was the most intelligent man I ever met," the nephew declared in an awestruck voice.

"How so?" I asked him.

"He had a small airplane," the nephew replied. "He would take it out on a field, and without ever touching the airplane, he could make it fly! I have never met anyone else as intelligent as that," he concluded.

The villagers knew how to make almost everything in their own environment. They made oil from wild nuts, rope from vines, and medicines from leaves. Even young boys knew how to make bricks out of mud and a house out of the bricks, which grass to gather for thatch and how to weave it into strips to create a roof. They credited us with the same intimate knowledge of our own possessions, but I could not possibly explain to them how our shortwave radio worked or what ingredients were used in making plastic.

Zeeay and Lasungo wanted "America," a glorious place they had created in their minds, a collage made up of radios and motorcycles and people who wore eyeglasses and drove tractors. Ironically, I wanted "Africa" in just the same way. My collage was made up of carved sculptures and brightly colored cloth and children raised communally.

But could either of us have what we sought? I could learn about Kalikaha. I could bring home, instead of souvenir masks, ways of doing things. I could learn to build an adobe house, to make pottery in the African way, to harvest rice, to dance at a funeral at dawn. But what did I really understand of their culture? And what did it really have to do with me? The villagers could not tell me who had witnessed my birth. They did not know where my father's family came from before Poland. Nor could they give me the closeness to my physical environment that they had with theirs—a closeness that deepened and enriched their everyday world. Another unsettling thought often haunted me—perhaps what I was learning about rituals and their meanings was equivalent to what the high school student had understood about his teacher and the airplane. Perhaps I had missed the point entirely and would never know it.

What about Zeeay and Lasungo? They sold their cotton to buy flashlights for new moon nights and matches to start fires. They had bicycles and kerosene lamps, but no running water, no electricity, no health care, no schooling—none of the truly valuable things our world has to offer. The modern world used their labor to grow cotton for its factories and gave them only a few trinkets in return.

At least, you might say that Zeeay and Lasungo had the old values: the tight fabric of the community, the sense of self-sufficiency from producing all they needed, the security that the woven network would hold their weight in times of need.

But they could not even count on that. I could see it unraveling at the edges. When Beh Tuo was initiated, he spent three months inside a small enclosure in the sacred grove with his age-mates, an experience that forged powerful bonds between the members of the group. Then the length of time was shortened to one month. Now the initiates spend two weeks together inside the grove.

Zeeay and Lasungo have their own fields and keep the money from the cotton they sell. They don't work for the elders in the big common fields that fed the entire village, as Beh Tuo did. Forced labor and forced cultivation ended the big fields because the French took so many of the men to work on roads and in the forests that the common fields could no longer be maintained. Nor could they manage to grow in the common fields, with so many men gone, the quota of grain and other produce the colonial state demanded. Now, everyone says that there is never quite enough to eat. The farmers grow cotton to have some cash, but in a bad year, although you can always sell the cotton, you still may not have enough food. In a bad year, the price of rice is high, and the cotton money won't buy enough. There are no more common granaries holding village reserves to feed the people in a hard year.

When Beh Tuo was young, seventy years ago, he invested his labor, giving it all to the elders, assuming that when he became an elder, he would receive the benefits of his investment. When the cold harmattan winds blew, Beh Tuo gathered firewood every day so that the elders could sit by a warm fire every night. Zeeay and Lasungo gather wood once a year and leave one piece by each elder's door in a symbolic gesture. When Zeeay and Lasungo are old, there may not be a *poro* group to show them even these token signs of respect.

Before I heard the people of Kalikaha tell their history, I thought of African peasants as people who had always been poor, who had lived always on the brink of famine. However, in Kalikaha, before forced labor and the demands of the colonial state took their toll, the villagers had enough to eat. It was not an easy life, and a bad harvest was always a possibility. There were dislocation and famine in times of war. When the French came, forcing villages to grow cotton for the textile industry in France and taking young men away from the villages to work on roads, regional famines occurred because the people who were left could not grow enough food. At the same time, the French brought peace to an area that had been decimated by the rival armies of Babemba of Sikasso and Samory Toure. After the French "pacified" the area, the people of Kalikaha were able to return home from a fortified village in the south where they had taken refuge from the bloodshed.

Beh Tuo mutters that he has been abandoned by the ungrateful young. Zeeay and Lasungo inherit neither the one world whole, nor a toehold in the other. Their grandfathers were beaten by the French if they refused to grow cotton. Not only were they forced to grow it, they had to grow it in rows, in the Western way, with no other crops planted between, although recent research has shown that the traditional system of intercropping in mounds was more efficient for their particular climate. Zeeay and Lasungo choose to grow cotton; it is the only way they know to acquire money. They grow it in rows and, barefooted, spray herbicides and dig fertilizers into soils ill-suited to their use. They sell their cotton harvest to the government cooperative at whatever price is offered. Even if their children go to school, Ivory Coast already has a surfeit of civil servants, and unemployment in the cities is high.

Sixty percent of the Ivorian population lives in rural areas and on farms, but the government continues agricultural policies similar to those that were begun under French colonial rule, encouraging export crops like cotton over food crops that could feed the people. The sack of rice that we bought for Donnisongui was printed with calligraphy that says it was grown in China.

127

The morning after the new roof was completed, I awoke to the sound of voices outside our house. Everyone has come to inspect our new addition, I thought to myself, but they'll just have to wait because I'm not opening the door one minute sooner than I have to. I lingered as long as possible over dressing.

When Tom pushed open the heavy wooden door, he nearly knocked down Donnisongui, who was waiting to thank us for the sack of rice. Then our neighbor Beh came to thank us and showered us with blessings, ending with "May Ancient Mother give you a harmonious marriage." Beh was one to appreciate that, since he and Sibatia were not on speaking terms. The chief of our quarter, who was both the head of the sacred grove and the land priest, thanked us formally on behalf of his lineage for what we had done for Donnisongui. Many other people were also waiting, not to see the new roof, as I had thought, but to thank us, giving us blessings for a long life and many children. I was surprised at how gratefully we were thanked by people who would never taste a grain of the rice in the sack that had come all the way from China.

Lasungo cemented the back courtyard, and while the cement was wet, Tom and I put our mark on Donnisongui's house—our own fetish, a shiny American quarter surrounded by a sunburst design of paper clips. We pressed it into the wet cement just outside the back door. "Look at this, Donnisong," I said. "Next year, when we're gone, you'll see this and you'll think of us."

He touched the quarter with the tip of one finger and nodded. I could see that the idea pleased him. But his face looked sad at the mention of our leaving, and he glanced at Tom with real tenderness. "When you go," he said seriously, "that won't please me at all. Not at all."

THE DRY SEASON

THE RAINY SEASON WAS ENDING. THE THUNDERSTORMS HAD become fewer and farther between, and when the wind did come up, hardly any rain came after it. I had not realized just how much the overcast skies had protected us from the sun. Now it beat down relentlessly, baking the red earth, and I was already soaked with sweat at nine every morning.

It was mid-October, and I was sitting on the bench under the mango tree on the funeral grounds. I had come up there because Tom was interviewing Beh Tuo at our house, and as soon as his questions touched on *poro,* I had been politely asked to leave. Next to me on the bench was the other Beh, our closest neighbor Beh Silue (Siluay), who was carefully sorting through a basket of kola nuts he had bought the day before at the weekly market in the nearest large town. Beh, who was no longer young, told me that he had ridden there on his bicycle, leaving

Kalikaha early in the morning and returning at dusk, a trip of about thirty kilometers each way over rutted dirt roads.

This particular market took place every six days according to the Senufo calendar, which has a six-day week. It was held on Wednesday one week, Tuesday the next, Monday the week after that. This meant that if we wanted to go to the market, we had to figure out first of all which day was market day. Not every town used the Senufo week, however. Kalikaha held its market on a seven-day system, every Saturday.

Beh carefully turned over several nuts before he chose a large red one, split it cleanly with his fingernail, and offered me half.

"No, thank you. I don't take kola."

"You don't *take* tobacco," he corrected me. "You don't *chew* kola. And you don't *drink* cigarettes."

I repeated Beh's lesson appreciatively. He always spoke Dyula slowly with me and had a knack of introducing a new word just when I would best understand its meaning. Beh and Donnisongui were my best teachers, so I often sought them out for conversations. Yardjuma, who could have explained things in French, was impatient with my constant questions. He seemed to think I asked them for the sole purpose of making him work more hours each day, and he would quickly turn the conversation back to village gossip.

"Kola is too . . ." I puckered up my mouth in a sour face and looked at Beh for help.

"Bitter," he said in Dyula, nodding in approval when I repeated the phrase.

The villagers nearly all chewed kola for the stimulant the nuts contain. They said that kola made you forget how hot the sun was and how thirsty you were. I found it too bitter, nor could I manage to spit out the juice that accumulated in my mouth the way they did, neatly, aiming at the ground ten feet away and channeling a stream of red juice through a gap in their teeth. They were amazingly good spitters. When I tried it, the red spittle ran down my chin and the pulp spattered my feet.

I had come up to the mango tree feeling left out and rather sorry for myself because I couldn't hear Beh Tuo's stories about his *poro* initiation in the old days. But Beh's companionable small talk and his obvious pleasure in my company soothed my disappointment. Every morning, as soon as I opened the door, Beh now called out my name as well as Tom's. "Carol, did you spend the night in peace?" "Peace only," I called back. And every night when he walked by our house on his way to take his evening meal with his brothers, he invited us to join him with the phrase, "Let's go eat." *"I ni chay,"* we replied. "We're full, thank you." When he returned a short while later, he gave us a blessing which meant "May we digest well the food we've eaten," and we both answered *"amina"* and tapped our foreheads to help the blessing sink in.

The night before, under the influence of a liter of *chapalo* that we had given him as a gift, Beh had made an unusual visit to the inside of our house. He only did this on the rare occasions when he was drunk. He had given an emotional speech about how much better life was now that we lived next to him. Our presence brought a constant stream of visitors to the courtyard. "This pleases me," he said over and over, grabbing my arm for emphasis. "It is not good for a person to sit alone at night."

His unusual display surprised me because he himself never joined the group that gathered in front of our porch every night. He listened to us from his porch and occasionally called over a comment. I thought of him as gentle but unsociable and probably too shy to join us. Only later did I understand the true reason for his solitude and why these words of his were so heartfelt. For the past five years, Beh had suffered from seizures, and the villagers had shunned him because they thought the disease was contagious. This was why Sibatia refused to sleep with him, and why she kept her chubby little boy carefully out of Beh's reach.

Yardjuma and I, for the first time since my arrival, were on excellent terms. No longer did he mutter resentfully, "Oh. So Carol's coming?" whenever I went with them to the bush. He had even stopped going on and on about the magnificent funeral he and Tom had attended before I arrived, compared to which the recent ones at Bohdanon and Kalikaha were "nothing."

The reason for this sudden turnabout was simple. I had rescued him from a miserable situation, and he was grateful. For several days, he had complained of a toothache that kept him from eating, drinking, or talking. "Life is no longer worth living," he muttered pitifully. "I may as well be dead." On Saturday, he drooped all morning, holding his chin in his hands and moaning melodramatically while Tom coaxed him through the interviews. It wasn't his tooth that was the problem, he insisted, but a bone that had gotten stuck between two back teeth when he was eating fish. Done in by your own gluttony, I said to myself, not without some satisfaction.

Tom sat Yardjuma down on the porch of our house

with a length of our dental floss and demonstrated what to do. But Yardjuma was not used to the floss and couldn't manage it. Tom tried to do it for him, but his hands were too large and he couldn't reach back far enough. Drawn in by the challenge, I offered to try. I flossed and flossed where he had indicated, but nothing came out. "Are you sure it's a fish bone?" I asked him. I suspected that Yardjuma had a rotten tooth and just didn't want to admit it.

Yardjuma was adamant. "This bone is ruining my life. If you can just get the bone out," he assured me, "I'll be my usual self again at once."

Although I wasn't sure that was the result I wanted, I sawed away. Yardjuma moaned and groaned as if I were killing him, and sure enough, a tiny bone poked its way out just far enough for me to grab it. "The whites are *so* intelligent," Yardjuma said with satisfaction when I handed him the bone.

He insisted that we come with him to his house, where he actually bought me a bottle of wine, the highest favor he could bestow. He also gave me a smoked goose leg from a wild goose Zana had killed the day before, a rare delicacy in the village. In fact, when Zana reached the village with his kill, Yardjuma had come running to our house for an advance on his salary. "Can you loan me some money? Zana has killed a *renard!*" he told us excitedly. "I have never eaten *renard.* They say it's the most delicious of all meat."

"A *renard?*" Tom repeated, pulling on his shoes. "I've never heard of an African fox. This sounds interesting!" He grabbed his mammal book as we ran out the door.

When we arrived, the two wild geese were lying on

the ground. "Where's the *renard?*" asked Tom. Yardjuma pointed to the geese. "Ohhhh," we both said together. "You mean *canard.*"

"*Canard?*" repeated Yardjuma. "Oh, yes, that's right. *CAnard.*" He shrugged. Who cared about two similar-sounding French words when a gourmet meal was at stake? Actually, *canard* means duck, which, according to Tom's bird book, this was not. At any rate, we didn't get any goose ourselves because Yardjuma had already spoken for one and Mama had taken the other. If it hadn't been for the dental floss, we would never have tasted smoked wild goose.

Mariam's year was up, and she had gone back to Korhogo. Her replacement, Mama, the senior wife, was considerably older, a short woman whose plump contours showed that it had been a long time since she had worked in the fields. She hired young boys to gather firewood and weed her fields for her, and she refused to sleep in the back room of the bar, as Mariam had done. She had a cement house built at right angles to the bar, where she lived with her youngest child, a little girl of about six. Yardjuma told me in an awed voice that she was very intelligent. I liked to watch her, selling the fried doughnuts she made every morning, giving advice to the young people, chastising the men who were too drunk, trading with the hunters for the choicest cuts of meat and with the traveling cloth merchants for a bright new pattern. She seemed to be always in command of the situation. Best of all, in my opinion, she was not the least bit afraid of me and treated me like a younger woman of equal status, chastising me because I called her Mama instead of Madame like everyone else.

It was Saturday, market day in Kalikaha, and soon the extension agent from a nearby village called Behvogo dropped in at Chez Mama's, and when he had heard the story about the fish bone from Yardjuma, he also bought me a bottle of wine. There were speeches and blessings all around. As we drank I saw a familiar figure coming down the road on a bicycle, a small man in a baggy suit coat and black felt hat. It was Wangolo, a friend of Yardjuma's who was also from Behvogo. Wangolo was a woodcarver as well as a farmer, and he had recently given me, as a welcoming gift, two small stools, each carved out of a single piece of wood. In thanks for the stools, I now bought a bottle of wine for Wangolo and made a speech about how much we needed the stools because of our many visitors. Wangolo had delivered the stools about two weeks before, so the timing of my thanks was just right. I was feeling rather pleased with myself for having mastered this much, at least, of Senufo etiquette, and unlike Yardjuma's other friends, I very much liked Wangolo, who hid under his rumpled felt hat and gave me occasional shy smiles. Yardjuma insisted that I eat another goose leg and some smoked fish while he repeated once more to Wangolo the story of how, with a piece of string, I had miraculously saved him and restored to him his capacities. Now once more, he could eat, drink, and spit. My head was whirling from the wine and the heat, and I felt as if I were on top of the world. I was tempted to quote Yardjuma. "Now all my problems are over!"

"If Tom is a Silue, what's your family name?" the extension agent asked me.

There are only five family names in Senufo, and Tom had adopted Silue because it was Donnisongui's name and because our quarter, Pempoho, was the home of the Silues, who were the traditional chiefs of Kalikaha.

"I'm a Silue, too," I said, "because I live in Pempoho."

"No, no!" this extension agent said emphatically. "A Silue can't marry a Silue. You can be a Yeo like me." Later, I realized that he had only been teasing me, but at the time I believed him.

Wangolo, the quiet woodcarver, was a Soro, as was Yardjuma. "Be a Soro," he urged me shyly, smiling at the prospect.

"Then we'll all be related," said Yardjuma magnanimously, gesturing to me, to Wangolo, and to himself. "All one family!"

"No, no, take Yeo!" insisted the extension agent drunkenly. We were all tipsy and the hot sun made me dizzy. I didn't want to be related to Yardjuma, nor did I like the sound of Yeo, which rhymed with *toe.* I was disappointed that I couldn't be a Silue like Donnisongui and gentle old Beh and nearly everyone else in Pempoho. It was the only opportunity I would ever have to choose my own relatives, and given my pick, I tried to think of another family to whom I would like to belong.

"I'll be a Tuo," I said quickly, to end the argument. If I couldn't be a Silue, then I would join Beh Tuo's family, for he fulfilled all my expectations of the dignified, wise African elder. Almost all, that is. His abiding interest in the necklines of my T-shirts still took me aback. Every time he sat down, gathering his robes around him, I expected to see the children come running from all directions for folktales.

"If she's a Tuo," Tom asked, "what's her name in Dyula?"

In Kalikaha, the five Senufo names were translated into Dyula ones, in an odd exception to the rule that one never translates proper names. In the Dyula part of the village, Tom Silue became Tom Kone (Konay).

"Traore!" yelled Yardjuma. "In Dyula, Tuo becomes Traore," and for some reason, they all burst out laughing. "Tom Kone and Carol Traore!" They began to joke in Senufo, and I heard over and over "Kone" and "Traore" and then peals of laughter.

"What's so funny?" Tom and I kept asking, but each time one of the three would start to explain, he would collapse in laughter as soon as he got to the two names.

It turned out, when they calmed down enough to explain it, that there were "joking bonds" between the two families, who were old rivals, and that they got along only by constantly teasing each other. "A Kone married to a Traore?" yelled Yardjuma incredulously, and once again, they all burst out laughing.

My choice of a name gave enormous entertainment to the Dyula part of the village, especially the Kones and Traores. "Traore *muso!*" (Traore woman) they would yell at me heartily whenever we walked into the Traore quarter of the village. "Where did you get that Kone for a husband and how much did you pay for him? You know that the Kones used to be our slaves."

"No, no," Tom would return. "It was the Traores that were the slaves of the Kones." But he couldn't put up a real fight alone. He was completely outnumbered. He bided his time until we crossed the alley into Konera. "Kone!" they would yell triumphantly at the sight of Tom. "How much did you pay for that Traore woman?" Tom and I were soon as bad as the rest of them and would start it ourselves as soon as we walked into "our" quarter and were surrounded by "our" relatives.

Even months after we left Kalikaha, we were in Bamako, Mali, where Bamana, the mother tongue of Dyula, is spoken. We walked into a shop and greeted the shopkeeper in Dyula. "What are your family names?" he asked us. Knowing that our real names would mean nothing, we gave Kone and Traore. He looked worriedly from one of us to the other, as if a fight might break out at any moment, destroying his small shop. "It's okay," I assured him quickly. "We get along."

"Well, if that's true, it's the first time ever!" he said in amazement, clasping his hands and looking upward, as if only Allah could be his witness to this strange event.

Hot winds blew all day long and the nights were cold, colder than I had ever imagined it would be in Kalikaha. This was the harmattan season, when hot desert winds blow from the Sahara during the day and bring cold desert nights. The winds dried our lips and our skin, blew dust everywhere, into every crevice of the house and onto every surface. Although the dust made us sneeze, we welcomed the coolness. But the villagers suffered from the wind and the cold. The harmattan winds bring disease, they told us grimly.

I had brought no clothes for cold weather, so when a used-clothing vendor passed through the village and spread his wares below the mango tree on the funeral grounds, I bought a red cotton turtleneck for a dollar, an American export that, like me, had found its way to Kalikaha. These clothes were probably donated by some American church group to be given away in Africa. But instead, they were sold at the dock in Abidjan in one-ton bales and then eventually bought by traveling peddlers. There was an entire section of the Korhogo market devoted to these hand-me-downs.

The range of T-shirts in the village was astonishing: from Kamp Wanakee Staff to the Deegan Funeral Chapel Bowling Team. One young man had a bright yellow one with a ringing phone on it that said in English, "It's for you!" And an old woman had a T-shirt which proclaimed in gold glittery script, BEE GEES. The white and pink sleeveless shells with stand-up collars that had been popular when I was in junior high school were common. The fabric, which had not a natural fiber in it anywhere, stood up amazingly well to the rigors of work in the fields. The women wore the zippers in the front.

Fanta sometimes came to work in a Girl Scout uniform, complete with troop number and shoulder patches, just like the one I had worn at her age. Remembering the skills I had laboriously practiced—lashing logs together to make furniture, baking meatloaf in underground pits—all a kind of play at rustic life, I would watch her approach in the green dress with the huge basin of heavy water balanced on her small head. A whole group of men wore nothing but used American raincoats, their bare legs sticking out underneath. Even if you wear them to the fields, they don't rip, they told me.

The nights were so cool that I was glad that we had finally given in and bought a woven blanket from Bazoumana the weaver, that old scoundrel. Yardjuma said that everyone was talking badly about Bazoumana. Here, we had bought an expensive blanket from him so that he could buy a sheep for Tabaski, the Moslem holiday when every family kills a sheep. "And did he send over a morsel of mutton for you, his enablers? Not, not even a chop!" said Yardjuma. "This ungrateful behavior of his I find personally despicable!" And for once, Don-nisongui agreed with him.

The hot winds brought not only dust and cool nights on their currents, they also brought migrants, the dry-season birds that had been in Kalikaha when Tom first arrived. The air was filled with hornbills, a bird the Senufo often depict in their carvings. I quickly learned to recognize their long bills and crazy looping flight. The carmine bee-eaters filled the trees with shimmering red. One day, as we drove along the road I saw my first Abys-sinian Roller, the bird that Tom said reminded him of me. It flew up from a marshy spot and landed in a tree near us, even more beautiful than the picture in Tom's book. Its wings were a bright deep blue, its back burnt orange, its tail very long and gracefully split. A sociable bird, it perched right above us on the road, seemingly un-afraid. The first time Tom had seen one, he had gotten off his moped and approached it cautiously. The bird's nutmeg-colored breast and deep blue wings reminded Tom of colors I liked to wear. And its uncanny willing-ness to let Tom stand quite near and pour out his feelings convinced Tom that the Abyssinian Roller must be a manifestation of my spirit in bird form. Once we came to know these birds, we learned that it was part of their nature to watch over roadsides and to let humans ap-proach them. It was their habit to fly up from their per-ches, spread their tails, flash their colors, and then settle again on the same branch. But knowing this did not make us marvel at them any less. Whenever I spotted one, or a pair cavorting, my heart leapt up, and I felt that they were signaling to me.

THE COTTON HARVEST

"GREETINGS ON YOUR RETURN FROM THE FIELDS," I called to Donnisongui as he rolled his bicycle past our porch late one afternoon.

"*Mbaaa,*" he replied.

"How are the people at the fields?"

"They are well, they all greet you," he answered, smiling.

"And your fields? Are they well?"

"Very well." Donni drew himself up. "Tomorrow the work party will be in my field to harvest my cotton."

"We're coming, too," I told him.

"That will please me," he said.

It was relentlessly hot when we finished the interviews at midmorning. The motorcycle ride to Donni's field brought some relief, since the movement of the bike created a breath of wind that lifted my hair away from my face and fanned my hot forehead.

When we reached Donnisongui's fields, the first thing I saw was his ox cart piled high with cotton, and on top, crowing at the sight of us, were his two children and his niece, jumping up and down to flatten the load. Twenty people moved up and down the rows, their fingers closing over one white boll at a time. Never before had I seen cotton harvested from green plants. The fields near Memphis, where I grew up, are sprayed with herbicide before the harvest so that the leaves turn brown and die.

No one wanted to order us around, so Tom and I stood awkwardly at the edge of the field, unsure what to do. After what seemed like a very long time, a woman called my name, and I saw Noupka, the young wife of our neighbor Domingeh, gesturing at me. Don't just stand there, her gesture plainly said. Follow me!

She led the way to the far side of the field and put me on the opposite side of the row, across from her. Her fingers closed over a boll, plucked it out clean in one sure movement, and then went on to the next. When her palm was full, she emptied the handful of fluff into the fertilizer sack that she carried on a strap over her shoulder.

"I ni chay!" called the women near me when I began to pick. *"I ni baara!"*

"N-say!" I returned happily. I could hear them exchanging comments and laughing. When I paused and looked back, I saw Tom standing in the very middle of the field, gesturing with his hands full of white fluff as he tried to pick cotton and ask questions at the same time.

Our neighbor Zanapay was harvesting the row behind me. *"I ni chay,* Carol! Thank you!" he called over. *"I ni chay,* Zanapay!" I called back. My cheeks were flushed and the sweat streamed down my face. I tried to keep up with Noupka's quick hands, but I had trouble getting the bolls out cleanly like she did, in a single pull.

When we were about halfway up the row, a little girl came out to us, bringing Noupka's baby because she was crying. Noupka put down the sack to nurse her, and I took it up. I had thought to myself while watching Noupka that the bag could not be too difficult to carry because it was already so full that it dragged on the ground. However, the large bag was extremely heavy, and although I didn't have to hold up its weight, I had to drag it after me with every movement I made. Not only that, but the bulky sack made it very difficult to maneuver in the small space between the rows.

My shoulders ached from the weight of the sack, and I looked longingly at the shade offered by a big tree at the end of the row. *"I ni chay,* Carol," Noupka would say every few moments, as if to encourage me. She moved faster than ever without the sack, despite her baby, which she tied in a cloth on her back and then swung around underneath her so that it could nurse as she worked. Finally, we reached the edge of the field. The shade draped us in welcome coolness, and we stood within it and helped another woman finish her row, loath to go back out into the sun. When the row next to us was finished, Noupka thrust her baby into my arms, threw the now-enormous sack up onto her head, and started off at a great clip for the cart. Tom was already there, and he laughed when he saw me hurrying to keep up, wearing his baseball cap, a baggy sundress, tennis shoes, and carrying Noupka's baby on my hip. When Noupka had emptied the sack onto the pile of cotton, she tied her baby onto her back and went off to do another row.

Donnisongui led us under a large tree and showed us the enamel basins full of fried fish and *toh,* a sort of corn pudding, that the women in his family had prepared for the workers' lunch. It didn't look like very much food for the work party in the field to me. "You've worked. You can't leave without eating lunch. Stay and eat," Donni urged us. But we declined. I knew that we would be given the largest portions and the choicest bits of fish. And I couldn't bear that, after picking only one row. Besides, to be truthful, neither of us liked *toh*.

A few days later, Tom was interviewing old Menergay about his farming activities when Noupka walked by with her baby. I was sitting on the concrete tomb of a former chief; the rectangular wall made a convenient bench. Noupka and I exchanged warm smiles, and she stopped. She handed me her baby, and the little girl, who was about seven months old, played happily on my lap. Her skin, always kept clean and oiled by Noupka, was as smooth as cocoa butter, and holding her soft little body warmed me all over. It occurred to me as I cuddled the baby that it must show on my face how much I longed for intimacy like this, how much I missed it. Perhaps the men were oblivious, but I knew that the women studied me closely all the time. And at that moment, as I held the child and felt that soft baby's skin against mine, I couldn't hide my feelings from the women. I couldn't pretend to be happy. I knew that my loneliness was written all over my face.

From that day on, a bond existed between Noupka and me. But outwardly very little changed. Sometimes, Noupka stopped by the house to greet us, and when she did, she always handed me her baby for a few minutes. The baby, in what seemed to me an odd reversal, was named Mama.

It was a busy time for Tom. Corn and rice were

being harvested, and we had to be everywhere at once in order to measure the yields. Tom depended a great deal on the farmers' cooperation to gather this information. Some, like Lonala's family, did everything they could to help the work along. When they were ready to harvest a remote field and couldn't find us, they carefully placed one pebble into a pot for each basket of corn that they harvested. Tom was able to measure one basket of their harvested corn, and by counting the pebbles, to reconstruct their harvest. That old scoundrel Bazoumana, on the other hand, harvested Tom's sample plots without telling him and added extra corn and rice to the piles of harvested food from the sample plots to disguise how poor his harvest had been. This ploy was obvious because we had seen the thin scraggly plots just a week before the harvest, so we knew that the one-meter plots could not have miraculously produced so much food in a week. Meanwhile, in his gruff voice, he was always asking us for something. "You didn't bring me any sugar?" he would say, his peg tooth protruding wildly from his mouth as he talked. "Not even a can of Nescafé?" He had a passion for coffee, which he looked to us to satisfy. Bazoumana had added to his yields because Yardjuma, it turned out, had told the farmers in the study group that there would be a prize for the best farmer at the end. Now that the villagers spoke to us directly, we were finding out just what Yardjuma had promised to the members of Tom's study to gain their cooperation. Tom was furious at Yardjuma and worried about how this would affect the outcome of the study. "The peasants are stubborn," said Yardjuma. "You have to promise them things. It's the only language they understand. But don't worry, we won't have to really pay up. When the work is finished, we can just leave."

145

Yardjuma, during this period of hard work, taught me a valuable lesson. "Express your negative feelings," was a Berkeley battle cry, but despite years of residence in Berkeley and many dollars spent on therapy, I stubbornly hung on to my antiquated notions of stoicism. I put great value on accepting whatever came along. Yardjuma, however, changed all that. "Don't say you're okay if you're not," my Berkeley friends always said to me. But somehow it took Yardjuma to bring this lesson to life. In only a few months with him, I made more progress than I had made in years of Berkeley life. Although I saved the word *suffer* for extreme events, Yardjuma used it daily. He suffered a great deal and was extremely vocal about these sufferings.

"We really work hard," Yardjuma would say, when we finished measuring a field. "And in this heat. *Ma vielle,* we have really suffered today. It's such a hardship this work we do. If I hadn't had that wine before lunch, I couldn't have stood it." Tom always winced when he heard his beloved research called a hardship.

Although we did work hard measuring fields, visiting Fulani herders, and chasing down people to be interviewed, our work seemed easy compared to that of the peasants. I could not easily forget that one hour we spent harvesting cotton in the suffocating heat at noon. But after months with Yardjuma, Tom and I finally relaxed our Spartan philosophy and began to suffer, too. Although I still couldn't bring myself to say these things in English, I felt a certain abandon in French. After Yardjuma was gone, we would commiserate together in French. "Oh, we certainly did suffer today," we would say, imitating Yardjuma's tragic tones. "What hardship it was to measure that corn field. *Comment!* And we had to wade through the mud to get to that herd. And then, just when we thought we were done for the day, Bazoumana came to visit. *Ma vielle!*"

One night, nearly a month after the cotton harvest in Donnisongui's field, I was reading next to the kerosene lantern on the porch when Noupka came by. I had given up the idea of getting closer to the women and resigned myself to the company of Tom, Donnisongui, and Yardjuma.

"Carol, we're going to pound the corn now for the workers tomorrow. Are you coming?" She spoke matter-of-factly, as if I always joined the women. But in fact, it was the first time I had been invited to take part in any women's activities. As I had done before when presented with Noupka's matter-of-factness, I got up and went without thinking too much about it. We walked together to Doh's house, only a few feet away. It was his field they would harvest the following day, and so it was up to his wife to cook *toh* for the work party.

The mortar was a hollowed-out tree stump that stood thigh-high. "Carol and I will pound," Noupka said calmly. We stood on opposite sides of the mortar and alternated strokes. One, two. One, two. One, two. One, two, three. One, two, three. A third woman had joined us without skipping a beat. Then a fourth. We four pounded our pestles into the mortar's open mouth, one after the other, keeping up a fast tempo that only lagged when I waited too long to strike my turn. One-two-three-four-*thunk*. One-two-three-four-*thunk*. I found it difficult to keep up with the rhythm as they did, always in perfect time, their pestles coming down just as the woman before raised hers up. Every now and then I missed my beat, and we all knocked into one another and ended up with pestles entangled in the mortar. When this happened, they laughed good-naturedly and started the

147

rhythm over. For the first time, I understood why the women often thunked their pestles against the side of the mortar as they swung them up. This extra beat gave the other women a signal and made the rhythm easier to follow, especially important since we were working in the dark. I put my total concentration on trying to keep my place in the sequence and to strike down as hard as they did. When Noupka struck down with her pestle, I could feel the heavy wooden mortar shudder with the blow.

In a few minutes, a woman from the group that was gathered around us came up behind me. Placing her hand lightly beside mine on the pestle, she struck once with me and then took over, spelling me without missing a single beat, entering into the rhythm with the same nonchalance with which we used to enter a moving jump rope when we were girls.

The women who weren't pounding gathered around me. They examined my long-sleeved plaid shirt, rubbed my arms, commenting on the hair, and then discovered on my wrist a copper Sando bracelet I had bought at the Korhogo market. Finely modeled on the antique Senufo bracelet were a mother and child.

"Why do you want to wear that?" they asked me.

"I think it's pretty," I answered.

"That? Pretty?" They laughed. "We think this is pretty," they said, pointing to my wristwatch. They called more women over and showed them the bracelet, as if to gather more witnesses to my folly. "You could really hit Tom with it," one of the women joked, and they mimed a fight between us in which I hit Tom with the heavy copper bracelet and laid him out cold.

When the laughter died down, Noupka got my attention. "Does Tom beat you?" she asked me.

"No!" I replied quickly, in a horrified voice. Noupka looked skeptical. "He doesn't beat you?"

"Absolutely not-*dé*!"

"Why not?" she asked.

I stood there, frozen for a long second, limited by my lack of Dyula words. What could I say? "If he tries to beat me," I said finally, "I'll leave. I'll be gone-*dé!*" And the vehemence in my voice made them all laugh loudly.

Although my tone of voice amused them, they didn't seem particularly convinced by it. Beating your wife was viewed as one of the prerogatives, even one of the duties, of a husband. The most popular song during our stay began with a conversation between a young woman and her boyfriend. He asks her why she didn't come to their rendezvous the day before. She says she was too busy. "Too busy?" he yells angrily. "Too busy!" A loud slap rings out and she cries out in pain. There are the sounds of more blows and her cries and wails. Then the song begins. She sings to the young man and asks why he will never come into her home and greet her family as he ought to do. Everywhere we went in Korhogo and later in Abidjan, this song poured out of the loudspeakers and out of the cassette players and radios people carried. I heard it on buses, in the discos, at cafés, at parties, in the markets. And each time I heard the cheerful, catchy notes that began the song, I winced, knowing that the slap and subsequent blows were coming.

I detested the song because I thought that it idealized violence. Now every young man will be hitting his girlfriend at the first opportunity, I said to myself in disgust. But an African woman friend tells me that the song had a very different effect. The song is a warning to young girls, says my friend. The young man refuses to come to the girl's house and greet her family because, if she becomes pregnant, he does not want them to know who he is. "It couldn't have been me," he will say. "Have you ever seen me at your house?" The young girls all heard this song, my friend explains, and they learned to beware of a young man who would not take any responsibility toward them. The young men all heard it, too, and she feels that although there are always a few who will take the song as a license to act badly, most understood its message as a denunciation of this type of violence. My friend says that young people were strongly influenced by the song, and that young men now are more likely to enter a girl's home and be introduced to her family.

This act of greeting the family goes deeper than mere etiquette. Once the boy begins to call on the family, he enters into a relationship with them, and interactions in the city then become more like those in a small village, where no one is ever anonymous. This mutual recognition brings with it responsibility, for the boy now has his own reputation and the good name of his family to uphold. He will have to accept the consequences of his actions toward the girl, just as he would in a small village, where everyone is linked in one way or another.

Interestingly, it was Yardjuma who first called this song to my attention one day as we stood measuring a large field. "There's a new song out that will interest you, Carol," he told me. "It's women's music."

I was intrigued and gladly loaned Yardjuma my tape recorder so that he could tape the song for me. I was shocked when I turned it on and heard the simulated beating of a young girl. Whether or not this song was "women's music," as Yardjuma suggested, I didn't know because I wasn't sure if the popular woman singer who recorded the song had written it or not. Yardjuma claimed she must have because no man would say the things she did about marriage. The part he liked was the sentimental refrain in which she longed for a return to the simpler, happier times now gone; he hummed and whistled it constantly. It wasn't women's music as I knew it in Berkeley, but the experience it depicted was certainly women's experience.

No one knew this more intimately than Noupka. Her husband drank whenever he could afford a bottle of wine, and from inside our house, I often heard him raging at his two wives. No one intervened, but he was not respected because he drank away all his money and could not feed his family.

When all the corn had been pounded and then sifted by two old women with sieves, and when what wouldn't go through had been pounded again, we had two large basins of corn flour. It amazed me, sifting the fine corn flour through my fingers (I had ended up sifting with the old women, a task I could manage better than pounding), that in just two hours of work, with only wooden pestles and mortars and a few round sieves, we had taken dried corn and made flour!

"The work is finished," Noupka said to me. The women began to bid one another good night. When I stepped outside the circle of women, Noupka was waiting for me.

"Where are you going?" I asked her.

"To take you home," she replied, taking my hand gently.

We walked the short distance hand in hand. As soon as we reached my house, most of the other women from the work party also arrived and surrounded Tom, who was reading on the porch. Tom looked taken aback, and the women started to tease him. "You go and make some friends and what happens?" Tom said in mock horror. "They all come to visit!"

Only later, when I went in to bed, did I notice that my hand was bleeding. The wooden pestle, worn smooth as glass, had given me blisters, which had quickly been rubbed raw. But in my excitement at working with the women, I had not even felt the pain.

The next morning, before she left for the fields, Sibatia came in to tell me good morning. "I'll see you when I get back from the fields," she called to me as she left. It was the first time she had ever come inside our house.

After that, Noupka came for me whenever there was a work party. I sifted corn and pounded a bit, but I could never harden my hands enough to pound for very long. Often, the women worked until midnight to prepare the large lunch that the cooperative work party would eat the next day. Teasing me was their favorite new diversion to speed the work along. My hair, my pants, the way I spoke English with Tom, all of it was comical to them. Noupka could do an imitation of me speaking English, with the inflections so close to my own style of speaking and yet no words, that even I would burst out laughing. I got back at her by imitating the nasal sounds of Senufo to howls of appreciative laughter. We compared everything about ourselves and made the differences into the subject of a hundred comic pantomimes.

Noupka was dark, almost blue-black, tall and slender, with a long muscular neck, strong shoulders, and a beautifully shaped head. Her features were too strong to be pretty; they were almost masculine; her nose and lips were wide. One night, Noupka examined my nose. "It's very long," she said seriously, with a note of sympathy. I imitated her flat nose, pressing mine in with my finger.

"That's right," she said, approvingly. "Mine's not long. It's nice."

After the work parties, the women always accompanied me back to our house. "These friends of yours always visit *en masse!*" Tom would say with pretended terror when he was completely surrounded by joking women.

One night, I sat up late with Noupka and Sibatia in our courtyard, feeding the fire under the pot of corn beer they were brewing together to sell. Tom and Beh had long since gone to bed. "Are you pregnant yet?" Noupka asked me.

"No," I replied. I tried to explain that I did not want to have a child just yet. I gave as my reason that I was alone in Kalikaha, far from my mother and my woman friends. For this reason, I preferred to wait, I told them. They got very serious when I said this. Noupka gave me a quick intent look. "Can you do that?" she asked me. "You really can?"

Noupka was silent, sitting and looking at her fire. She never asked me anything more about it. Later, I realized that she probably thought I had some powerful fetish to prevent pregnancy and that it was too secret to discuss. She wasn't far off, although I would have tried to talk about it had she asked. At that time, I had come to think of my diaphragm as my personal fetish, something that protected me. Sometimes, when I saw it sitting by the bed in its case, I felt like laying sacrifices of chicken and kola nuts before it.

Sibatia fastened on another aspect of my excuse: my aloneness. "Noupka's your woman friend," she protested. "She would be with you when you gave birth." Noupka indicated Mama, who was asleep in my lap. "Well, anyway, you've found a girlchild now," she said, in that matter-of-fact way of hers. "From now on, Mama is your girlchild, too."

LEARNING DYULA
FROM SCRATCH

I FEEL LIKE THE HARE IN A DYULA FOLKTALE WHO ASKS THE hyena to "throw me as hard as you can into that field of tall grasses, to clean the sand off my fur." This sounds like a good idea to the hyena, who is about to make his lunch off the hare, and he gladly complies. The hare, an ancestor of the Brer Rabbit I knew from childhood, hops off happily through the tall grass. Just throw me into a strange land where no one speaks English and give me a small notebook and a pencil. Nothing will make me happier than to have to learn the language from scratch.

During the year I spent traveling with a backpack through the Mediterranean countries and North and East Africa, I developed my own method for learning languages quickly. This is not to say that I learned any language fluently or even proficiently. I didn't. But I knew exactly what phrases I would need most often, and I learned those.

Whenever I arrived in a new country, after the customs official had finished asking me questions, I asked him a few. "Excuse me, how do you say *thank you* in Swahili?" After that, I was always on the alert for someone who spoke English or any language I understood better than Swahili. Whenever I found someone, I pulled out my little notebook and seized on the situation. "How do you say *hello* and *good-bye, yes* and *no, good morning* and *How are you?* How do you say *please* and *more* and *tomorrow?* Can I buy you a cup of tea? Now, how do you say *Please speak slowly.*" In this way I learned quite a bit of Arabic, Greek, Berber, and Swahili, all of which I promptly forgot again. Yet, even these small scraps of language have generated huge amounts of goodwill from native speakers I met.

I once stayed for a month on a Greek island where hardly anyone spoke English, and in a month, I could make myself understood in Greek. But in order to learn a language quickly like this, I have to feel desperate. It can't be a luxury.

I know that I will understand only as much of a strange language as I expect to understand. When someone is speaking a foreign language, if I say to myself, It's no use. I don't speak Greek, and I turn off all the brain cells that help me understand language (even when someone is speaking English), I hear only a Babel of noises. But in a fix, if I can relax completely, focusing not on specific words but on comprehending, I have discovered that I do have an inkling of what the person is trying to tell me. Without understanding any of the words, I have sometimes comprehended the gist of entire conversations.

But doing only that was not my goal in Kalikaha, for I knew that I would be there a year and that Dyula was a simple language grammatically. This was my first real chance to stay in a place long enough to grasp a language beyond the rudimentary level.

Dyula was a giant puzzle. Each word or phrase was a piece I needed. The entire puzzle, when put together, would be a picture of me having conversations with the people around me. I wanted badly to fill in the missing pieces and complete this scene.

I worked on the puzzle at every moment of every day. I bought a small spiral notebook with an orange cover and I began to enter every new phrase I learned. But I soon realized that it was not enough to enter the phrases in the book. I needed to be able to retrieve them again at will, and so I devised a simple system of indexes, gluing colored cardboard tabs onto certain pages so that I could find them again quickly. I started with sections for Verbs, Nouns, and Adjectives. Then I added Time, Geography, Agriculture, and Pottery. The verbs were simply listed because it was difficult to subdivide them, although often they were listed again under other subject headings. The nouns I divided into other categories: Food, Animals, Clothing, People (kin terms and identities), Parts of the Body, and so on. I had special sections for Housework, Blessings, Farm Work, Livestock, The Passage of Time, Social and Cultural Life, and Trading at the Market. Nearly all the words I knew fell into one of these categories.

Since I had lots of time and one box of colored pencils, I decorated each section—there was a market scene, a Fulani herder with his cattle, and small drawings of pots and utensils and people. I worked on the notebook constantly, expanding and refining the divisions. In all the village, it seemed that only two things were completely in my control: my journal and this Dyula notebook. I lavished care and attention on both of them, feeling that they had to take the place of my house, my study, my garden, and my friends. I could not shut the doors to my house, so I kept the private sides of myself between the covers of my journal. The care I normally lavished on my house and garden I put into my notebook of Dyula words, decorating the dividing pages with colored designs and carefully reinforcing them with tape.

There were a number of reasons why it was so important to me to put the puzzle together and speak Dyula well. I wanted to get free of Yardjuma and to have my own connection to the villagers. I also have a competitive streak, and I wanted to speak Dyula better than Tom. I chafed at the wifely role everyone cast me in, at the way Yardjuma treated me, at the way I was never consulted in discussions that concerned both of us, at being in Kalikaha for Tom's research and having to put the needs of that research before anything else. Having come three months after Tom, I lagged far behind him in knowing the villagers and in learning the myriad paths around the village and the fields. I saw that I would never catch up with him in these two areas, for they were important to his research. Nor would I ever win Yardjuma's respect, for he alternately despised and feared me.

I felt beleaguered in the village, attacked by Yardjuma, and treated by everyone else as an appendage to Tom. I wanted to prove myself to all of them, and I wanted to be superior at something. Speaking Dyula, I decided, was what I could do best. I knew that I had never met anyone who learned languages as quickly as I did. Nor was learning to speak Dyula as vital to Tom as it was to me, for he usually went places accompanied by an interpreter. Whereas I, if I wanted to do anything besides tag along, had to fend for myself. What obsessed

Tom were the questions he had come to Kalikaha to ask, and they were more accurately asked and answered via an interpreter. What obsessed me was the way one could put language together to ask those questions. I swore secretly to myself that whatever else I did while I was in Kalikaha, I would learn Dyula so quickly that not only would I catch up with Tom, I would soon be translating for him.

I didn't realize until later just how much my determination and quickness threatened Yardjuma. The more I talked to other people, the more I began to notice the gaps in his stories. When he made arrangements for us, I pricked up my ears and listened. If the talk was in Dyula rather than Senufo, I often noticed discrepancies between what Tom wanted and what Yardjuma was actually arranging. I pointed these out to Tom, sometimes foiling Yardjuma's plans.

I sought out people like Donnisongui, our neighbor Beh, and Mariam because they were patient and had the knack of putting things simply for me. I didn't care what we talked about—Donnisongui's farm work, Mariam's lectures on how a wife should treat her husband—I would listen to anything as long as it was simply put and I was encouraged to reply.

We also had a Dyula dictionary and grammar, which I studied night after night by the kerosene lantern. I searched the dictionary for useful words and then listened for them in people's speech. Dyula varies so much from region to region that any dictionary is an approximation at best, but if I heard the word I was listening for, I wrote it down in my notebook and tried to work it into my own vocabulary.

As soon as I had acquired a limited vocabulary, I began to try to express complex ideas using only very simple means. I never tried to translate my thoughts directly into Dyula; that led only to frustration. Instead, I had to be content to distill my ideas down to their most basic and childlike form.

"That pleases me. That doesn't please me. That's bad. *O ma nyi.* That's good. *O ka nyi.* That's difficult. *A kag bele.*"

These were the only opinions I could express when I first arrived in the village, and they had to somehow encompass the sum of my experience. It was frustrating, and yet, when I understood Donnisongui or Beh and I could express one of these opinions in response, I felt immensely more satisfied than when we had long conversations that passed via Yardjuma's translation.

Soon, the villagers themselves began to comment on my improvement. "If Carol had come when you did," they told Tom, "she would understand everything by now." They teased Tom at every opportunity. "Carol just got here and she understands more than you do." The villagers fueled the competition, and it became a sore point with Tom, for they never let a day go by without pointing out my progress to him.

"Of course Carol speaks better Dyula than Tom," Mariam said sagely. "Men and women are not the same."

When Yardjuma disappeared for a week without warning, it was clear that my help as a translator was essential for Tom's work. Both Tom and the villagers acknowledged my skills. They still addressed Tom when they spoke to us together. But when they finished, they would turn to me. *"You* understand what I'm saying don't you, Carol?"

The obsession with words and how they fit together is a prerequisite for learning any language quickly. But it is not the only requirement. The state of being not quite articulate is a childlike state. To learn a language well and quickly, one must be willing to play the child. Whenever I chafed at acting childish and criticized myself for it, the learning process did not yield very tangible results.

It is in the first two years of life that we learn most quickly and intensively. Never again will we learn so much in so short a time. In Kalikaha, I was, in many senses, like a child, for I had to be taught the most rudimentary lessons about language and manners, lessons any six-year-old knew well. The two were inseparable: To learn to speak Dyula was to learn to be Dyula.

And yet I came to this childlike state as an adult who had already matured in another society. In this paradox lay the most interesting part of the village experience for me. I was very conscious of what I wanted to learn and why. And although the phrases I used to express my emotions were childlike in their simplicity, the feelings that I compressed into these phrases were the complex emotions of a grown woman. In this paradoxical state of being the adult child lay much of the charm for me of the process that anthropologists call participant observation. Psychologically, it was even a kind of revenge on the adults of my own society, for I was once again a child, but I was not powerless.

Mariam became a kind of mother figure for me in the village, stern and gentle at once. Yet the messages she gave me about my role as woman and wife (who should be a mother) were so extreme that I could easily dismiss them and yet appreciate Mariam's motherly concern. This is the ideal I would like to achieve with my own mother—to accept her love in intent but not always in content. I was no longer a child hearing Mariam's injunctions to serve and obey. I was already a young woman, and this maturity, as well as my outsider status, gave me the power to weigh what she said and to accept or reject it as I wished. I did not have this power when I was socialized in my own society to be all the things Southern women are taught to be: gracious, yielding, creative, and strong but in a backstage sort of way, prompters and prop mistresses rather than actors. As I weighed the pros and cons of my role in Kalikaha, curiously, I was also weighing the pros and cons of what I had absorbed in Memphis and later in Berkeley. It was a winnowing process, one I did unconsciously every hour of every day as I compared life in Africa and America. As the time approached for me to leave Kalikaha I seized on the opportunity to jettison many hulls and husks that weighed me down, and as I stood beside Noupka as she winnowed the last of the rice, I winnowed, too, and watched the light husks float upward from her bouncing basket while the grain landed again and again, with a soft staccato patter.

To winnow. I noted the verb in the Housework section of my Dyula notebook. *Ka flay. Noupka ka malo flay bi.* Noupka winnowed rice today. It was a word I had never thought that I would need to know.

 # THE AMBIVALENT
INTERMEDIARY

IT ALMOST SEEMED AS IF YARDJUMA HAD KNOWN WHAT WAS coming and had left to escape it, for the now-familiar landscape of Kalikaha was being transformed into something strange and ominous. All around the village, people set fire to the grasses. The herders hoped to force one last spurt of green growth for their cattle. The farmers feared real bush fires that would rage out of control, so they set small ones to protect the village and the sacred grove. The hunters set fires and then waited for the fleeing animals.

Hot winds blew all day, and the nights were cold. The land was parched and burnt, the grass stalks like porcupine quills where the fires had scorched them black. When we drove past the lines of fire, we could have been driving straight into hell. The flames crackled loudly, and the smoke filled the sky with dark clouds. Just beyond the line of fire, cattle egrets shifted from one black foot to the other, their delicate white bodies in sharp contrast to the orange flames, their beaks poised to snatch the insects that fled the fire. Overhead circled the hawks, watching and hoping.

On Monday, Yardjuma didn't come to work, and we couldn't find him anywhere in the village. He had left no word about where he had gone or when he would come back. But Tom's research couldn't wait for his return. All around the village, the rice was being harvested, and if we didn't get to every field in Tom's study in time to harvest the sample plots he had staked out, this information would be irretrievably lost.

On Tuesday afternoon we heard from Kwadjoe Kwadjoe, the Baule agricultural extension agent, that Yardjuma had borrowed his brand-new moped to go to Korhogo. Yardjuma had gone, he said, at the request of the other extension agent, Tenena, a Senufo, who was in the hospital in Korhogo after a serious motorcycle accident. Tenena was having an affair with the very young wife of a very old man. The old man had never married her properly; he simply took her from her husband. No one said anything to the old man because he was a powerful sorcerer and people were afraid of him.

When the girl took up with Tenena, the old man was furious and went to a powerful fetish for a curse. The curse would kill anyone who spoke to the girl. If it worked, the old man would have to pay the owner of the fetish the enormous sum of seventy-five dollars. If the old man did not pay up, the fetish would turn on him and begin to kill his family members, one by one, until he paid.

Shortly after the old man put the curse on the girl, Tenena had a serious accident on his motorcycle. The girl felt responsible and disappeared. That was where things

stood, Kwadjoe Kwadjoe told us, when Yardjuma received a note from Tenena in the hospital asking him to
come to Korhogo.

"Why didn't he take his own moped?" Tom asked
Kwadjoe.

"You mean La Crosse? It's broken down again, as
usual." Yardjuma never said "my moped." He always
referred to the old vehicle as La Crosse, the name of a
racy model of Yamaha motorcycle that was everyone's
dream bike just then.

The next morning, Wednesday, Kwadjoe Kwadjoe
came to call on us early, angry because Yardjuma had
still not returned with his new moped. "I only loaned it
to him to help out Tenena because Tenena has so many
problems," Kwadjoe growled. Kwadjoe Kwadjoe had
gone over to see the mechanic, Dotrugo, hoping to get La
Crosse to use until Yardjuma came back, but La Crosse
still wasn't working. "Dotrugo is waiting for Yardjuma
to bring him a cylinder from Korhogo," Kwadjoe told us.

"I loaned Yardjuma the money for a cylinder," Tom
told him. "And he told me he bought it and gave it to
Dotrugo last week."

"Madame Mama is right," sighed Kwadjoe with the
air of someone conceding a point. "He is truly a bandit."

The two of us were worried about how we would
manage the household interviews, but the people in the
sample had never been so patient. They spoke slowly and
used words we knew well. To our surprise, we saw that it
mattered to them that the interviews continue, and this
response touched us and kept us going.

The longer Yardjuma was gone, the angrier Tom
felt. "I feel like firing him," Tom said to me that night.
This surprised me coming from Tom. Yardjuma owed
Tom a large sum of money, which he could only pay back

by more work, and Tom's grant gave us nothing to spare. Even more important, Tom was still grateful to Yardjuma for his help in those first crucial lonely months.

The next afternoon, Tom woke up from a nap with a clear-eyed, determined expression. "I'm going to fire him," he said. "The consequences can't be any worse than this."

The question remained of how to find a new interpreter. Only one villager really had a command of French and that was Adama, a young man from the potters' quarter, which was located just outside the village proper. In many ways, Adama was ideally suited because, although he was Senufo, he belonged to the potters' subgroup, which made him both an insider and an outsider in the village. He was ethnically Senufo and spoke Senufo as his first language, but around the time of Adama's birth an Islamic marabout had passed through the area around Kalikaha. The potters had been particularly responsive to his preaching, and in five or six nearby villages, they had burned their sacred groves, changed their Senufo names to Islamic ones, thrown away their brass ornaments, and converted. The marabout had not come to Kalikaha, but the potters, who had their own separate *poro,* found themselves suddenly isolated. When someone died in their quarter, no other *poro* groups came to the funeral and so, several years later, around 1950, they also converted to Islam and gave up their *poro.* Adama was the first child born after this conversion.

This gave him the bond of religion with both the Dyula and the Fulani, and he spoke Dyula fluently as a second language. Adama also satisfied Tom's other criteria: He had a good móped and he had done the *poro.* Despite his conversion to Islam, Adama's father had wanted

165

Adama to undergo the formality of a cursory initiation into the Kalikaha *poro*. Most importantly, although we didn't know him well, we both liked him a lot. Tall, with long lanky legs, he sometimes came by to greet us if business brought him to our end of the village. He had the same education as Yardjuma, the sixth grade. He had been one of the first students when the primary school was built at Kalikaha.

After he completed the sixth grade, Adama wanted to go on to high school, but his father fell ill and was unable to work for three years. During this time, Adama, as the oldest son, stayed at home and farmed. Instead, when their time came, his younger brothers went to high school in Korhogo in his place. Now that his father had recovered and his brothers were grown, he was free to leave, but he was in the same position as Yardjuma. The agricultural extension agency no longer hired extension agents without a high school education, and he was too old to attend high school. When Adama told us this story, he gave a sad smile and said frankly that he did have a few regrets, but Allah must have intended it and so he had come to accept his fate. Despite his literacy, he would remain in the village with his family and be a farmer all his life.

That night, we went to call on Adama. He was very interested in working for us, he replied immediately. But he was the president of the Kalikaha cotton cooperative, and it would be hard for him to resign in the middle of the cotton market. "What interesting work," he said thoughtfully. "To go around and ask the elders how it used to be in Kalikaha. I would learn a lot of things about my own village that I don't know." He asked for a day to think it over.

Tom decided that to minimize his financial loss he

would take Yardjuma's decrepit old moped, La Crosse, as payment for Yardjuma's debts, have it repaired, and sell it. As we talked, we realized that if Yardjuma returned the next morning and was fired, he would take off right away on the old moped, and that would be the last we would ever see of him or of La Crosse. So, despite the late hour, we walked across the village to see Dotrugo, get La Crosse from him, and store it at our house as collateral.

"If it belonged to Yardjuma, I would certainly give it to you," Dotrugo replied. "But it belongs to Kwadjoe Kwadjoe. La Crosse is his moped, not Yardjuma's."

"He's lied to me about everything," Tom said angrily.

On Friday morning, we faced the problem of how to complete the week's interviews. We had done the interviews with the Dyula households first, hoping that Yardjuma would return to translate with the Senufo farmers. But the week was nearly over, and he hadn't reappeared. As far as we knew, none of the Senufo women spoke Dyula. With trepidation, we walked over to Nofigay's house. If Nofigay wasn't in the mood to be interviewed, she would chase us off without a moment's hesitation; she had done this frequently to Tom and Yardjuma before I came to Kalikaha.

I always remembered my first morning in the village when we had gone to Nofigay's house to interview her. She was sitting in her doorway, picking through a gourd bowl of tiny red peppers she had just harvested. Every few moments, she would look at me, sitting on a stool in front of her door. What in the world are you doing here? her dark eyes seemed to ask me, and the absurdity of it doubled her over in laughter. Out of everyone I met in those first confusing days, Nofigay stood out, for she seemed to see things in the same perspective I did. What the heck was I doing in Kalikaha? It was a good question. When the interview was over, she gave me a handful of her small red peppers.

"Be careful!" warned Yardjuma. "They're the very hottest kind. Make sure that you don't touch your eyes."

To our surprise, when Nofigay understood that Yardjuma was gone, she sat down immediately and gave us her full attention. We nearly fell off our stools when she spoke to us in excellent Dyula and made every attempt to help us understand. Her cowife, Wahdonan, did not speak Dyula, but her small son patiently translated her Senufo into Dyula for us. Everyone tried to cheer us up, even Menergay, their taciturn old husband. "Don't worry," Menergay told us, "he'll come back."

That morning, Kwadjoe Kwadjoe had come again to see us. "Where is he?" he demanded. "He left on Monday on *my* brand-new moped and hasn't come back!"

We told him we had no idea. Kwadjoe Kwadjoe confirmed that La Crosse was indeed his. "Yardjuma came to me and begged me to loan it to him until his work with you was finished. I'm not even Senufo. I'm Baule. But I felt sorry for him, so I agreed. But I never would have loaned him my new moped if it hadn't been for Tenena. I wanted to help Tenena because we work together. And what have I got for it? Now I have work to do and no moped. Not only that, but he borrowed six thousand francs from me, so he owes me that, a cylinder for the old moped, and he has my good moped! And I'm not even Senufo!" Kwadjoe struck himself on the side of the head in frustration and went off, muttering.

We didn't return from the fields until afternoon, and after a late lunch, we lay down for a quick siesta. The sound of a moped coming into the quarter woke me.

There was a loud knock at the door. "Who is it?" called Tom.

"It's me. Yardjuma."

When we were dressed, we opened the door. "Would you like some coffee?" Tom asked him formally, offering him the bench.

"Sure. While you're making the coffee I'll just go ahead and start telling you my story," he said casually. He was wearing a long, very faded yellow cotton boubou that I had never seen before and thick tortoiseshell glasses that hid his eyes and made him look like a different person.

"On Monday, I got a message from Tenena that Siata's mother wanted to see me right away, so I borrowed Kwadjoe's moped and went to Korhogo."

We had gone no further than this and there was already one contradiction in the story. Kwadjoe thought that Tenena himself wanted to see Yardjuma. If he had known that Yardjuma was going to see his mother-in-law because of a message from Tenena, he would never have loaned Yardjuma his brand-new moped.

Siata's mother told Yardjuma that it was the elders in her natal village that wanted to see Yardjuma one more time in order to finalize the divorce. So, Yardjuma said, he went to the village and met with the elders.

"When I got back to Korhogo," Yardjuma continued, "there was only one thing on my mind and that was how I could get back here to my work as quickly as possible. Unfortunately, I had given every single cent I had to the elders. I didn't even have the money for gasoline.

"I went to see my friend, the one who rents from Siata's mother, but he didn't have any money either. I even spoke to his manager, but he wouldn't give my friend an advance on his salary. He said he was already drawn out to the limit. At that moment, I felt desperate. I didn't know how I could get back here to do my work. I went to Quartier Soba, hoping that I might run into someone I knew who would loan me the money for gasoline." (Quartier Soba is the red-light district of Korhogo.)

There, Yardjuma ran into a schoolteacher he knew who taught in a town not far from Kalikaha. The schoolteacher agreed to loan him the money as soon as the bank opened the following morning. Meanwhile, to pass the time, they did up Quartier Soba, drank, ate, had a wonderful time, and the schoolteacher paid for all of it.

"The next morning," Yardjuma continued, "I was so anxious to get back to work that I woke up my friend, and we went together to the bank. But when I had the money, he told me that I couldn't just leave like that without going with him to eat, so we had something to eat and drank some beer, and then my friend asked me not to leave Korhogo yet, but to wait until afternoon and we would ride part of the way together. Since he had loaned me the money for gas, I couldn't very well say no, so I had to wait. We barely reached his village before dark. So, he told me not to go on but to stay and spend the night and offered me all sorts of things to eat and drink, so I couldn't refuse that, it wouldn't have been polite at all, so I had to stay. You know how we Senufo are about hospitality. You can't refuse. Today I left there, and I've just arrived. I'm sorry, I give my apologies, and there's no excuse really. Then, too, when I arrived, I saw that your door was shut and I was sorry to bother you, but I was so anxious to let you know that I was all right that I knocked and woke you up. Now I've ruined your siesta. I apologize for that, too."

All during this long story, which sounded oddly pat, all I could think about was what was coming and how Yardjuma would take it. He looked tired and subdued, perhaps from all the drinking and the late nights. And the new glasses altered his appearance so much that I couldn't stop staring at them. They were tortoiseshell, very heavy, with clear lenses. There were tables of these glasses for sale in the Korhogo market, near the sunglasses and the cassette tapes. Although they had no prescription in the glass, they were popular as jewelry, to give one the educated look.

"There are several things I want to know about," said Tom. "I heard that you were at the meeting when the committee came to estimate the damage that Moumouni's cattle did in Bayma's field. Is that true?"

"Yes. I was there."

"I had specifically asked you not to go to that meeting. They are both in the study, and it's important for us to remain neutral." Tom paused and then burst out, "What about the money that I loaned you to buy the parts to repair La Crosse?"

"After it is repaired, I'll pay Dotrugo," replied Yardjuma. "He hasn't finished the work."

"But he says he can't fix it until you bring him a cylinder and pay to put gas in it."

"When the work is done, I'll pay him," Yardjuma said stubbornly.

"What have you done with the money I loaned you to buy a cylinder?" Tom asked him outright.

"I wasted it," Yardjuma said flatly.

"What about the fifty thousand francs I loaned you to buy a used moped? I thought you had bought one, and now Kwadjoe says it's his."

"Well, I do intend to buy it. He's going to write the

person it belongs to and if they are willing to sell it, I'll buy it. If not, I'll give it back to him."

"What did you do with that money?" persisted Tom.

"Well, you're right," Yardjuma said suddenly. "This is a serious matter and it is better to speak frankly."

"Where's the money?" demanded Tom.

"I have it. On me."

"On you? But you said you didn't have enough money for gasoline."

Yardjuma hung his head. "I wasted it all," he said remorsefully. "This time I have no excuse. I can only offer my apologies. The other times I was absent I had valid excuses, but this time, I have no excuse at all. I apologize."

"That won't do," Tom said quietly. "You're fired. The only question is how you're going to pay me back the money you owe me."

For an instant, Yardjuma sat suspended, disbelief frozen on his face. Then he collected himself as the meaning of Tom's words sank in. He was too proud to argue. I thought he might throw himself on Tom and plead for one more chance. His mouth quivered, and then he pressed it together and composed himself.

"Fine," he said. "I'll pay you back. I have family. I didn't just drop out of the sky, you know."

"Carol and I have work to do now," Tom said, not knowing how else to reply. "Come back at seven tonight and we'll talk about it then."

I looked at Tom, shocked, despite our talks, that it had really come to this. Tom looked pale. I remembered the first letters he had written me about Yardjuma, how Tom had seen it as a piece of great good fortune to run into Yardjuma in Kalikaha and how happy he was when Yardjuma offered to leave his job to work for Tom. Tom had described him in his letters as friendly, open, and honest.

"Carol," Tom said in a small voice. "Could you please just hold me?" I put my arms around him and squeezed as tightly as I could.

All the farmers in Tom's study were harvesting their rice, and it was necessary to visit every field to weigh a sample. Yardjuma's absence had put us behind schedule, and a few problematic fields still remained, their locations unknown, their perimeters unmeasured, and their yields uncalculated. Tom stopped to rest only when it got too dark to see at night.

Looking for Wahdonan's field, we drove down a small path, and by luck, we found her in it and almost, but not all, the rice harvested. "Wait, wait!" we yelled, running out to her, waving our arms. She watched us as we crazily staked out a one-meter square plot, pulled out our pocket knives, and harvested the rice in it. She gestured to beautiful heads of rice just outside our square. No, no, we gestured back, only these. She didn't speak any Dyula, and without Yardjuma we couldn't explain. She watched quizzically as we weighed the sample of rice and then handed it back to her. You keep it, she gestured, since you need it so badly. No, no, we insisted and gave the rice back, hoping she understood our Dyula thanks. As we rode off she shrugged her shoulders and turned back to harvest the last of her rice.

Nofigay, in her peppery way, had refused to tell us where her rice field was. "I'll take you there some day," she always said, "but today isn't a good day for that." If we didn't find her that afternoon, it would be too late. Luckily, we met Wahdonan's little son on the trail and squeezed him between us on the seat of the motorcycle. He directed us down one remote twisting trail after another. Ambushed, Nofigay laughed and welcomed us, grudgingly acknowledging our victory.

As we returned toward the village the setting sun glinted on the golden fields, and for the first time, they looked more beautiful to me dried than they had ever looked when they were green and the harvest was only a distant hope. Sunset tinted the stalks of rice a luminous pink, and over the fields flew the white bodies of cattle egrets, their black legs trailing. Boys struggled to pedal bicycles too big for them, heavy sacks of harvested rice tied to the bikes. Long lines of women and girls shared the trail with us, their heads loaded with basins of rice, the stalks tied into bunches like fat golden bouquets, the bunches almost spilling over the basins' edges. The women walked quickly under the heavy loads and the sweat streamed down their faces, yet they called out to us and laughed as we passed.

That evening, Yardjuma returned. Tom told him the amount of his outstanding loans, more than Donnisongui or the other farmers made in a year from their cotton. There was no way Yardjuma could pay back such a sum.

"What about my *préavis?*" he asked Tom. In one day, we had learned the French and Dyula verbs for "to fire," but this we had to look up in our French-English dictionary. It meant "advance notice." He said there was also a payment that anyone received when he was fired.

"We usually give two weeks' salary," Tom replied, and he subtracted two weeks of Yardjuma's original salary from the total.

"But in Ivory Coast," Yardjuma persisted, "the amount of the payment depends on how long you have worked." The way Yardjuma figured it, he had worked eight months and he should receive eight months' salary. Was it some proportion of that? We were in the same old bind as ever—we didn't know what was normal. Yardjuma had been fired a number of times, and in his accounts, he was always the victim of French racism. We had listened to these stories with a great deal of sympathy for Yardjuma, and Tom had met one of Yardjuma's former employers, an arrogant and rather brutish Frenchman. But now a seed of doubt crept into my mind concerning the circumstances of these firings.

"I didn't fall out of the sky, you know," Yardjuma said again to Tom. "When you have found out the payment and subtracted it, you and I will go to my village and my family will pay you."

Tom would never have returned to Yardjuma's village to ask his family, who were dirt-poor, to pay us back what Yardjuma had borrowed. The idea was absurd. But not knowing what else to say, Tom agreed.

Yardjuma wrote down the address of the store where his friend in Korhogo worked and shook our hands.

"What about the pocket watch that Carol loaned you?" Tom asked him.

One day we had all been in a market town and had eaten lunch in a small restaurant. A woman came in, and Yardjuma ordered a large bowl of meat for her, the most expensive dish, and paid for it himself. Later, he explained to us that she was a distant relative and that

175

once, when he was a boy, he had been sent to stay in her father's house in the city. The father had converted to Islam, and he told Yardjuma, "If you want to eat in this house, you have to pray." Yardjuma refused and went hungry.

"Then why did you buy meat for her if her father treated you so badly?" I asked him.

"So that he will hear about it," Yardjuma replied. "When he hears that I fed her well, he will remember how I went hungry in his house and he will be ashamed."

Remembering this story, I told Yardjuma to keep the watch. It was my revenge. He left us, looking almost relieved that it was over, reaching his arms above him and stretching in the old catlike style before he went out the door. On the porch, he met Donnisongui coming in and greeted him as if nothing had happened.

Donnisongui approved of what Tom had done, and the three of us were sitting companionably on the porch when Adama drove up on his moped. As if our house were the stage set for a play, the principal characters kept entering and leaving through the granaries, as if they had become the earthen wings of an adobe theater. Tom asked Adama to translate for us, and he explained to Donnisongui in detail everything that had happened. We reassured him that Tom's work was not ruined and that we would hire someone else as soon as possible.

"I can't think who there is except Adama," Donnisongui said, in complete innocence of our plans. Tom and I almost chuckled out loud. I searched Donni's face for any sign of disapproval, but found none. Although the two men did not know each other well, they spoke to each other with mutual respect. Tom, Donni, and Adama were all born about the same time, age-mates.

"Adama was my teacher before you came," Donnisongui continued. "He taught me French."

Adama looked embarrassed. "I tried to start a night school for the adults," he said. "I wanted to teach them to add and subtract at least, so they could tell if they were being cheated on their cotton. In the beginning, all the men came and I had great hopes. In the end, it was only Donnisongui and one or two others. I got discouraged and gave it up."

"Why did the men quit coming?" Tom asked.

"They were afraid that other men would sleep with their wives while they were at the school," replied Adama.

"Why didn't they take their wives with them?" I asked. "The women could have learned French, too."

Adama was too taken aback to even reply. It was obvious that this had never occurred to him. Donnisongui, however, smiled at me with affectionate tolerance. He had become accustomed to my eccentric notions, and true friend that he was, he accepted them as part of me.

When Donnisongui had said his good nights, Adama announced his errand to us. He had come to give his final answer. He very much wanted to work for us. However, he could not start for two weeks. His family depended on him, and he had to get the rice harvested and stored in the granaries. He left us with a blessing: "May Allah give each of us a good daybreak."

Still later, another figure walked into the silent courtyard. Lasungo looked very nearly bowed down by the responsibility he carried on his muscular young shoulders. He used the traditional Senufo manner, never speaking to Tom directly, but addressing his plea to me so that I could "pass the words" to Tom. Lasungo was, in a certain sense, Yardjuma's *jatigi* in the village, but Lasungo was not really in a position to sponsor anyone. He was still a youth, still *tyolo,* an initiate who had not yet graduated from the *poro.* His family was unusually small—his mother, Zele, his married sister, who lived near us, and himself. That made him practically an orphan in village terms. He badly needed a sponsor himself and had looked to Yardjuma, like an older brother or an uncle, to fill this role. In the grim sad way he carried his shoulders there was more than just responsibility. What weighed him down was the shock of lost innocence. Yardjuma, who could tell such wonderful stories, who knew the world beyond the village, who had stood up to policemen, to French bureaucrats, to the elders of his own lineage, who gave advice, who had even promised to find Lasungo a job, could never again be the hero he had been. And yet, seeing him more clearly, Lasungo still came to speak in his behalf.

"Carol," he began, "I have come to speak about my friend Yardjuma. I know he has done wrong. He has not taken his work seriously. But I have come as his friend to ask you to give him another chance."

"Tom," I said, passing the words, "Lasungo has come to speak for Yardjuma as his friend. Have you heard and understood?"

"Yes, Carol, I have," replied Tom, "and I ask you to thank Lasungo for me. Yardjuma is fortunate to have him as a friend."

"Carol," Lasungo continued, "Yardjuma knows he has done wrong. And when a person knows that what he has done is wrong, surely he deserves one more chance. That is all I ask for him."

"Carol," Tom replied, "I thank Lasungo for coming tonight. But I have given Yardjuma many chances. You will have to tell Lasungo for me that I am sorry. I cannot give him one more."

Lasungo told me good night and sorrowfully walked out of the quarter. I could see that he bore us no ill will. He had simply done what he felt was right.

The next morning, very early, Kwadjoe Kwadjoe arrived at our house. "What did you decide to do?" he asked Tom at once.

"I've already told you," Tom replied. "I fired him."

"You can't do that!" Kwadjoe retorted. "If you fire him, how am I going to get my money? What you have to do is keep him on and every month subtract a portion of his paycheck and give it to me as payment for his debts!"

"Koko!" came a voice outside the door, and Noupka's husband entered and announced that Yardjuma owed him the price of a guinea fowl. He asked hopefully if Tom were going to pay him back.

Tom looked from one to the other worriedly. "I'm not responsible for Yardjuma's debts," he said adamantly. "Look, he owes me more money than anyone else." Tom showed Kwadjoe the figures.

"If he owes you so much money," said Kwadjoe, "why are you firing him? You should keep him on, and then you'll get your money back and so will the rest of us. You can subtract some each month to pay us all back. This is selfish of you to fire him. We will all lose our money!"

"But he's ruining my work!" Tom burst out. "Listen, I've fired him and he stays fired. I'm sorry about your money. We're in the same boat."

"Yes, but you're rich," said Kwadjoe Kwadjoe. "You can afford to lose so much money."

"I'm not rich," said Tom. "I'm a student. I came here on a scholarship."

Kwadjoe stared at Tom in disbelief.

"Here are my papers to prove it," Tom said, bringing out his letters from the university, the Ivorian Ministry of Education, and the foundation that had funded his research. Kwadjoe read them and admired the gold embossed seals.

"Then you're really not rich?" Kwadjoe Kwadjoe shook his head in astonishment. "Truly, the world is a very strange place!"

Afraid that more creditors would appear, Tom and I fled into the bush. All over the savanna, plants that looked like wild frangipani bushes had suddenly burst into bloom. Their bare, brittle branches were crowned with waxy, cream-colored, star-shaped blossoms that smelled more sweetly than the most exotic French perfume. While Tom stalked birds with his binoculars I wandered like a lotus-eater from one bush to the next, sticking my nose into every blossom. As for our problems in the village, I simply wanted to forget them.

When we returned in the afternoon, the Saturday market was loud and lively. Yardjuma had told us that he intended to leave on the bush taxi that took the vendors of bicycle parts and enamel basins back to Korhogo on market afternoons.

So we were surprised to hear from Mama that Yardjuma had snuck out of Kalikaha at daylight. He had gotten someone to give him a ride on the back of a moped to the main road so that he could flag down a bush taxi to Korhogo and be gone before anyone could hear the news. He wanted to escape his creditors, who would have descended on him at once when they heard he no longer worked for Tom. Frustrated, they descended on us instead. He owed Tugawo four thousand francs for credit at the postage stamp–size store, someone else for a sack of rice, the transporter another three thousand francs, hunters for meat, women for corn beer. It amazed me that he had managed to run up so many debts in a village as poor as Kalikaha.

"What will happen now?" Mama asked me. "Yardjuma said Tom would have to come to Korhogo, and the affair would be judged there."

"Judged?" I burst out. "Judged by whom? Yardjuma's fired and that's that. It's over!" Mama and I laughed, but I didn't know that I spoke too quickly.

"Listen," Mama said, with the air of someone unburdening herself. "About that moped he told you he sold for his marriage. Well, a Senufo marriage never costs more than a few chickens. Men don't buy women here. They work for them or they are given them. He sold the moped to pay off his creditors in Korhogo because they were after him. He's nothing but a liar and a bandit, and he had to sneak out of Kalikaha before daylight like a thief!" And she laughed with mischievous pleasure at the thought of Yardjuma sitting nervously on the bush taxi when his creditors in Kalikaha were just getting up and learning the news.

"There's something else you should know, too," she said, motioning us into the privacy of her house. "Do you remember when your American friends came from Abidjan? And they brought a Baule woman with them to take care of their baby? And she came and slept here at my house with me? Well, Yardjuma wanted to sleep with her. He was drunk, and he said that he had a right to sleep with her because he worked for you. I told her to run in the house, and I locked the door. He was furious, and he called me names and banged on the door and threatened all kinds of things if I didn't open up. He spent most of the night out there, trying to persuade me to let him in." Mama folded her big arms over her chest and nodded with satisfaction. "He yelled and threatened and wheedled and coaxed, but I never did open that door."

I laughed with pleasure at the picture of Yardjuma locked out and Mama at the door, stoutly defending her guest. But I winced when I thought of the delicate young woman who carried the little white boy on her back and taught him to greet her in Baule so gently.

Beh Tuo came into Chez Mama's yard and sat down in one of her large wooden chairs. Yeo, a friend of ours who was a livestock extension agent in a nearby town, was with him. Tom asked Yeo to do him the favor of translating to Beh Tuo his explanation of what had happened, since Beh Tuo was a kind of *jatigi* to us and we wanted to give him a formal accounting.

"I'm glad he's gone," was old Beh's raspy reply. "Good riddance. Before you came, he was just hanging around the village trying to borrow money. I've always wanted to tell you that he was no good. I'll be happy when you find someone else and we can continue our work."

"The old man is a good judge of character," said Yeo. "He knows." Instinctively, I had always trusted Beh Tuo, but Yardjuma had called him a schemer out for his own ends.

"When Yardjuma found something to drink, he forgot everything in front of him and everything behind him for days at a time," Yeo told us. "All his problems came from drink. I could tell you a lot of stories about Yardjuma and drinking," he offered, but we had heard more than enough, so we thanked him and went home.

The next afternoon, we were measuring Kolo's rice field. Donnisongui and a number of our friends belonged to Kolo's reciprocal work group, and they were all in the field that day, working to harvest the rice by hand. Kolo and his family were hard workers, and the field was so tightly packed with golden rice that the delicate stalks held one another up and only the stalks on the very margins of the field fell over.

Everyone looked away from us. They didn't tease us. They didn't even try to badger us into helping them harvest. Finally, unable to stand the gloomy looks any longer, I went over to the line of workers and whipped out my little rice harvesting knife, made by the blacksmiths of Kalikaha.

"Where's the *chapalo?*" I demanded. "If I harvest Kolo's rice for him, he'd better have a big pot of *chapalo* for me!"

There was no response. They looked at me as if I were joking at my mother's funeral.

"Since I'm helping you today, Kolo," I tried again, "I expect to see you in my rice field tomorrow!" Donnisongui gave me a sympathetic smile, but everyone else looked away. I had never before had my banter go unreturned. The villagers thought that our work was ruined and that this reflected unfavorably on Kalikaha, as if the village was responsible for Yardjuma's behavior. Tom and I went home so depressed that we closed the door, drank too much beer, and tried to forget our troubles by playing poker for hours.

The next morning, we left early for Korhogo. Between hands of five-card draw, we had realized that Yardjuma now knew every agricultural researcher in Korhogo, both French and African. They had all come to visit us in Kalikaha at one time or another. It would be very easy for him to go to one of the researchers who did not know us well, say that Tom had finished his work early, and get himself hired as an assistant. If he didn't ask for a job, he could ask for money, saying that we had gone down to Abidjan and been detained and that he needed to borrow some money until we returned. We felt it was imperative that we go into Korhogo and tell everyone we knew that Yardjuma no longer worked for Tom and that whatever he might say, he spoke for himself alone. As it turned out, Yardjuma did make the rounds of our friends and acquaintances, asking for both jobs and loans. But by that time, everyone had heard the news.

At the Ministry of Labor, Tom inquired about the facts of firing. An employer must give his employee three written warnings before firing him, the official there told us.

"Don't leave in a hurry," the man said. "First, tell me what you are doing in this area." With great interest he questioned Tom about his research and wanted to know our reactions to everything in Senufo country. Tom's remark that he had been initiated into a *poro* group pleased him immensely.

"Have you done the *poro,* Madame?" he asked me. "Oh, you should! You should!" This man was completely different from other African bureaucrats I had met, who

184

had mostly been contemptuous of traditional African culture, at least in front of me.

"I did the *pòro* the same way you did," he told Tom. "I paid to be initiated and to be taught a few things because I was sent to school and couldn't take part in the true six-and-a-half-year initiation. My knowledge of *poro* is really very superficial. When I go back to the village for funerals," he said sadly, "the young boys who are now initiates can speak to the elders about certain things, and the elders understand, but I, who am a grown man, cannot discuss these matters with the elders."

What he wanted to do more than anything else, he confided to us, was to return to his village at the beginning of the next six-and-one-half-year cycle and spend a week in the sacred grove, learning along with the young initiates. I had never heard an educated Senufo man express a desire like this before. I imagined him at a funeral in his natal village and knew that the villagers would envy his portly figure and Western suits. Undoubtedly, he was the pride of his lineage, a "big man." "I truly hope you will do the *poro* before you leave Senufo country," he urged me.

Before we left Korhogo, we decided to visit Mama's husband at City Hall and let him know what had happened. Outside City Hall, on the beaten earth parking lot, beggars and hangers-on waited to ask favors of the politicians when they left the building. Inside, secretaries with intricately braided hairdos regarded us haughtily. Luckily, Mama's husband walked out and gave us a cordial welcome, which made the secretaries look at us again, as if to memorize our faces. We went back to his office, where another man shook our hands, an older man with a gaunt, lined face.

When our friend heard that our business was about

Yardjuma, he gestured to the older man beside him. "This is who you should talk to if it concerns Yardjuma. This is his *jatigi.*" I couldn't imagine who would sponsor Yardjuma until our friend continued. "This is Baba."

I couldn't stop myself from turning to look at the older man again. I was surprised to find that he really did exist. Once again, it seemed as if we were characters in a play. The bustling, decrepit old City Hall was the next stage set, and all the important characters were present for the next act.

"In my position," Baba said somewhat apologetically, "I am afraid that I will have to take the part of asking for a bit of clemency for Yardjuma."

Tom nodded before he explained what had happened and how many times this had occurred before. Both men said they regretted Yardjuma's tendency to drink too much.

"I saw Yardjuma myself during the week," Baba said regretfully, "and I asked him about his work, but unfortunately, he told me that you had given him two days off."

"I wish it were true," said Tom, "but in fact he didn't even tell me he was leaving."

Baba said quietly that he thought that Tom was doing the best thing and that there was nothing more he could say in Yardjuma's defense. He was just sorry that Yardjuma had such a problem with alcohol. It was his downfall. As our friend paid us the courtesy of accompanying us out to our motorcycle we encountered the mayor of Korhogo himself, wearing an elegant tweed three-piece suit and glasses. It seemed that something had gone wrong. The mayor looked irritated, and at that, our friend looked worried. Underlings scurried away to set things right. The mayor took time out to greet us graciously, however, and looked casually down my dress the whole time our friend was explaining Tom's research.

Before we left, we added that Mama had been very helpful to us during this crisis.

"It's true," he agreed. "My wife knows the village and the people. She may be a woman, but she does know a few things." We laughed as we drove away. Of all Yardjuma's creditors, and more were turning up daily, only Mama had gotten anything out of him. Yardjuma owed her two thousand five hundred francs, and she had convinced him to give her, as payment of the debt, a handsome new piece of cloth worth three thousand francs!

After we had returned to Kalikaha, one of the schoolteachers brought over a letter addressed to "Monsieur Tom, Researcher at Kalikaha." Inside, there was an official summons. Tom was convoked to the Ministry of Labor by Yardjuma. The hearing was to be the next Monday morning at ten.

Monday morning, when we rode up to the building, Yardjuma was standing at the door, his legs spread wide apart and braced, as if readying himself to hold on to the ground he had gained. We were ushered into the same office, and I was relieved to see behind the desk the friendly official who wanted to do the *poro.* He shook our hands warmly and explained the procedure. Yardjuma would speak first, since he had brought the complaint, then Tom would have a chance to respond, and then they would try to settle the matter.

Yardjuma told the official that it was true that he was two days late for work and that he knew that he had been wrong, but nevertheless, his employer was not entitled to fire him without any written warnings. This was his complaint.

Tom replied that Yardjuma had actually been gone

for five days without leaving any message and that it was actually the fourth time that this had happened. Tom cited the others, having kept a special file, a village log of his frustrations as Yardjuma's employer.

Yardjuma replied that Tom had no right to fire him because he had been hired until the following March. It was then December.

"Is there a contract?" the official asked.

Tom produced the contract. In it, Yardjuma agreed that if he had to leave the work for any reason, he would pay back what he had borrowed at the outset. The termination date was given as March.

"Do you have a copy of this contract?" the official asked Yardjuma.

"Oh, yes, I did have one for a while but I threw it away. I didn't have anywhere to keep it," replied Yardjuma. The official looked seriously offended. He obviously held contracts in great esteem.

"I was hired until March and I want to work until then," Yardjuma stated in an injured voice.

Tom refused point blank to take Yardjuma back. "If I have to, I'll terminate the post and have no assistant at all. But I won't have him working for me."

The official asked Yardjuma how he intended to pay back the money he had borrowed from Tom.

"I can't," replied Yardjuma honestly. "That is why I want to work until March. That is the only way I can pay back the money. He has no right to deny me my work."

Then the official did something that absolutely took me by surprise, which is to say that he asked my opinion of the matter.

"What do you advise, Madame?"

I thought that the point had been reached when it

was too late to try again. As if it were a divorce, which it was, I counseled separation.

"How can I pay back my debts if I am not allowed to keep working?" Yardjuma asked. "You know how it is when you work for a salary," he said, appealing to the portly official as one of his own kind. "You just naturally accumulate debts."

"Oh?" The man gave Yardjuma a sharp look. "Your personal debts are your own problem," he told Yardjuma. "You can't blame your employer for them just because he gave you a job."

"When a final date is specified on a contract, both parties have to agree to break the contract," the official said, sounding worried. Yardjuma didn't want to give up the job. Tom refused to take him back. And to fire him, Tom had to give three written notices, which he hadn't done. The official picked up the enormous leatherbound volume of regulations and the contract and went to see his superior.

When he returned, he said that Yardjuma had the right to take his complaint to court in Bouaké. "You could be prevented from leaving the country," he told us. "It takes months, probably years, for a case to come up."

"All right," said Tom. "In order to end this, I propose that I'll erase Yardjuma's debt if he agrees not to go to court."

"Well, if Monsieur Tom can make such a large sacrifice, I suppose that I can sacrifice, too, and accept this solution," Yardjuma said dramatically. He didn't look at all pleased. The stuffy room was as cool as ice at that moment. We never so much as shook Yardjuma's hand farewell. It was over, and we were free of him. We drove sadly back to Kalikaha.

When we got there, Mama looked grim. Yardjuma

had come the night before, in our absence. He said that he intended to go to Mama's husband and tell him that Mama was sleeping with Kwadjoe Kwadjoe. He claimed that it was these two who had put Tom up to firing him. (Actually, they had both urged Tom to keep Yardjuma on so that he would pay back the villagers.)

The next Saturday, at the market, we were approached by the oldest Fulani herder in the Kalikaha area. Although the Fulani had no chief, Samboya was acknowledged as their leader and was respected, not only for his age but also for his dignified demeanor. In fact, he was so utterly reserved that his face, largely hidden by an enormous conical Fulani hat, rarely showed any expression. However, I never felt put off by this because, oddly enough, his eyes flickered with light and life, and when he turned them on me, I felt a great warmth. When he did not want to communicate, he simply pulled his hat even lower over his face and sat impassively.

"I have come," he said slowly to Tom, "to speak about that man who used to work for you. When you were gone to Abidjan to meet your wife, he came to me and asked to borrow ten thousand francs. He said that he would repay them when you returned, but he never has."

Tom was really angry when he heard this. Only through interpreting for Tom could Yardjuma have known how wealthy Samboya was, for the Fulani all lived in the same grass shelters and they carefully concealed how many cattle they owned. It had taken Tom a long time to gain their trust so that they would answer his questions about their herds. It made him furious to think that Yardjuma had taken advantage of Tom's connection to Samboya and risked this progress.

Our friend the transporter was standing beside us as Samboya spoke. In reply, he told Samboya the amount that Yardjuma had borrowed from Tom and never paid back. With those long expressive fingers of his, Samboya made the gesture of washing his hands. "Never mind then," he said at once. His eyes flickered ever so slightly with what could have been disgust. He, Samboya, seemed already above these earthly desires, as if by virtue of his age and his piety, he were already halfway to heaven and to Allah.

Tom apologized and said that this was why he had fired Yardjuma. Samboya nodded slightly, adjusted his hat, and drifted silently away.

The only sign of Yardjuma left in Kalikaha, besides his unpaid debts, a negative space that recalled him to many minds, was his puppy. Mama adopted it, and it quickly grew fat on her scraps. Its name, of which Yardjuma had been very proud, was a play on words that means in Senufo, "The One Who Has the Last Word."

AFRICA

Perhaps I had to brave certain trials to proceed on my path nearer to Africa. I had to prove that I wanted it badly enough. That was what I said to myself after Yardjuma was gone. For in a certain way, the worst possible thing had happened. I had come to Africa hoping to like all Africans, and instead I had ended up locked angrily with one in the intimate act of hand-to-hand combat. Under the pressure of this moment, I almost gave up and got angry at Africa herself. I saw this happen to many foreigners, especially the technical advisors. The first time they were cheated or robbed, they got angry and bitter and blamed Africa. They got disillusioned, for they had come under the illusion that Africa would get down on her knees and thank them for their beneficence and benevolence toward her, would acknowledge their power over her. They had all come in positions of power, to decide how to change the face of Africa herself, where to dam rivers and flood valleys, where to build bridges and roads, which new crops to introduce. Most arrogant of all to me was the process they called sedentarization, whereby they tried to convince nomadic herders like the Fulani to give up the nomadic life and move into houses that the government built for them. It wasn't very different from colonialism except that they worked for African directors.

What these technical advisors got in return was simply the flow of human life on earth and, in particular, the flow of African life on African earth. They got delinquents as well as hard workers as employees, they attracted beggars and con men because of their money, they found devoted friends and also flatterers who wanted to use them for their own designs. Some of their students were dull and many of their dams refused to hold water. But this was not what they had envisioned, and so they blamed Africa and called her ungrateful and recalcitrant and an impossible place to work.

It was impossible not to feel powerful and wealthy in Africa if you were white and educated and came from the industrial world. A black American would have felt powerful on the last two counts as well. Uneducated African villagers offered up power every minute of the day, proffered it with deference in the gourds of water they gave you to drink and then expected you, after you had drunk, to turn around and work miracles. "A calf has been born with three legs," they said to us. "Will you come and bring one of your medicines to fix it?"

Under the pressure of this distortion, I nearly gave up on Africa. But just in time the fog cleared and I saw Yardjuma for who he was—an alcoholic tottering on the brink of Senufo society who was trying to turn us into a lifeline with which to pull himself back up. I saw Tom when he first arrived as a desperate climber, ready to grab any rope that was willing to haul him up the rocky cliff of Africa, where his work waited. He didn't test the rope's strength; he simply tied it around his waist. When I arrived, I was willing to step out on any bridge, no matter how shaky it seemed, if it crossed the river that separated me from Kalikaha.

When I was free of Yardjuma, I had the feeling that the demons within me and the demons without me had been exorcised at once. Gone were my expectations and hopes, and instead I was filled with a comfortable, pregnant emptiness. Never again could I see the people around me simply as "Africans." They were all as individual as Yardjuma himself. I hadn't come all the way to Africa to stand on the opposite bank and watch the villagers through binoculars, like the technical advisors. But I understood now, more clearly than ever, that if I wanted a bridge, no one else could provide it for me. I would have to construct it myself, log by log, one Dyula word at a time.

After Yardjuma left, I felt a great freedom that I hadn't felt before, and I wandered around the village greeting people, going to visit Mariam and Nofigay, and carrying Mama on my back, which made everyone laugh. I could speak Dyula with them now, for in the crisis, my Dyula had suddenly blossomed, and I realized with great excitement that I could make myself understood. I felt freer and happier than I had since I had come to Kalikaha. It was as if a great obstacle had been removed from my path, from all my paths: both the ones that twisted and turned through the village and the paths inside my head that presented what was possible and what was not. I felt grateful to the villagers who had reached out to us, grateful for their kindness and concern. I also had felt, once, their shame, and I knew them better for it. For the first time, I felt connected to the village of Kalikaha and to the people in it. It was a very sweet feeling, like a bud bursting open inside my chest. It was at this time that I finally met the women potters.

THE WOMEN POTTERS

I HAD BEEN EXCITED WHEN TOM HAD WRITTEN ME THAT there was an active quarter of potters at Kalikaha, and I hoped that during my year there I would be able to learn the local pottery techniques. Pottery in West Africa is made almost entirely by women, and I wanted to know more about the association of women, earth, and fire. So it was a disappointment to learn, when I arrived in Kalikaha in August, that the potters were hard at work in their fields and would not even dig the first clay until January. Just at the time the women were finally ready to dig clay, Tom and I spilled off our motorcycle on an unfamiliar sandy road and I burned my leg badly. Walking was painful, and for a week, I stayed close to the house.

The first day that I felt better, I went to Kafongon, the potters' quarter, which was about a ten-minute walk from the village proper. As soon as I arrived they took

me to Adama's wife, Nafini. She was sitting on a small
stool behind a shallow bowl filled with sand, which functioned as her potter's wheel. Nafini was in the midst of
making footed bowls for serving sauce, deftly throwing
large feet onto the bottoms of the already formed bowls,
using one hand to turn the wheel and the other to form
the foot.

Nafini sent a young girl to fetch a stool for me and
gestured for me to sit down. We smiled at each other
self-consciously. When Nafini smiled, the gap between
her front teeth gave her a girlish look. Although I didn't
realize it until later, with that gesture and smile, Nafini
had just become my *jatigi-muso* among the potters.

All around me sat piles of gray clay in hard lumps.
Wet clay soaked in huge ceramic vats. And in every direction, wherever I looked, I saw women making pots.
Some were coiling large water jars, others were kneading
the clay with their bare feet. When they saw that I
wanted to learn the names of the different pots, they
scattered the children like a flock of chicks through the
quarter. The children returned with a parade of pots for
all uses. Jars with holes were made to be used as sieves or
for smoking meat over a fire; wide shallow basins with
flaring rims were for washing clothes, dishes, and children. For grilling peanuts there was a bowl that had a
large clay tab attached so that you could grab it and remove it from the fire quickly. A griddle for making little
millet cakes had many round indentations, lids like
breasts, and handles like nipples. The women seemed very
pleased to show me all the pots they made and to teach me
the names. When we got to the last pot, they said, "This
one is very powerful. This old woman will tell you its
name, but you will have to pay something to learn it." I
handed over a coin, thinking to myself that I was setting

a bad precedent for my first day on my own as a researcher. Tom said that if you paid for the answer to one question, you would soon have to pay for every answer. But, in fact, I needn't have worried. This was the only time that any of the potters ever asked me to give them anything. This pot, the old woman explained, was used for making very powerful medicines, ones that rendered people invisible or that caused bullets to bounce off a warrior or that could make anyone who slept with your wife become impotent. The jar was decorated with aggressive-looking bumps.

The old woman who gave me this information was named Mawa. She was tall and thin and had a large goiter in the front of her neck, like an overgrown Adam's apple. Nafini introduced me to all the women straight off, in a way other women in the village never had. "This is Carol. And this is Salimata, this is Naminata, this is Ma and Na and this is Sita, Adama's mother."

They even introduced their children to me by name. Nafini's three-year-old son, Salifou, ran a safe distance away and watched me from around a granary. Her daughter, Nawa, who was five, flashed me a quick look of shy delight and then was off, skipping through the quarter, rolling an old bicycle wheel with a stick as she went, kicking up her heels in a flippant good-bye. From that moment, I was taken by Nawa. She was a sprite who never stood still. She would appear from around a granary and flash me that hot look of delight; our eyes would meet in the intensest recognition, but before I could bring her form into focus, she was off and running, skipping, hopping, gone, a wild little gazelle with big eyes and her father Adama's long legs. Even when she ate, she remained in motion, hopping in circles on one foot as she fished rice from a calabash tucked under one arm. If I ran after her, she ran in earnest, partly in delight, giggling, and partly in wild animal terror of being caught. Only much later did she let me catch her to tickle her. In the beginning, even when I tried hard, twisting and turning and doubling back through the granaries, she always got away.

As I left that first day Sita, Adama's tiny old mother, called to me, "Come here and see this." She led me behind her house to show me two enormous water jars, waist-high, the sort of jars I imagined that Ali Baba's thieves could have hidden themselves in. The clay was still damp. "This is the work of Namwa," she said proudly, introducing me to the older woman who lived behind her. I walked around the jars admiringly. They were round and robust, decorated with textured designs and a line gracefully placed to mark the upper third of each jar. The rims had been smoothed until they were thick and soft, and they were perfectly round, as if they had been thrown on a giant potter's wheel. But the potters made these rims by walking around the stationary jar, holding on to the rim with a large folded leaf and smoothing it as they went, so that the jar stood still and the potter herself became the moving wheel. It took a perfect sense of symmetry and a light, even touch to produce a perfectly round rim. When I tried, mine came out roughly oval, lumpy, and uneven.

The older women often finished the difficult rims for the younger potters. They all helped one another. If Ma got tired, Salimata would finish her pots for her. If Yacouba cried to be fed, Ma might take over for Nafini so that her pots wouldn't dry out and have to be thrown away.

"Do they cook with pottery or metal where you come from?" the women asked me that first day.

"Metal," I replied after a moment's thought. The women clucked sympathetically and welcomed me as one who shares a common dilemma. I felt at home with them in a way I had not felt in the rest of the village. Physically, all the houses were placed in a circle, their doors facing inward. This gave the quarter a warm, contained feeling. The potters were somewhat isolated from the rest of Kalikaha, so they had rarely seen how many of the villagers deferred to Tom. Therefore, these women took me for what I was—another woman with a free pair of hands—and gladly put me to work. When Yacouba was fed, Nafini would hand him to me to hold while she worked. When the pots were ready to be burnished, I helped. When mealtime came, if I was there, they fed me. When I took off my sandals and joined in stamping the clay, they laughed and called out, *"I ni chay,* Carol!" They all spoke excellent Dyula because they were Moslem, the entire quarter having abruptly converted in the fifties. Usually, they spoke Senufo among themselves, but when I was there, they would pay me the courtesy of speaking in Dyula so that I could understand. I came to know them very quickly, these women who formed a circle as round and as close as the houses they lived in. I never thought of them singly, for they did everything in two's and three's. The women of Kafongon, the potters. Like flowers, they came in clusters.

There were the young ones: Nafini, Salimata, who loved to tease, and tall, big-boned Na, who lived next to the entrance to the circle. Then there were the older women, Nabuna and Naminata, who were short and squat, and tall, thin Mawa of the goiter, who loved to joke and sing, and Namwa, quiet and self-assured, always patient and welcoming with me. In between these generations, there were Ma, thin and with the look of someone who perpetually works too hard, and Fatimata, Adama's sister, who was tall with a long neck and a constant nervous energy that turned to sharpness when she wasn't joking. Only later did I sort out their relationships. They were all related. Mawa, who loved to dance and joke, was the mother of teasing Salimata, of course. Squat Nabuna and Naminata were sisters. So were tall Namwa and Mawa, who often worked side by side.

To be a potter one had to be born into this particular Senufo subgroup, and members of this group married only within the group. If there was not a suitable spouse in Kafongon, a young girl would be married to a man from a potters' quarter in another village. When the women began to teach me their techniques and they saw that I knew how to work clay, they took me in, as if I must be a very odd and distant long-lost cousin, for they had never met a potter who was not related to them.

As for the men associated with these women, they seemed peripheral to the daily life of the quarter, at least as I experienced it. Although I knew all the potters and all their children, their husbands remained vague to me, glimpsed occasionally returning from the village or from a fishing trip to the river. Sharp-tongued Fatimata was divorced, and teasing young Salimata was already a widow. Sita and Naminata were both married to Adama's father, one of the two elders of Kafongon and one of the few men I did come to know. He was always seated at his loom under the mango trees just outside the circle of houses, and I always stopped and exchanged a few words with him as I passed.

"Come with us," Nafini said to me one day, "to greet the mother of us all." This was Tene, an enormous old woman who lived next to Na at the entrance to the circle. She was the only fat person in all of Kalikaha, and it wasn't really fat so much as just sheer bulk. She was Adama's father's sister and the aunt of Mawa and Namwa. After they introduced me to Tene, I would often bring her a packet of snuff, and this pleased Nafini and the younger women more than any gift I ever gave them. I did it to win their proud, approving looks as much as for Tene's gap-toothed smile and blessings.

Once, when I was at the potters' quarter during a wedding, there was a dance in which the younger women went to the house of each elder woman and danced before her as a sign of respect, getting down on their knees. They danced before Tene last of all, and she came out and swayed her enormous bulk in front of them like an old she-elephant, grinning, her mouth red with kola nuts, in old elephantlike delight. In our culture, we would have laughed at the sight of this fat, toothless old woman, and that is why I can never forget the looks of the younger women as they beheld her. They beamed up at her with faces of proud joy and love.

Time after time, I woke in the night to see if dawn had come. The potters had told me that they were leaving just after sunrise and not to be late. I was relieved when the dark night finally softened to gray and I heard at five in the morning the call to prayer at the mosque.

When I arrived at Kafongon in the first cold morning light, Salimata was already pounding corn. Nafini opened the door of Sita's large round house, and I slipped inside. For light, they had only one small candle stub. Sita and the children slept in a row on the packed dirt floor, wrapped only in cotton cloths against the cold harmattan night. While I watched, Sita got up and spread out the tanned hide of a small duiker. Facing the east, she began to pray. Her forehead touched the ground easily despite her age. She was a tiny woman, as birdlike as the chickens she raised, with sharp, watery eyes that saw everything. She rocked back on her heels and raised her small face upward, toward Allah. Her hands opened and closed eloquently, as if to say, Here I am, Sita, frail and old. You may take me when you like. Her lips moved and her small hands closed and opened like praying leaves.

When her prayer was finished, Sita went back to the children and wrapped herself in several of the thin cloths. Nafini heated water and bathed three-month-old Yacouba and then dressed him warmly. The other women were already waiting for us outside. Ma took Yacouba, and Nafini, as the youngest, took the empty metal basins for all the women and carried them in a stack on her head. Before we had gone far down the path, two young girls ran up, out of breath from the effort to catch us. Nafini passed them the stack of empty basins, now that they were the youngest members of our party.

We walked quickly, single file, on a small path through the bush, which glowed tawny gold in the first sunlight. The stalks of dried grass caught the light and reflected it back like thousands of yellow-gold spears. In half an hour we reached Chowga, the bottomland where their clay pits were located. During the rainy season, rice was grown here in the naturally flooded fields. The older women remembered the old days at Chowga before they converted to Islam. Then, before any clay was dug, the entire quarter—men, women, and children—came to Chowga carrying cooked chicken and rice. They ate together and left offerings for the bush spirits of Chowga. Only after that did the potters dig the first clay of the season.

While the women filled their basins with the dry chunks of clay Nafini sat down on a pile of dried clay and nursed Yacouba. I had brought an old backpack of Tom's and so I filled that, which made the women laugh. "You can't carry all that clay on your back!" they protested. "It's too heavy. Put it on your head."

"If I do that, it will fall off," I retorted. I had tried to balance things on my head before, always with disastrous results.

Namwa and Mawa, the tall sisters, bent down and took hold of the two sides of a metal basin. They lifted it up slowly and settled it onto a softly curled rag on Namwa's head. Then Salimata helped her mother, Mawa, lift hers up. Everyone's basin was up except Nafini's, so I ran over to help her. This gesture always touched me for it symbolized so concretely a woman's need for other women. No woman could raise to her own head the load she could carry for miles. And arriving at the village, she would once again need the help of another woman to lift it down. Nafini's basin of clay was very heavy and the last bit—from shoulder height to the top of her head—took every ounce of strength I had. The line of women set off down the path single file. Under the heavy loads, they walked even faster than before, anxious to reach home. When I dumped my pile of clay beside Nafini's, they were astonished that I had carried that much weight on my back. They carried everything except their children on their heads.

"When are you going to fire the pots?" I asked the potters every day, as the quarter filled up with dried jars and basins and bowls. The pots were stacked against all the houses, and we had to keep a close watch on Nawa's wild games and on the goats with their rambunctious little hooves.

Finally, one day, they answered, "Tomorrow!" clapping their hands and laughing when they saw my excitement.

When I arrived the next afternoon, the women were already assembled on the low plateau outside the quarter, which was built up of the ash from hundreds of firings by their mothers and grandmothers. At the sight of me, a chant went up. "Carol's come! Carol's come! *Caro-way! Caro-na!*" Mawa did a little dance, and they all clapped their hands. I felt wonderful to be so welcome.

They had already laid a round bed of small branches on the ground, and on top of the branches, they were arranging the pots, the largest in the middle. The smaller basins and cooking pots were put around the edges, their mouths turned outward and upward. Nabuna and Naminata, the short squat sisters, were firing their work, and what struck me most about their mountain of pots was how large it was. Two women had made this mountain of pots in only two weeks without a potter's wheel or complicated tools!

The older women consulted together, then rearranged the pots, adjusting one here or there, placing stones or shards under the largest pots to steady them and then conferring again. Only when the arrangement finally satisfied them did we begin to lay sticks over the pots, placing each stick on the pile gently, one at a time. There was something magical about this act for me, all of us in a circle around the mountain of pots, facing one another, as if we were all dowsers.

Then they began to carry out the thatch that Nabuna and Naminata had gathered and lay bundles of it over the sticks. "It will make your arms itch!" they warned me when I reached for a bundle. At a later firing, a young potter picked up a large bundle of thatch and was bitten on the stomach by a scorpion that was hiding inside.

When the mound was entirely covered with thatch and the older women had approved its placement, they threw baskets of garbage from the dump heaps on top. A little girl came running from the village, carrying a broken piece of pottery in front of her, and I realized with excitement that she was bringing hot coals to light the fire.

Salimata chose a long bunch of thatch, held it to the coals, and fanned it until it burst into flames. Then she divided the flaming torch, giving half to Nafini. Standing side by side, they touched their torches to the giant haystack. It was a race between the two young women and the fire! Quickly, they ran around the mound, touching their torches as they ran, so that a chain of flames encircled the mound, for they wanted the haystack to catch evenly. When they reached their starting point, they ran away quickly because at that moment the mound of hay and pots broke into one glorious mountain of flames. We all stood, our arms folded, a short distance away, enjoying the excitement. All potters have a red-hot streak of pyromania in their blood, and it only takes a firing to scratch the surface and bring it out.

An hour later, Nabuna and Naminata began to carry huge basins of water out to the fire. In the water were strips of pounded bark that were dark red inside, as if they had been soaked in wine. With eight-foot-long wooden poles that had iron hooks on one end, the women began to poke at the glowing mound. Neatly, they hooked the small bowls and lifted them out. Without ever dropping one of the glowing red pots, they plunged them into the basins of water and pounded bark. Then, using the long poles, they spun the pots around and around in the water. I watched in amazement. For according to everything I had learned during four years of art school, in the course of which I had earned a degree in ceramics, the pots should have exploded from thermal shock then and there! The pots were red-hot, and each time one was plunged in, the water boiled furiously. Clouds of steam rose up over the basins. By this time, it was dark, and the darkness added a sense of mystery to the scene. The mountain of pots glowed softly, and the wood that was left gave off a gray-white light of its own.

What I had been taught at an American university was that to stack hundreds of dried pots in a pile, place sticks and grass over them, and set the mound alight would certainly result in thousands of broken shards. We would never even have attempted it. We thought we knew better. Nor could you fire pots this big for only one hour—that would never work. Worst of all, to dunk the red-hot pots in water was madness itself! Yet very few pots broke. The firing was a success. As I stood and watched I resolved that I would apprentice myself to these women and learn from them just how they did this impossible feat.

When Adama arrived and joined me, Namwa immediately came over to ask me, "Is this how you fire pots where you come from?" I explained a bit about kilns and letting the pots cool for a long time, usually until the next day. Satisfied, Namwa nodded and went back to her work. Her curiosity was striking because women in Kalikaha proper had never asked me questions about where I came from. It seemed too distant even for them to imagine.

"When I was a child," Adama told me, "and our women fired, the pots extended in a circle way out to there," and he indicated the farthest perimeters of the cleared area proudly. "But now people don't buy as many pots, so the women make fewer."

When only the big water jars were left, like so many giant eggs laid by some gargantuan prehistoric bird, the women pulled them out into a wide circle. Using hand brooms of straw, they slapped the bark and water mixture on the large pots and then left them to cool.

In subsequent firings, I tried to pull out the pots myself and learned how difficult a task it was. I could spear the red-hot pots in the fire easily enough and land them in the water but then, to balance the long heavy pole, keep the pot hooked, and spin it round and round in the dark water without so much as a flashlight or a kerosene lantern to light my way—impossible! Inevitably, I would drop the pot into the water and then be fishing in the dark to find the opening again. When I watched Nasou, the youngest potter, I saw that she had the same problem I did. Later, I would bring my flashlight with me, and although the older potters took no heed of it, the younger women would call to me to come where they were and light up the dark basins.

The potters fired at dusk because the wind was calmest then. On the night of a firing, Tom would ride over on the motorcycle about ten o'clock to pick me up. He was as fascinated by the scene as I was.

"Is Tom coming tonight?" the women would ask me as we sat around the fire, waiting for it to burn down. They saw him so rarely that his arrival always caused something of a sensation in Kafongon. He always greeted the potters in Senufo, and because he never stayed very long, they all believed that Tom spoke Senufo. This pleased Tom because the villagers were always pointing out to him that my Dyula was better than his.

When Tom did arrive, the women clustered around me, pushing me down inside their circle so that I was hidden in the dark.

"Good evening, Tom!" they chorused, in response to his greeting.

"Where's Carol?" he asked them, looking around for me.

"She left already," they told him. "She's gone home."

"Gone home?" The first time it happened, they caught Tom in a moment of confusion. Had I really walked home alone in the dark without a flashlight? But their giggles gave them away, and Tom came closer and spotted me, hunched giggling, in the middle. After that, it became a game.

"Carol's gone," they would begin each time, having hidden me as soon as they heard the *putt-putt* of the Honda.

"Oh? Where'd she go?" Tom would ask in pretended innocence. "To Korhogo?"

"That's right," the women would reply, stifling giggles. "She said to tell you she'll be back day after tomorrow." My destinations got farther and more far-fetched each time. I went to Abidjan and even to *Ameriki* to visit my mother, whom the women knew I missed. But what the women said to me as they hid me was very different from the stories they made up for Tom. They told him that I had gone on long journeys alone. What they said to me was, "You can't go home with Tom. We're going to keep you here with us. We're going to build you a house next to ours and you'll live here with us for a long, long time." And at the moment when the game was over and I stood up to join Tom, I always felt a twinge of sadness that I couldn't have the house next to theirs and live with them for a long, long time.

 BLESSINGS

Before Adama became our interpreter, the constant exchange of blessings made me a little uneasy. After all, the one I received most frequently was "May Allah give you children." In Berkeley, having a child was a weighty personal decision, something one pondered for years and went to therapy to resolve, not something one wished lightly on others like, "Have a good day." When the blessing was given in Senufo, the deity was Kolotyolo, and so I could translate it, "May Ancient Mother give you children." I preferred the Senufo version because I thought that Ancient Mother was more likely to understand my feelings on the matter: children were desirable, but there were better and worse times to receive them. As far as Allah was concerned, I imagined him to be the Grand Old Patriarch with a white beard who had never actually carried a baby on his back or wiped a runny nose, and I figured that his main concern in the matter was the production of more little Moslems. If this were true, an infidel like me was probably safe from his schemes for the grand design of things. Nevertheless, the constant collective desire of sixteen hundred people to see me become pregnant as expressed through frequent fervent blessings gave me pause for thought.

Whenever I gained a few pounds or was sick to my stomach, I could see their eyes light up hopefully. Against this strong a collective desire, I worried that my diaphragm would prove too weak. After all, it was designed to repel mere matter. Could it really stand up against something as powerful as the collective faith of an entire village who daily invoked two different deities to aid them in their desire to see me bear a child? Did a man-made scrap of rubber, an upstart human invention, have a chance against a desire that strong and that ancient? This is what I asked myself uneasily as I muttered *"amina"* to their blessings.

Whenever Adama translated the blessings, he always used the French word *Dieu* for God, and this also made me feel uneasy. I wasn't sure I believed in one. Certainly I believed in vague "forces" or "powers" in the universe, but I felt more comfortable if I left my forces in an unnamed state of spiritual ambiguity. Like many people I knew, I claimed to believe in Something. I just didn't want that Something defined too clearly.

But the forces I felt in the universe were not something I invoked as personally and specifically as the people of Kalikaha invoked theirs. When Sita prayed at dawn, she seemed to open her heart to Allah in a way I had never considered doing. And when my neighbors gave me blessings, they were always concrete and specific. They asked God to give me a good afternoon or a peaceful night or to help with my work that day, to give me a child, a harmonious marriage, a safe trip back from Korhogo, and a long life. At first, I tapped my forehead to help the blessing sink in and muttered *"amina"* as a matter of course. I was pleased that I was able to catch the first word, *Allah,* and that I could respond appropriately by saying "amen."

Being around Adama changed me. When we went into the village to do interviews, Adama gave out blessings to everyone. This was something Yardjuma had never done. If someone told Adama of a death or an illness, he immediately responded with a heartfelt blessing. *"Allah ka nagoya kay.* May God make it better. *Allah ka hinara.* May this person go to heaven." The blessings soothed the roughness of the moment. This did not mean that Adama did not try to help. He did. But first, he always invoked God's aid.

"May God give your children life," Adama said fervently to every mother. And they all, no matter how young and hopeful or how old and wizened, whispered intently, *"amina"* and their eyes thanked Adama for expressing the concern that they lived with daily in their hearts.

This giving out of blessings was more than polite utterance. It was a way of sharing hope, for people in Kalikaha needed hope to survive. No abstract relationship with deities who lived far above, this was a gritty daily contact with two deities who seemed, through people's words, to be always present in the village with us. Nor were the deities themselves estranged in enmity. Sometimes Adama spoke in Senufo of Ancient Mother, sometimes in Dyula of Allah; to us he spoke in French of *Dieu.* When I questioned him about distinctions, he said it didn't matter, that God was always the same.

Tom and I, at the end of interviews and conversations, found ourselves making up our own blessings and asking Adama to translate and deliver them for us. I didn't do this unconsciously, the way I sometimes picked up new words. Rather, I found myself wanting to hand out blessings and feeling sincerely touched and, in the most appropriate word, *blessed,* when I received them.

I started a page in my Dyula notebook for blessings and began to learn the hundreds of different ones that applied to particular situations. "I need a blessing to help the potters with their work," I would say to Adama. "One that says 'May the firing turn out well.'"

"Allah an jayma," replied Adama instantly. "May Allah help us in our work."

Adama regarded my new relationship to blessings with obvious approval, and the page of blessings in my dog-eared Dyula notebook was quickly filled. There was a blessing for the young Dyula girls who wandered through the village selling bits of soap or bouillon cubes. "God help the alleyways to please you." When someone bought a new piece of cloth in the market, you said, "May it wear out before you do," a pragmatic blessing if ever there was one. At about three-thirty, I could bring smiles to the stony faces of even the most proper Dyula elders by saying as I passed them on their way to the mosque, "May the afternoon prayers be good."

When I gave out my favorite blessing, I could never keep a totally straight face—a certain irrepressible delight in the phrase itself always came out with it. It was so idiomatic, so absolutely, essentially Dyula in character, that villagers crowed with delight at the absurdity of hearing it from me. I could astonish Dyula guests in the village by casually saying as I told them good night, *"Allah yan kelen kelen wuli."* Literally, it means "May everyone here wake up one at a time."

"Do you know the value of waking up one at a time?" the Dyula man who taught me this blessing asked me. I had to admit that I had no idea.

"If there is some disaster in the night," he replied, "like a fire or a death or a war, someone will call out, and we will all wake up at once. But if the night passes in peace, each of us will wake up in the morning at our own moment, one at a time."

When someone gave a gift, everyone present showered the giver with blessings. The most frequent was *"Allah i baraji."* "May God give you something even greater than what you have given me." This blessing represents most clearly the sense in traditional African thought of the communal good. For it will probably not be me who will repay you. Life is not that neat, and Africans do not pretend that it is. To assume the responsibility for equity yourself is a form of arrogance in Kalikaha. You receive from those more fortunate than you—older, wiser, or wealthier. You give to those less fortunate. The age class system is based on these precepts. Somehow, the gift will be returned. It will not come back in the same form. Nor will it come back from the same hand. Years may pass.

It was not only knowing the blessing which was important but also saying it at the proper time, with (of utmost importance) the proper pauses. If I blurted out a blessing at the wrong moment, no one understood. They didn't say *"amina,"* even though I was sure I had gotten the words right.

Not only did I need to know the right words. I needed to know the appropriate situations in which blessings were given and the appropriate moments at which to give them. Once Tom and I had mastered that, we progressed to multiple blessings. Blessings flowed nicely

215

when they came in three's. "May God heal you. May God grant you happiness. May God give you a long life." We learned to pronounce them one after another with just the right pause between. Then we were rewarded with a long chorus of head-tapping and the soft sound of *"amina, amina, amina here be."* The best reward of all was seeing the soft look of appreciation, that moment of *blessedness* that came over people when they received a string of heartfelt blessings.

The sound of the three blessings reminded me of services when I was a girl and how, at the end, the rabbi always raised his arms. We were supposed to bow our heads, but I always looked up to see his black bell-shaped sleeves stretched out like wings as he gave three singsong blessings in Hebrew and English, with a long pause between each one—the same long pause they used in Kalikaha. But in Kalikaha, I didn't need to be a rabbi and I didn't need a long black robe.

I do not feel nearly so powerful nor so rational as I did before I went to Kalikaha. There, I saw my good intentions go awry too many times. In Kalikaha, I tried to save a child, a month-old baby. I failed. The baby died. And when Adama said, "It is God's will. May the child go to heaven," I felt a little bit comforted. Not everything is within our will or understanding. Not everything can be harnessed by our rational powers. In Kalikaha, I felt a spirituality that was threaded through every small encounter. I no longer hesitate to call on the help of other powers and to wish that help on my friends. When I speak to myself, I call these blessings what they truly are: prayers.

BOOK VACATIONS

IN KALIKAHA, THE CHARACTERS IN THE BOOKS I READ SEEMED very real. They became friends, and even after the book was finished and put away, I would summon them up for a talk or an argument. They were an odd crew, all jumbled together, because I read anything that anyone gave or sent me. In addition, before I left, I spent one night combing the used bookstores of Berkeley buying up old paperbacks that cost fifty cents or less, trying (in vain) to imagine what subjects would interest me six months hence in a mud house in an African village. I found all the Don Juan books for a quarter apiece and Jane Austen for thirty-five cents and a book of narratives of spiritual experiences collected in Tennessee from former slaves. All these books I put into a box and shipped by boat at the cheapest rate, calculated to arrive sometime in the middle of my stay when I was desperate for printed matter. And despite the vagaries of African mail, they did.

Sometimes I had to get away from Kalikaha. I simply could not stand the differentness a minute longer. I could not leave physically, but if I had a good novel stored away in a box under the bed and if the termites or the mice had not eaten it, then I had the ticket I needed for a brief vacation.

Of the book vacations I took in Kalikaha, I look back with fondness on my stay with Emma Woodhouse at Hartfield and on the year I spent in a village in Iraq with Elizabeth Warnock Fernea. I used to imagine Emma in Kalikaha, scheming away to win the red hat of chiefdom for her favorite. In Fernea, I felt that I had found a comrade-in-arms, for she accompanied her husband, an anthropologist, when he did fieldwork in Iraq. I discussed with her how to deal with the benchsitters and the women who came in to greet me but whose real interest was my empty oil bottles. Some days, when the bench was filled from dawn to dusk, when there were requests for Nescafé, for aspirin, for watches to be wound and wounds to be bandaged, when the goats wailed and the children howled and the guinea fowl squawked and honked and chickens came in the door as soon as my back was turned, sometimes I longed to enter the village in Iraq physically and change places with Fernea, for she had spent her days isolated behind closed walls except for visits to other women. On those days, a long black robe to cover my face and high walls did not seem too high a price to pay for one day of complete quiet and solitude.

One night, Tom was sick all night and I felt terribly helpless as there was nothing I could do but sit by. At midnight, I remembered a copy of *Shogun* that a friend in Abidjan had urged on me just before I left the city.

The perfect ticket for a round-trip excursion to medieval Japan. I bailed out.

Although I may have been physically present for the next four days, sitting on the front porch of the house and even responding automatically to greetings, mentally, I was learning Japanese and watching out for black-garbed assassins with knives. On the third morning, recovered but desperate for company, Tom shook my shoulder and announced unhappily that neither Yardjouma nor Fanta had shown up for work. "No interviews and no water," he said adamantly as he looked directly into my glazed eyes. He was determined to get through.

"No loyalty in the ranks," I muttered in disgust. The samurai code stressed loyalty above all other virtues.

Once, when we returned from a trip to Korhogo, we found that termites had built their earthen tunnels up our walls and right to our shelf of precious books. In three days, they had done an amazing amount of damage! The tunnels had been built straight up the wall and then over the edges of the books, like fat adobe worms. When we broke open these tunnels, they were swarming with red termites, and when we shook the books, showers of termites fell to the floor. Donnisongui came running in, and as he did whenever anything bad befell us in his house, he immediately took charge. His guests invaded by termites. *"O ma nyi!"* He would take care of that! Donnisongui did not lack for the samurai spirit.

Tracing the tunnels upward, he found that they led to the wooden rafters and striking the rafters with a stick, he made it rain termites! With a spray can of insecticide, he attacked them so vehemently that I ran outside, gasping for air. The smaller rafters had been eaten nearly through, and most of our books had their edges bitten away. Had we stayed in Korhogo a few days longer, they would have devoured the text as well. Our return confined the destruction to the margins, as the termites were working their way in from the outside. Tom looked down in amazement at his only hardback book, an old range management textbook. He eyed the handsome red binding ruefully. It was all chewed up, its edges ragged and tattered. "It's a classic in its field," he said in disbelief, as if that alone should have saved it from the termites' destruction.

On my little table, the termites had ignored all the books and gone straight for fifty pages, carefully typed, that I had written just before I left. The stack of pages resembled a piece of bread when a child has eaten all the crust but ignored the middle. As if a novice writer didn't have enough to contend with already, now I had termite critics who came into my study when I was away, read, judged, and then devoured.

A few hours before leaving New York for Africa, I had been wandering through the bookstores in the Village with a friend, and Adrienne Rich's *Of Woman Born* had caught my eye. I left the bookstore without it, but suddenly turned around on the sidewalk, went back into the store, and bought a copy, having a strange but very strong feeling that despite my overloaded luggage, I needed this book. This long conversation with Adrienne Rich kept me sane when the blessings and the pressure mounted, and gave me a perspective other than the one in Kalikaha, where woman was synonymous with mother.

Books like this one were the only discourse I had that did not deal with everyday events. There were no movies or billboards or radio programs to distract me from the ideas in the books, so I turned them over much more thoroughly than I ever had at home.

Over and over, as I read, I was struck by the way in which we, in modern society, have lost the root meaning of our own metaphors. We talk about lighting the way, about plowing straight lines, and bridging distances. We compare people to animals, consider foxes to be wily, deer to be gentle, and mother hens fiercely protective. Yet for the most part, we know nothing of the realities upon which these metaphors are based, for they come from a life close to the land, a life most of us have never lived.

Books I read in Kalikaha had a particularly intense effect on me. The metaphors struck home in a deeper way than they had before, for now I had experienced more of the realities to which the metaphors referred. I had watched Tom take the handles of Donnisongui's plow and try to guide the oxen in a straight line. I had cared for chickens and seen one of mine change overnight into a fierce, single-minded creature the moment she laid her first egg.

The metaphor I came to appreciate the most strongly was light. It occurred to me as I sat on the porch night after night that I was in an ideal position to learn the stars. They spread over us like a clear-eyed carpet. I wrote my mother and asked her to send me a book about the heavens. Miraculously, this book arrived very quickly, and after that, I often sat on the porch, craning my neck upward until it ached and searching to place names on small points of light. Unlike the other books, which I read and put away, the *Peterson Field Guide to Stars and Planets* could be read again and again. Because the night sky changed continuously, I could never finish it. Never before had I been able to see specific stars so clearly, and the shapes of constellations were complete, so that the Greek names no longer seemed quite so arbitrary and far-fetched, as they always had before. I came to know stars like Rigel and Procyon, Betelgeuse and Sirius, Vega, Altair and Arcturus. I saw falling stars so bright that it seemed as if the star had fallen just behind Zanapay's house and must be lying there on the packed dirt, quivering. In West Africa, a falling star means that somewhere someone has just died. A soul has fallen.

On dark, new moon nights, I watched the stars in silence, but on full moon nights, the village became transformed. The alleys and courtyards were brightly lit, and it was easy to find your way. Taking advantage of the natural lighting, the young people danced in all the quarters. Young Zeeay and his friends would play *balafons* and drums in the courtyard next to ours and dance until a cloud of dust rose up and surrounded them. In Kalikaha, without electricity, it was impossible not to notice the waxing and waning of the moon. Each full moon rose like a blessing over the village, making it bright and safe. Each time the moon disappeared altogether, I felt disappointed, even punished, and not even the strongest flashlight could make the alleyways feel safe again. Shadows lurked behind every granary, and people went to bed early. My own body and spirits waxed and waned with the changes in light, and my period synchronized with the full moon. No wonder that Moslem festivals begin when the first thin crescent of moon reappears after darkness. Once, I came upon the Dyula elders staring into the sky at dusk, watching hopefully for the crescent to appear so that they could announce the beginning of a holiday.

Today, if you were to ask me where in the moon's cycle we are, I could not tell you. Only when I see the moon rise full over the Berkeley Hills do I notice it. The rest of the time, one night sky seems the same as any other. We use light as a metaphor for clarity and safety a hundred times a day, darkness for ignorance and evil. Yet we forget that the metaphor is based on sun and moon, night and day. Most of us have never experienced a truly dark night without lights. In the village, day is light. Night is dark. The two are not the same. A fire, a candle, a flashlight, or a kerosene lamp make small circles of light in the darkness, but their spheres are limited. Yet the full moon creates a miracle two or three nights each month, a double blessing, an oxymoron—a night that is not dark.

I, who learned this at Kalikaha, have already forgotten, in the electric lights, what it means to have to curtail my activities at sunset and to seek out other people for comfort and to sit with them talking in the darkness. Only when I see the full moon rise and hang in the sky, do I remember that the full moon in itself, in a dark village, is cause enough for joy and for dancing.

WHERE THERE IS
NO DOCTOR

Where There Is No Doctor IS A BOOK WRITTEN BY DAVID Werner for community health workers, and the edition we had was formulated to be used, in particular, in Central and South America. Our copy was given to us by two friends who were both veterans of their own fieldwork in Africa, and inside the front cover, Marie-Hélène had inscribed a quote from Saint-Exupéry.

On ne voit bien qu'avec le coeur;
l'essentiel est invisible pour les yeux.

One doesn't see well except with the heart;
the essential is invisible to the eyes.

How we would have survived without this book I cannot imagine. The book itself is written in a straightforward, no-nonsense yet sympathetic tone of voice and has line drawings done by the author to illustrate nearly every point. For the most part they depict Latin American farmers who live in small houses and raise corn and pigs. Lest you envision the charming, naive drawings often done of peasant life that portray it as a pastoral idyll, let me hasten to assure you that these drawings were nothing of the sort. They were executed in a thin, wavering line, which symbolized for me just how tenuous was these people's hold on life and health. No clear strong black outlines these, no simplified, folksy forms. In these drawings, life in Latin America was relentlessly real, down to the scrawny babies with puddles of diarrhea coming out of their bottoms.

Each time I opened the book and confronted the babies, my complacency was shaken to the core. I read the entire book through countless times and came to know the symptoms of tetanus, polio, smallpox, yellow fever, and cholera. Only then did I appreciate what we have accomplished by eradicating these diseases from America through good hygiene and powerful vaccines. In the late nineteenth century, the city of Memphis, for example, was entirely depopulated twice by yellow fever epidemics. Yet I grew up there in the fifties and sixties without the slightest threat of that disease.

The book was on our shelf when the termites attacked and thus bore signs of having survived that natural disaster. The edges all the way around had been gnawed in tiny bites, but fortunately, the termites had not had time to eat the text itself or any of the Latin Americans who lived inside. When we were out in the village, we were often asked for help concerning illnesses. Tom and I would note the symptoms and then go home and consult the book. The book also saved our own health with its explicit explanations of the two different kinds of dysentery and how each must be treated.

We liked having the book to go to for advice. It helped us not to feel so alone, and the book's folksy tone and real-looking peasants were comforting. After all, those that followed the book's advice were plumped out ever so slightly, the lines that outlined them became slightly firmer, and they were smiling. It was another kind of research, one that gave very tangible results. However, there were two sections we dreaded having to consult. One was called Serious Illnesses That Need Special Medical Attention. Unfortunately, many diseases in Kalikaha fell into this category, and the only medical attention that was available came from our inexperienced hands. These were illnesses that I had never heard of people actually having before I came to Kalikaha: tuberculosis, meningitis, tetanus.

The other section we dreaded was on skin diseases. The people on these pages were depicted in graphic drawings, and many of the sufferers were children, their conditions the results of malnutrition. We had to sit down together for courage and brace ourselves to face these children.

The attitudes that the book encouraged were not always easy to remember, especially in times of stress. Talk *with* people, not at them was one of the book's maxims. In one drawing a man on a soapbox shouted and gesticulated at a group of people who sat in front of him passively. In the next drawing, the people sat in a circle and spoke together. Of course, I said to myself, I'll be like the person in the second drawing. But this was more easily resolved than accomplished. Once, a woman who lived near us came in and told us that she had stomach problems. We blithely handed her two Alka-Seltzer tablets and promised instant results. The next day she returned. Our medicine had *seemed* very powerful, she said, but it hadn't worked. "What part of your stomach hurts?" I asked her. She drew a wide band across her abdomen. "If Tom leaves, I'll show it to you."

When Tom had gone, she unwrapped her waistcloth. All across her stomach was a wide patch of flaky grayish skin. No wonder the Alka-Seltzer hadn't cured her! After that, I learned to ask our patients more specific questions before I jumped to conclusions.

Our most famous cure, the one that firmly established our reputation as healers, was the removal of a kernel of dried corn from a young girl's ear. She was one of our closest neighbors, the sister of young Zeeay of the snappy salute. How she got the corn that far down into her ear I do not know, but by the time they brought her to us, her ear was bleeding from the attempts to remove the kernel, and she was shaking with fear. We seated her on a stool in our back courtyard with only her mother to hold her hand. The kernel was too far down to dislodge with instruments. We could poke and poke but we would only push it farther into her ear. I was totally at a loss, and for once, the book failed us. Although it had an ingenious method for removing stubborn specks out of eyes, there was nothing that could be applied to kernels of corn in ears. Luckily, Tom's experience stood us in good stead because he had once had his ears irrigated to remove compacted wax. He assured me that water would work if we could get enough pressure behind it. I ran next door to Sibatia's and borrowed the little red rubber pump she used to give red pepper enemas to her child. We washed it well and began to pump water into the girl's ear. Suddenly I had a terrible thought.

"Tom, what if the corn swells and gets stuck even harder?"

A moment of doubt passed over Tom's face, but

before he could answer, on a spray of water, the kernel came flying out! The entire quarter had assembled outside our house, and when they saw the girl emerge and our smiling faces, they broke into cheers and clapping.

Later, we cured pneumonia and third-degree burns, but our most acclaimed cure was always the girl with the kernel of corn in her ear. It had the neatness of an insoluble medical puzzle, and perhaps that is why it became a legend of sorts. Ironically, like the shaman in curing ceremonies I had read about, Tom handed the girl the corn to keep as a souvenir.

Health care in Kalikaha had gone from one tradition to another without any intermediate phase. They had gone from traditional herbs to penicillin, but unfortunately, they had bypassed soap. Over and over, the same thing happened. Someone would get hurt and they would apply the traditional medicine, cow manure mixed with other things so that it looked like asphalt. Then the foot or hand would become infected, and when it was red and swollen, the person would come to us and ask for antibiotic pills or go to the infirmary thirty miles away for an injection of penicillin.

The government provided free clinics, and the people saw that the injections worked, but never had there been any sort of rural health program where workers came to the villages and taught basic hygiene. Not only were shots being given unnecessarily, the nurses who worked in these remote clinics took advantage of the peasants and sold them medicines, which were supposed to be provided free of charge. This enraged us, for every time we went to the clinic, whatever we needed—if they weren't out of it—was given to us free. When the villagers were seriously ill, they were afraid to go to the clinic for fear of being charged an exorbitant amount that they did not have. So they put off going until the last possible moment, and then it was often too late.

I became, despite the book's good advice, blindly evangelical about soap and water. It became an obsession with me. Determined to spread the gospel, I took to handing out little pieces of antiseptic soap wherever I went. Children and babies were bathed at least once a day, and they were soaped and scrubbed down so thoroughly with such quantities of suds that I rarely saw a child with an infected cut. It was the adults who had the infections. The antiseptic soap I brought back from Korhogo and handed out I explained as being a special soap for cuts and burns.

One day, near the end of my stay in Kalikaha, I was visiting Mariam, when her young son and his wife came out to speak to me. They had been clearing a new field and both had burned their feet while burning out stumps. Both of them had red swollen feet coated with the thick black paste. Mariam wanted me to give them antibiotics. I felt totally defeated. If Mariam, whom I saw frequently, hadn't gotten my message about soap and water, then no one else had either.

"What about washing wounds with soap and water?" I asked in a hurt voice. "I thought you agreed it was a good thing to do."

"Yes, Carol, you have said many times to wash the children's cuts with soap and water, and now I do that. But I did not think it was good to wash burns."

I should have remembered what the book said, but instead, I went straight off the deep end in frustration. Day after day, I treated swollen feet and hands and saw bad cases of blood poisoning that could have been prevented. Day after day, I handed out ampicillin to people who had put mud and manure on their wounds instead of washing them. This was the last straw. Exactly as the book very graphically warned not to do, I climbed up on my soapbox and began to rant and rave about the wonders of soap and water with more fervor than I ever had before. "From now on," I ended, adamantly shouting *at* them, "I refuse to give pills to people who haven't bothered to wash their wounds!"

Mariam watched my outburst with sympathetic interest, but I could see that she was simply not convinced. It was my belief system against hers. About everything else, I retained a sort of cultural relativism, believing nonjudgment to be essential to living in the village. But somehow I just couldn't maintain this attitude when it came to the case of the traditional black gunk they put on cuts and burns. I had seen too many bad infections. I admit it. I had become positively and blindly evangelical about soap and water. I believed implicitly, probably irrationally, in its powers. This belief ran deep inside me, beyond my conscious control. I was determined that I was not moving from that spot until I had converted Mariam, the devout Moslem. It was the last stand of my soap and water jihad, and I was desperate for at least one convert.

"Remember when I burned my leg?" I asked her. About a month before, Tom and I had hit a sand pit on the motorcycle and gone over. I had burned my calf badly on the muffler. Mariam nodded. "I didn't put any medicine on it, I didn't even bandage it. I just washed it with soap and water several times a day. And what did you think? Did it heal well?"

Mariam nodded. "That is true," she said, sounding almost convinced. "Everyone talked about how quickly it healed. From now on," she said slowly, "I will wash the burns with soap and water. But Carol," she added, her eyes full of wounded dignity and reproach, "we were taught never to wash burns and that is why it was difficult for me to believe what you said."

Chastened, I went home immediately and brought back antibiotics for the infected feet. I felt ashamed of my outburst. Over the ampicillin, Mariam forgave me and we remained friends.

But this was not the end of my soap evangelism. Most people didn't really believe that mere soap and water had cured my burn, for everyone knew that the whites had very strong medicines. Of course, like the Senufo and Dyula themselves, we kept them well hidden, just as Donnisongui kept his secret medicines hidden in our house. So whatever we possessed that had cured my burn, it couldn't have been the soap I handed out so freely.

This belief in secret medicines permeated village life. Adama assured us that if we wanted to pay a very large sum he had some relatives in another village who would sell us a medicine that would render us invisible, and then we could walk around the village and spy on people to our heart's content without ever being seen! For another large fee, they could give us something to make bullets bounce right off us. Adama was amazed when I told him that we didn't have any medicines that could do this.

Other people in the village were extremely surprised that we ever got sick at all. Once, Tom threw his neck out and went around with a stiff, painful neck for a week. This amazed the villagers. Why hadn't our medicines, if they were so powerful, prevented this misfortune? What about my famous soap?

As far as the soap itself went, many of them did not much believe in the pieces I gave them. The power, in their eyes, lay in the ritual of having the wound washed.

If soap was our particular brand of medicine, as they had herbs steeped in pottery jars, then part of its efficacy came from being administered by us, the soap healers. An old grizzled hunter came to our house and held up a cut foot, filthy from hours of tramping in the bush. When I offered him soap, he refused. He wanted me to wash the foot. "It won't matter," I told him. "It works no matter who washes it." But the old hunter didn't believe this for a minute. I was simply trying to keep the medicine's efficacy for myself and my own. He stuck his filthy old foot in my face. "Wash your own dirty feet!" I yelled in English, "and I'll wash mine!"

Other patients were more appealing. One of these was the four-year-old son of the chief of our quarter. He was brought to us one day with a gash in his cheek. The wound was so infected that one side of his face was swollen as hard and as round as a tennis ball and his eye was shut tight. Boys this age were charged with herding the teams of plow oxen, and he had been gored by the long horn of one of these oxen. The boys always looked tiny to me behind the enormous animals; it seemed an awfully large responsibility for such small children.

I cleaned out the wound and put him on a schedule of ampicillin four times a day. For the children, I had to break open the capsules and divide the white powder into small doses, which I twisted in bits of paper. The first few times an older child brought the boy, but after that he came alone. Each day, four times a day, exactly at the appointed hour, he gravely presented himself on our porch. I would pull out a stool for him and take out a paper of the white powder. Mixing it with water in a large spoon, I would hold it out for him. He always licked every white grain from the spoon and drank the glass of water I handed him with a rich sense of his own

importance. Both of us came to look forward to the ritual; it bound us together. The day I told him that the
medicine was finished, he looked at me in surprise before
he clambered down from the stool. After that, I rarely
saw him anymore. He went back to following the oxen. It
was not until weeks later that his father came to thank
us. It was done in the best Senufo manner. The father
handed us a bowl of the freshest eggs and said only that
the boy was very well. As soon as we accepted his blessings, he turned and walked away.

Four women we knew gave birth while we were in
Kalikaha. The first baby was a girl born to Jeneba, a
Dyula woman in Tom's study group. The morning after
the birth, we went into the dark house where Jeneba lay
with the baby. Dyula women spend a week sequestered
inside their houses after they give birth. Anyone who
wishes may visit them, and bringing a small gift is the
custom. However, some people who have strong secret
medicines for working sorcery may not want to visit a
woman who has just given birth, for the place of recent
birth has a power of its own which could ruin their medicines.

I took the tiny girl in my arms, her features still
squashed flat from birth. How difficult this is, I
thought, to conceive, to bring the pregnancy to term, to
give birth to a healthy child. I was overcome by the miracle of it. "This pleases me, this pleases me very much,"
was all I could manage to say. "May Allah give you one
of your own soon," replied Jeneba's cowife.

I should have known at that moment that the strug-
gle was not yet over. Tom and I had compiled statistics
which showed that 34 percent of all children born in
Kalikaha never reach puberty. Jeneba's baby cooed at us
each time we visited, and soon, all the little girls of the

quarter were carrying her around on their backs. But one day, Tom came back to the house with a serious face and reached for the book. "Jeneba's baby is sick. She has fever and is having trouble breathing. I told them we'd be back with medicine as soon as possible. They're really worried."

It sounded like pneumonia. There were guidelines in the book for the doses one gave to a child, but from there I had to extrapolate to figure out how much to give a month-old baby. I divided a capsule of ampicillin into doses and wrapped each one in paper, hoping that I had the dosage right. I had never before seen Jeneba look tense and frightened. She was usually hale and hearty and had a smile that reached out and embraced everyone near her—her cowife, her old husband, Tom, me, all her neighbors, and every child in the quarter. She had been pregnant the whole time I had known her, but she had worked in the fields as hard as the rest of the women up until the week she gave birth.

The baby sucked in each breath with difficulty. The force of the effort pulled her skin taut, outlining each tiny rib. Jeneba carefully spooned the ampicillin into the child's mouth and nodded at our instructions for the other doses, which we synchronized with the Moslem prayer times. We promised to come back first thing in the morning. The next day, Jeneba's smile beamed at us the moment we reached the compound, and she showered us with blessings. She was radiantly happy. The child had turned for the better.

Each day that week, I sat at home, opening the capsules and dividing the white powder into four equal piles, careful not to breathe too hard, lest I waste any. This is life itself, I said to myself. The paper I used came from an old *Newsweek* that contained interviews with Vietnam veterans. "All that killing," said one. "So many people died and it meant nothing." I twisted his statement at both ends like a candy wrapper and carried the precious parcels across the village to Jeneba.

After the child recovered, Bayma, her father, thanked us profusely, and we were always greeted with grateful appreciation in his compound. Jeneba's smile shone on us even more brightly than before. For the first time, I felt the tremendous rush of power that comes from having healed another human being. The power inherent in that act frightened and fascinated me at the same time. For the ego, it was a passage through Sirens.

But if that time I made it through triumphant, my next experience as a healer quickly reminded me just how small I really was against the forces of death. The other baby born about this time was also a girl, born to Nofigay's cowife, Wahdonan. Wahdonan was shy and did not speak Dyula, and we didn't know her as well as her peppery cospouse. For a long time one of her legs had been swollen very large, and there was talk that she was a sorcerer and that the swelling was really a pot of dangerous medicine that she kept hidden in her leg. According to the villagers, a sorcerer could remove the pot anytime, use the medicine inside to do harm to someone, and then return the pot to be stored away again inside the body. I could never believe that shy Wahdonan, with her small heart-shaped face, would cause harm to anyone, and I knew that when her leg was swollen, she suffered more than anyone else because she could not tend her fields. In addition to the pain, she had to bear the brunt of the village rumors.

The father of the child, old Menergay, came to our house one afternoon and told us that the baby, now about a month old, refused to nurse. Did we have any medicines that would help? Had we known more about babies, perhaps we would have realized that this was serious. But we simply said we didn't have anything, so he thanked us and went away. Menergay was an important Senufo elder, and because of his *poro* training, tended to be taciturn. When they are initiated into the *poro,* Senufo boys are taught to speak briefly and to the point. They must never be thought to be garrulous. It is women's speech, in the Senufo world, that is rambling, vivid, and embellished with details. Perhaps this is why he didn't tell us more about the baby's illness.

The next morning when we arrived at his compound to do interviews, the place was very quiet. Only old Menergay and his son were outside. Menergay sadly informed us that the baby was gravely ill and that no one could speak with us. All of the women were inside Wahdonan's round house keeping watch.

We asked Menergay if he had thought of taking the baby to the hospital in Korhogo or to the clinic. His reply was that since the baby had not drunk anything in a day, they were afraid to take it out of the house for fear that the heat would kill it.

We asked if we could go inside. At least, Tom said to me, even if we don't know what to do, we can show our concern. The house was full of women. Nofigay held the baby. It was very quiet inside the round dark room. The only sound was the baby's breathing—very fast and labored. There was mucus in her nose, and she breathed with difficulty but did not have the symptoms of pneumonia, with which we were now familiar.

The only thing I could think to do was to make a steam tent. Perhaps the baby just had a bad cold or bronchitis. If she could breathe better, maybe she would nurse again, I told myself hopefully. With Adama's help, I explained what to do. "Please, Adama," I whispered, "please explain that it won't cure the illness. It will only help the baby to breathe."

After he had explained in Senufo, I tugged at his arm again. "Are you sure they understand that?"

"Yes," he said gently. "They understand. And they want to try it."

When we came back half an hour later, one woman sat on a stool holding the baby. A large pot of very hot water was carried in. I held one cloth and another woman held another and we closed them at the top until the woman inside sat in a steamy tent.

"I saw them do this once at the clinic," one of the women told Adama. "But the nurse dropped the baby into the water."

The tent worked well and the steam lasted a long time. They said that they would put the baby into the tent every hour. If only the baby would nurse, perhaps we could somehow get her to the hospital.

It seemed a million things happened that day that demanded Tom's and my attention. A new livestock extension agent arrived in the village, placed there because Tom's work had called the government's attention to the need for such a person. Tom was completely occupied with introducing him to all the elders and arranging for a house for him. Our friend Jean-Baptiste from Korhogo, a French veterinarian, suddenly appeared with a carful of German researchers who were visiting the area, and I spent the afternoon taking them on a hot, sweaty tour of the Dyula part of the village, stopping to greet everyone we knew, including the old marabout El Hadji Traore, who shook the men's hands but politely refused mine because he was reading the Koran and mustn't touch a woman.

It was evening and we were both very tired by the time we returned to Menergay's compound to ask about the baby. Her breathing is better, they told us, but now she stiffens up and rears back. As we sat there the baby did this several times, contorting her tiny face, stiffening all over and arching her back, her small fists clenched tightly. Wahdonan held her own child now.

Tom and I walked home sadly to consult the book. It sounded like tetanus, probably from the razor blade used to cut the baby's umbilical cord. The disease could have been avoided if Wahdonan had been vaccinated during her pregnancy. Tom always urged the men to take their pregnant wives to the clinic for vaccinations, but now we remembered that old Menergay, who believed firmly in the herbal medicines, had refused. There did not seem to be anything we could do. We had antibiotics but no way to inject them, and the baby would not drink even a drop. This, then, was the meaning of tetanus's old name—lockjaw.

We hardly slept that night. It was so hot that my hair was soaked with sweat, and when I did fall asleep, I had a strange dream and woke up badly frightened. In the dream, a dying man came and stood over the bed, leaning over me, calling out to me.

In the morning, we got up tiredly. I was inside making tea when I heard Tom, out in the back courtyard, make a terrible sound—part moan, part cry of pain, part stifled exclamation. "What is it?" I called out frightened. "Are you all right?"

"Oh, no," he moaned again. "They've got Wahdonan's baby on the funeral grounds."

Over the back wall, I saw a small group of women. A man dressed only in a *poro* loincloth was holding a very small bundle. I could see the shape of the baby's head and feet, all tightly wrapped in a white cloth. They laid the bundle down in the center of the funeral grounds on a woven cloth, and a woman came and placed a vessel of water a short distance away. Then each of the women walked up and threw cowries down beside the small body.

I don't remember moving, but somehow, of one accord, Tom and I found ourselves standing at the edge of the funeral grounds, watching sadly as they carried the baby past us and placed her into a grave that had already been dug. The grave was next to a large pit in the earth into which I had once thrown garbage during one of my first weeks in the village. Donnisongui had come to me and asked me never to throw garbage there again as the pit was sacred to women. Two men in loincloths placed the baby in the grave and covered it up, building up a large mound. When this was finished, the men washed their hands and arms in the vessel of water. Nofigay picked up the tools they had used and put them into the sacred house where the *poro* stored things. Wahdonan was not present at the burial. Three younger women went into the house and took the tools out again and then everyone left. In contrast to the celebratory quality of the funeral of an older person, this one had been tragically sad.

Tom and I still stood there, unable to move, staring at the mound of fresh earth. Several women passed by us carrying water from the pump, but not one of them smiled. I didn't hear a woman laugh all day in the Senufo part of the village. They murmured greetings sadly. Sibatia arrived carrying a heavy basin of water, but she was so absentminded that she did not even acknowledge it when I ran over to help her. The only women who smiled that day were the very oldest women, and perhaps they had lived long enough to know that life would go on and more children would be born.

A short while after the funeral, Menergay's son arrived at our house to ask for medicine for his father. In the night, desperate to try to help his baby, which was surely the last child of his old age, he had gone out to gather leaves to make medicine. He was in a tree when a branch broke, and Menergay fell and hurt his shoulder and arm. He was all right, nothing was broken, but he was in pain. Before he left with the painkillers for his father, the young man told us that the baby had died about five that morning.

When Adama arrived for work, we walked over to Menergay's compound. Menergay was sitting in front of his house, leaning on a stick. He looked terribly sad and kept his head bowed as Adama gave him our blessings. Then he thanked us for our efforts to help the child the day before. Even though we had not succeeded, he wanted us to know that he knew we had done what we could.

Wahdonan was sitting on the porch of Nofigay's house, her eyes swollen from crying. Adama addressed our condolences to Nofigay, who was washing all of Wahdonan's clothes.

"I saw you come out for the burial this morning," Nofigay replied, "and you stood there for the whole thing so I knew you came not just to watch but to be there with us. Thank you for that."

So often, I feared intruding on the private moments of the villagers, and yet here I was being thanked for standing up with them. It was a lesson to me not to hold back but to act as I felt. When I did that, it seemed that they always understood.

Adama gave many blessings to Wahdonan for more children, health, and a long life. They had taken every single thing she owned out of her house and had washed the walls and floor and coated them with fresh cow dung. Her stools stood outside to be scrubbed down. When a child dies, the mother leaves her house, and her friends wash the child and wrap it in cloth. Then they clean the house and all her possessions. Only when that is finished does the mother re-enter her home. In that end of the village, everyone went about their work in slow motion, with a sad, subdued air.

MARRIAGE
IS VERY DIFFICULT

FOR WEEKS, THE DYULA WOMEN HAD BEEN TALKING ABOUT the wedding. For the past two days, guests had streamed into the Dyula part of the village, arriving on foot from small villages in the bush, tired and dusty, their heads loaded with food and bundles, or grandly, swathed in expensive cloth as they stepped out of taxis from the city. Others came on mopeds, the women sidesaddle on the back, miraculously not falling off without appearing to hold on. On every cooking fire a thirty-gallon pot of rice simmered. Mariam, who had to count each franc with care, had bought twice as many spices as usual just to feed her guests. As for me, I walked the long way around to the potters' quarter, going twice as far in the afternoon sun, just so that I could pass through Dyulaso and observe the bustle.

"Come and cook with us!" the women called. "There's lots to do."

"I can't today," I called back. "I'm going to make pots."

"All you do these days is make pots. But we haven't seen you at the market selling them. You must be selling them in the other towns and getting very rich. When are you going to give us some of your pots?"

"Soon," I promised vaguely, as I went on my way. When I was put on the spot, the important thing was to give an answer; any answer was better than none.

The next day was the first day of the week-long Moslem wedding. Three brides were being married at once, two from my adopted family, the Traores, and a third girl who was a Silla from Sillera.

As soon as we heard the drums start up in the afternoon Adama and I walked over to watch. A large crowd had gathered. In the middle of the crowd were the three brides. Matching cloths were twisted around their waists to form long skirts, but to my surprise, they were barebreasted. They wore necklaces of brightly colored plastic beads, and on their heads, like crowns, were hats made of origami-folded foil, as if they were going to a New Year's ball. They also wore sunglasses with heavy black frames. I hadn't expected white eyelet, but these outfits took me completely aback.

"Why don't they wear shirts?" I asked Adama. "I thought Moslem women always wore shirts."

"Not on their wedding day," replied Adama. "It's to prove they're virgins."

"How can we tell?" I asked.

"Because their breasts are small," he said, giving me an odd look. "They aren't pregnant."

"What are the glasses for?" I persisted.

"To make them beautiful," he replied solemnly, gazing at the brides with rapt satisfaction.

Behind each bride danced a supporting chorus of her younger sisters and friends. They carried towels to wipe away the sweat and the tears, both of which were shed copiously as the afternoon progressed. Some held aloft full-length portraits of the brides' boyfriends, large black-and-white photographs about sixteen inches tall, framed in glass with red tape on the edges, taken by a photographer who came to Kalikaha sometimes on market days.

The institution of boyfriends and girlfriends is a traditional custom in Dyula society. When a girl has accepted a boy, he goes to her parents and presents them with a gift of kola nuts. If the kola nuts are accepted, he is officially recognized as her boyfriend. She is allowed to spend nights with him in the house he shares with other youths at the edge of the quarter. Sexual intimacy is encouraged, but intercourse is strictly forbidden. The boy must protect the girl from other boys and men, and if, on her wedding night, she is found to be a virgin, this is held up not only as a credit to her family but also as a sign of the good character of her *petit ami.* It is his reputation that is on the line, not hers. One day, perhaps with very short notice, she must forget this young lover that she chose and marry the man her family chooses for her, a man who is often twenty or thirty years older than she is.

Several young men played drums and the older women shook gourd rattles, but the bulk of the music came from the three brides as they sang continuously in a repeating rhythm that rose and fell. The young men swarmed around them with jumbo-sized bottles of baby powder and toilet water, dumping both on their bare shoulders. Admirers ran up and attached thousand-franc notes to their foil crowns. The women who followed the brides had on their best outfits, and the giant, brightly colored designs seemed to swim through the village, as if they moved independently of the women who wore them. Multi-colored butterflies and flowers, black and yellow television sets with rabbit ears, alphabets and inkpots, papaya trees, cotton bolls, and huge geometric motifs striped and dotted and $x$ed their way along the paths in red, purple, black, and orange. If I had thought that this part of the wedding had anything to do with the solemnity of marriage or their future husbands, I was totally mistaken. At midnight, the girls would be given to their grooms, dressed in white from head to toe, prayed over and blessed with solemn chanting. But this afternoon was the final fling, the last revelry of youth. It reminded me of a parade in New Orleans at Mardi Gras.

The three brides sang their way from quarter to quarter, and I followed in the crowd, feeling like a sparrow who has wandered into a flock of peacocks. The girl from Sillera, who was cross-eyed, didn't sing with the same gusto as the other two, yet she hung on to a picture of her boyfriend, sang as best she could, and cried constantly. I did not know her name, but the two Traore girls were named Biba and Jiata. Biba was to marry the tailor, a young man of twenty-five. Jiata would be given to a man in his fifties, a cousin, who already had two wives. Cross-cousins are a preferred marriage among the Dyula.

Many of the women stared at me with odd, curious, even distrustful looks, and I realized that these were the guests from other villages. I had already forgotten how it had been when I first came to Kalikaha and was regarded like that by everyone. For gradually, I and the villagers had drifted into a mutual acceptance, and my presence was now more or less taken for granted. "She lives here with us. She speaks Dyula," I heard the women from Kalikaha whisper over and over with a proud, proprietary air that surprised me.

From quarter to quarter we paraded, the brides singing the same tune over and over, the crowd following after, the young men sprinkling baby powder and toilet water until the brides turned white. The young men handed out candy and cigarettes to the spectators, and when something especially pleased them, they threw handfuls of candy into the air, and all the children scrambled after it. Young girls meandered through the crowd selling fried dough balls and paper cones of peanuts.

One of the brides pulled a young man out of the group and danced sensually in front of him, flipping the hair whisk she carried across his face playfully. Everyone laughed, candy flew into the air, and Mariam told me that he was her boyfriend.

The older women, dressed in flowing robes and scarves, formed a benevolent chorus on the steps of the mosque. The young girls came to them and asked for blessings, which the women chanted softly in unison. I stood near Mariam, who looked saintlike in flowing white, and let the soft chants of the choir roll over me.

From time to time, one of the brides would go up to a woman and sing to her, standing very close, their faces nearly touching. Then, inevitably, the older woman would break down and cry. Tears, in odd contrast to the carnival atmosphere, flowed everywhere. The brides cried often. Everyone cried except the young men who were having their last day of fun before their childhood friends left them to become wives and mothers. Adama and I had become separated in the crowds, so I couldn't ask him what it all meant. I thought that they cried because, as one traditional song went, "marriage is very difficult" and because the brides did not want to leave their boyfriends for husbands they had not chosen.

Finally, in the dusky light of evening, Biba and Jiata broke off and headed for the house of the elder of their family, El Hadji Traore. Everyone must have known this was coming because the cement terrace of his house had emptied of people, and he was seated there alone, as if on a throne, an enormous man bedecked in white robes and red hat, holding his prayer beads in his plump hands.

The two brides made their way toward him singing and waving their black whisks. What remained of their voices was hoarse and strained. They had started singing at one in the afternoon and it was now after six. They could barely get out the words, but they sang on determinedly, supported by the young girls behind them. They sang sadly, their tired voices raspy and broken. I couldn't understand the words, but I imagined that they were pleading with him not to marry them off to strangers, not to send them away from the tight circle of the family. They went down on their knees in front of him, swaying and brushing him with their whisks, chanting the same refrain over and over. El Hadji's face was pained; he didn't look directly at them; it was as if he could not bear to. He kept his eyes fixed on the prayer beads in his lap. Finally, he raised his hands slightly, his palms toward them, as if to say, Enough. Please, no more.

But they kept on, their hoarse voices rising and falling. Finally, I saw one single tear flow out of his eye and roll down his cheek and it fell on his hands, bedecked with silver rings, where he wiped at it. At this, Biba and

Jiata turned and danced, tired but triumphant, down the steps. All of the old women and many of the young ones were crying freely.

I stood not far away from the corner of his terrace and stared at El Hadji. It was a strangely moving sight, the old patriarch who wields so much power over the lives of his family, who could by a word marry these girls to whomever he chose, brought to shed a tear by the pleas of the hoarse, sweating young women with supple shoulders and dark, ripe breasts. I couldn't take my eyes off the old man, although everyone was leaving the quarter and I knew that I would soon be conspicuous, staring at him like that. He pushed back his heavy sleeve, glanced at his watch, and then bent his head and stared intensely once again at his prayer beads. He looked strangely satisfied, although why this should be I had no idea.

Adama and I walked home with Noupka, who had been in the crowd. Wherever there was music and dancing, you could be sure Noupka would be there, no matter what the event. "You should be ashamed," Adama admonished her, "to come to the wedding without a shirt. It isn't right. You were the only one." Noupka shrugged and handed me Mama, who was trying to jump off Noupka's back into my arms. Mama had spent the afternoon tied onto Noupka's back, being jogged up and down, and she was ready for a change. As for me, I was sweaty and tired and my T-shirt and my hair were coated with baby powder, sprinkled on me by way of salute from the young men.

The next day, I went to see Mariam to ask what it all meant. Each bride makes up her own songs, improvising on the spot, Mariam told me. When she sees the young men, she sings, "Come and dance! Today is my great day!" When she sings before the chorus of elder women, she asks them to give her blessings, to ask Allah to give her health, children, and a harmonious marriage.

When she sees a woman she knows, she sings of the woman's sorrows, the children she has lost, for example. That is why all the women cry when the brides sing to them. Then the brides give blessings to comfort the women. Through the brides' songs, the tragic events of the past year are brought forward and remembered. On that afternoon, when they are no longer children and not quite women, the brides have the power to bring forth tears. After the tears have been spilled, they give blessings for solace.

When the brides want to end, they sing before the elder of their family. It seemed to me that they pleaded with him not to marry them away, but I was wrong. They sang to him of his life and of the tragedies of the last year, the wife who died, the babies that were lost. And then they gave him benedictions to console him. "It is Allah's will," they sang. "Be comforted." And that is why he cried.

CARRYING STONES

After dinner, Tom and I walked over to the courtyard of the Traore family. We were greeted warmly by Bamasouri, a handsome man in his thirties. Like all the Traores, he was a scholar and had studied the Koran, but he also farmed and had a farmer's muscular body. When he spoke, he used an educated Dyula that was much more complex than the market language. Although he slowed down for my benefit, he steadfastly refused to simplify his vocabulary. He would explain a phrase to me in Dyula, but he would not demean his native tongue by reducing it to baby talk or the ungrammatical market patois that we used. He seemed to have perfect confidence that I would somehow transcend the limitations of my own basic Dyula and rise to his level. Underneath the beautifully framed sentences and the schoolteacher's tones, there was so much unspoken warmth that it seemed to radiate out of Bamasouri's broad chest in a luminous glow.

Bamasouri presented us with three red kola nuts. He apologized for pressing them on us when we didn't like kola, but, as he explained, it was his obligation as host to give kola to the guests during the wedding. Tom and I didn't want to be rude so we split one and chewed some to keep awake. I found that if I took just a little piece in my mouth, the bitterness was manageable. This was the first time that I chewed kola and didn't spit it out right away. Eventually, I even came to like it and would share a nut with Tom and Adama as we walked around the village. But I never did learn to spit the pulp out neatly in a thin red stream.

Once I had handled kola myself, I could more easily understand how it had symbolic value for so many African peoples and why, in earlier eras, the kola trade had been so important in West Africa. Kola from the forest region south of Kalikaha had been traded for salt and slaves as far north as the Sahel. Ivory Coast is still called in the Dyula and Bamana languages "The Land of Kola." A kola nut looks mysteriously like a human heart, and when you split one open with your fingernail, the nut opens cleanly along an interior fault. The inside texture has a curiously pristine look that is difficult to describe. In Dyula, to marry is called "tying the kola" because the elders put kola nuts into packages of leaves, wrap them with string, undo them, and then retie them as a symbol of the marriage contract.

Tom and I thought we might need the kola to keep awake, and we were right. As usual in the village, the nighttime ceremonies began very late. Hours passed, and we were still the only guests. Finally we heard gentle

singing, and a procession of women came into the courtyard. In the middle were Biba and Jiata, still dressed in
their matching skirts, jewelry, and foil hats. The foil hats
glittered dramatically in the lanternlight. The women
moved slowly past us, and we followed them to the courtyard of El Hadji, where that afternoon the old man had
sat on his terrace and cried his single tear. The courtyard
in front of his house was full of older women seated on
woven mats. The area was busy with women coming and
going, dressed in their best clothes, all light and flowing
in the dark night.

"They are washing the brides now in the courtyard," said Bamasouri. "Carol, you can go in and watch,
but Tom must stay here with me. Men are forbidden to
attend."

I walked hesitantly into the courtyard and looked
around for a woman I knew who could act as a *jatigi-muso*
for me. But despite the fact that I had adopted the name
Traore, there were no Traore women that I knew well,
for not a single Traore family had ended up in Tom's
random sample. I sat down with some older women on a
woven mat near the wall and tried to be as inconspicuous
as possible. I wasn't used to going out in society without
a *jatigi* of some sort, someone to whom I could attach myself. Without one, I felt vulnerable. From my mat, I
could see nothing except the backs of the circle of women
who surrounded the bride. These were older women, and
they chanted softly, the same refrain over and over. Very
near them, against a wall, I saw a line of younger women
watching whatever was going on inside this circle. Gathering my courage, I went and stood near them. A wave of
whispers went through the strangers and I heard several
of the women whisper to their guests, "She's a Traore.
And she speaks Dyula."

One skeptical stranger greeted me to find out if this were true. "Traore woman, good evening," she said with a testing tone to her voice.

"*Nsay,*" I replied in perfect pitch. The guests all laughed in surprise, but they seemed satisfied and made room for me to stand near them.

The bride was seated on a stool inside the circle of older women, and as they bathed her, they sang softly in sad, gentle tones. When the bath was finished, they called for her clothes. She made no move to help them as they lifted her feet and fitted sandals onto them, and then they wound a white cloth around her head. They stood her up and dressed her all in white. Last of all, they put a white veil over her head, a veil made of the same white cotton as the rest of her clothing, so that we could not see her face at all. When she was all dressed, the chant became quicker, and the women all clapped in time to the music.

Now the second bride was carried in on the shoulders of older women, completely nude. There was only one kerosene lantern in the far corner of the courtyard so I could not tell whether it was Biba or Jiata. Again, the bride sat stiffly while they bathed her. When they wanted to wash her arm, they lifted it themselves. She never moved of her own volition. Then, she, too, was covered up like a white ghost and led away. All this time, the high voices of the older women sang on, sadly and sweetly, chanting verses from the Koran and blessings.

The girls were seated on mats at one end of the courtyard, and while everyone chanted, they prayed, bending like sheets folded over a line and touching their foreheads to the mat.

When the prayers were finished, the mood lightened. Everyone sang to the two girls, and sisters sat behind them, their arms draped around the brides. Some of the old women made bawdy jokes and laughed loudly at their own wit. Near midnight, the women lifted the first bride up. She stood stiffly and made no move to help them. They carried her, laid flat like a corpse, on their shoulders.

"Marriage is very difficult," the brides' pallbearers sang, "because you have to ask your friends from time to time to give you red pepper, some salt, a little flour. That's why marriage is not always good."

Outside the courtyard, the men fell in behind our procession. The women carried the bride, who never moved, to her groom's house, where he waited. Still singing, they carried her up to the door and put her down on her feet. Even now, she stood like a statue that has not yet been unveiled. Several of the oldest women went inside to make sure everything was all right. Then they pushed her inside and went in after her. The crowd remained outside for hours, chanting and singing.

"We're going to wash you, too, and give you to your husband," the old women teased me.

"I've already been married," I lied.

"That doesn't matter," they replied. "We'll give you another wedding, a Dyula wedding. We'll wash you and give you to Tom," they cackled. "You'll have to stay in his house for a week."

This idea made me wince all over. In a Dyula marriage, it is so clear that what is being given is the woman's body, for it is ritually bathed, dressed, blessed, sung over. One cannot say in Dyula, "They got married." One can only say, "He married her" or "She was married to him." The man is the actor. The woman, in language as in ritual, remains passive. Whenever we talked about it, I unconsciously switched the grammar around to make myself active, and this gave the old women enormous merriment.

Of all the Dyula ceremonies I witnessed, none had the solemn and sacred air of the washing of the brides. The gift of a bride from the elder men to the younger ones and the alliances formed by these marriages are the mortar that holds Dyula society together. But none of the women said anything to me about keeping it secret. I assumed that men could not attend because the brides were nude. After all, the men sat just outside the courtyard and overheard everything. Only by chance a month or so later did I learn about the need for secrecy.

This time, twenty-one brides were being married at once in Dyulaso, and we invited our French friends in Korhogo, Claude and Jean-Baptiste, to come for the afternoon dancing. When I told Adama that Claude might stay for the evening and go with me to wash the brides, he looked doubtful. "You had better ask the old women about that," he told me, "because I have heard them talking about it a lot. They don't like foreigners to see that and especially not a white woman. 'If it wasn't Carol,' one said to me, 'we would not have let her attend. But since it is Carol, it was all right. After all, she lives here with us and we are all the same now.' "

"Still," Adama continued, "they are worried that you may write something and give away the secrets of what happens."

"But what could I say?" I asked Adama. "Just that the old women wash the brides and everyone knows that already. Everyone hears the singing. Why didn't they tell me this? How can I keep a secret if I don't even know it is one?"

"I really don't know," Adama replied. "It's a big secret between the men and the women. They don't speak to us about it, and I don't know what happens, so I don't know what you could say. But it is something very serious and important for the women."

What Adama said touched me. I was happy to hear how they felt toward me. So often, I felt a bond with the women of Kalikaha, but rarely did I know if they reciprocated that feeling. I have done just what they feared and written about parts of what I observed. I hope that by describing these events in these very general terms I have not betrayed their trust in me.

I describe the scene that night because I want to convey the feeling—the soft singing of the older women, the faint glow of lanternlight in the darkness, the gentle drip of water, and the young brides who stand like statues and are carried to their grooms like corpses. For as women, it seems to me that we have so little mythology of our own, so little ritual. We so often bathe the sick, the young, the dead, but are so seldom bathed ourselves. I was reminded that night of the wedding of Psyche, who is garbed in ashes and rags and set upon a high crag, not to the tune of wedding hymns but to the sound of a funeral dirge.

A Dyula girl is buried that night and a woman is born. In the past, her clitoris would have been excised in the year preceding the wedding to rid her of any maleness, for the clitoris is perceived as a "male" organ. Totally female, she can now marry and bear children. This has changed in the recent past, and girls are now excised at a much younger age so that the connection between excision and marriage is no longer such a direct one.

It is the older women who excise the girl and bathe and prepare the bride and who carry her to her groom, sometimes as unknown to the girl as Amor was to Psyche. This often seems to me a cruel paradox—what older women do to younger ones in any society. As they carry the girl to her groom, they sing:

Marriage is very difficult
because you have to ask your friends
from time to time
to give you red pepper, some salt, a little flour.
That's why marriage is not always good.

They do not send her away with promises of an easy life. They do not bribe her by telling her that her husband will give her gifts and take care of her. She hears the wedding song all her life and it says that even after she is married, she may lack for the most basic necessities, for salt and red pepper are necessities to a Dyula woman.

Where should she turn? Who can she count on? It is not her father or her brothers that are invoked, despite the patrilineal structure of Dyula society. It is the other women, her sisters and friends. They will give her a little red pepper and a little salt so that when it is her night to cook for the family, her meal will not be criticized by the men. We take spice in our food for granted, but the Dyula do not. They say that without salt and red pepper, a sauce is not a sauce, and is not worth eating.

In Dyula society, a girl must be excised to marry. She must marry to remain a member of society. Only after she is widowed or legitimately divorced does she have any choice. Then, when she is past child-bearing age, she can marry whomever she likes or she can choose not to marry at all. But only a few women ever reach this moment of choice and it is often made by economic necessity. An older woman alone could not raise enough food to survive. She must be attached to a household. For the rest of the women, they marry the men their fathers choose and hope to have a husband who treats all his wives fairly and cowives who are kind and help each other.

The night that the bride was carried into the groom's house was by no means the end of the wedding. It was only the beginning of the week-long affair. During this week, the bride must not step outside the door of the groom's house. In theory, the groom was supposed to be inside with her. But in reality, he could go out and stroll over to the houses of his men friends to be entertained, as long as he didn't go too far or stay away too long.

The bride's week of confinement was anything but dull, as I discovered several afternoons later when Adama and I went to pay our respects to Jiata, who was now the third wife of a man in his fifties.

"Bride!" shouted Adama over the din. The inside of the house was crammed, every meager square inch of it, with young men and women dancing to cassettes of Bob Marley and popular Zairean groups like Franco and the OK Tip Top Jazz Band. The air was thick with sweat and smoke.

Jiata danced out of the crowd. She was dressed in a beautiful new outfit made of green tie-dyed cloth with a shawl of the same green tie-dyed cotton draped over her head and shoulders. Brides always wore shawls over their heads. "Bride!" Adama yelled over the hubbub. "We've come to give you your greeting!" Dark lines of kohl outlined Jiata's eyes, and her lips and cheeks were rouged. She looked very queenly and seemed very pleased at our visit. I gave a gift of money to the friend beside her and then Adama and I fled outside where we could breathe.

The day that the week-long wedding ended, I happened to go over to Dyulaso in the afternoon to visit Mariam. I had bought two new halves of gourds at the market to use as bowls, and Mariam had offered to show me how to stain the insides white. I used the gourd bowls, which were at least a foot in diameter, for my sponge baths, and also to clean our rice, which had to be carefully washed and rinsed and picked over, an operation that took hours and had to be done during daylight. If I didn't do this, we ended up eating tiny stones that could break our teeth and wreck havoc on our digestive systems. If your gourd bowl cracked, there were specialists at the market who would fill the crack with reeds and then carefully sew it together with grasses, making each tiny hole first with a pointed tool and then drawing the crack together like a tightly sewn seam. I always bought ones that were already repaired because the mending jobs were so beautiful.

"Mariam is gone to the dance," her little daughter told me, putting the bowls inside the house for me. "She's over there, where the women are dancing and singing."

Curious, I headed in the direction she had indicated. Under the mango trees that separated one Dyula quarter from another, I saw Mariam, dressed in her best flowing white clothes. Other women were drifting quietly, in two's and three's, out through the mango trees and away from the village on the path that led to the tobacco gardens and the two potters' quarters. "Can I come with you?" I asked Mariam. She hesitated before she said yes.

When we reached the mango grove outside the potters' quarters, some of the women sat down on the roots of the big, spreading trees. Others, including Mariam, walked on. "Sit down here and wait," Mariam said to me before she left.

"Sit here by me," said an old woman who had come

259

all the way from Mali for the wedding. "I have never talked to a white woman before. Are you married? And children? Not yet? May Allah give you one soon."

"Amina," I replied and tapped my forehead.

"Aaaeeeeeeiiiii!" said the woman, in one of those unreproducible African sounds that express surprise. "This white woman speaks Dyula!"

While we talked the women were hunting on the ground for stones. They seemed particular about the size they wanted, discarding one after another until they found one that suited them. One young woman made everyone laugh by pretending to choose a very large stone that she could barely lift.

After we had waited for a time, I heard the sound of singing, and a procession of women came toward us from the other side of the mango trees. The procession was led by a very small old woman dressed in white and carrying a staff. On her head, each woman carried a rock the size of a tennis ball. When Mariam passed, she gestured to me to get in line in front of her and she handed me a rock, too. I had taken to wearing a baseball cap against the sun and this was very fortunate, as the rock sat on top of the cap and didn't fall off.

Mariam and I were in line about a third of the way from the front. Ahead of me stretched the line of women single file on the dusty red path, each one carrying a reddish stone on her head and singing. Once, I looked back, and although we had nearly reached the village, the line of women stretched all the way back to the grove of mangoes, from which women were still emerging. It was a beautiful sight, the billowing bright dresses, the colorful headscarves and turbans all lit up by the afternoon sun. Above the women's heads, the line of red rocks formed a procession all its own.

When our long procession reached the village, we wound like a multi-colored snake through the building where the Dyula men met for ceremonies, the place where the elders had "tied the kola." I climbed the steps carefully, crossed the room balancing my stone on my head, and then went down the steps on the other side and out again.

In a large courtyard, a hearth of three stones was set up. Here, the women stopped, and each of us placed our small stone next to the hearth. All around it were arranged the brides' new cooking utensils—baskets, pots, stirrers, and gourds—all brand-new and all traditionally crafted out of straw and leather and pottery. There were no metal pots or plastic basins. I understood now that we had carried stones to help the new brides establish their hearths, for every woman needs three good stones on which to rest her cooking pots.

The three brides were carried out of their grooms' houses, again on the shoulders of other women. Over their heads, they wore bright orange woven cloths. The first bride was carried to the hearth, where a large stool waited. An old woman sat on the stool and held the bride on her lap. Oil was heated in a cooking pot, and then cut-up pieces of chicken were placed in the hot oil. The old woman took the bride's hand and together they stirred the chicken until it was cooked. The bride never moved of her own accord, nor showed any expression. She remained totally passive while they bathed her hands and feet and then once again holding her hand in theirs, they made her stir the large pot of *toh* that was cooking on the hearth. As she stirred they sang, and one old woman dressed in a billowing dress of see-through yellow net played a drum. When each task was finished, the women watching all clapped their hands in a fast rhythm.

I watched uneasily as one after another the brides acted out in ritual exactly what I had been taught as a young girl: accept your role passively, cook for others, live the way your mother did. An old hand over a young one on the wooden stirrer speaks volumes. It says: *Don't fight against what is larger than you are. You will only be destroyed. Accept it, as I did. Accept, if you love me. Accept and care for us in our old age. Cook for us and carry our water, and when you are in pain trying to give birth, we will not abandon you. We will come with herbs to make it easy.*

The next day, the brides were paraded through the village by the older women. Once more, they wore the woven orange cloths over their heads. Anyone who wanted to see how beautiful the brides were had to give a small coin to the old women, who would then lift the cloths and show their faces. "Brides!" the people yelled at them delightedly wherever they went. "Good morning brides!"

The older women who accompanied the brides were dressed to the teeth. The older Dyula women favored a layered look with long full dresses over long waistcloths. They loved white turbans and headscarves and ample flowing headcloths. But the ultimate in fashion for the older Dyula woman, the one thing that truly marked her as a woman of means and distinction, was a parasol. Any sort of umbrella would do.

When the procession of brides and their guardians approached, the sight was unforgettable. The brides were dressed in new outfits, but their heads and shoulders were hidden by bright woven cloths. On their heads, they carried traditional baskets, the edges bound in leather. In front of them, behind them, and to every side were their guardians, determined to use the occasion to show off their own finery. Those who sported parasols made bright circles of color, even from far away. Very slowly, the parade made its way from quarter to quarter.

The next time I went to see the potters, Sita fixed her sharp watery eyes on me the moment I arrived. "I heard you went to carry stones," she began. I had the feeling I was in for a lecture. "That's true," I said noncommittally. "I went with Mariam Jiabate." Mariam was as upright as they came and widely respected. With Mariam as my *jatigi-muso,* I couldn't have done anything too wrong.

Sita nodded approvingly at Mariam's name. "But you didn't go with her past the mango trees, did you?" she asked me sternly, leaning forward and keeping her sharp eyes on mine.

"Oh no, I only went *to* the mango trees and I waited there with the other women until they came out."

"Very good," said Sita, satisfied. "If you go again to carry stones, you must be sure that you never go past the mangoes. Do you understand?"

"But why not?" I asked her. "What do they do past the mangoes?"

"Hmph!" sniffed Sita. "Just make sure you never go there."

In one of the later weddings, two girls from Logonso, the second potters' quarter, were married. A girl from Kafongon, beautiful Nasou, was supposed to be married as well. Nasou was Ma's daughter and the youngest potter of all. She could make only the simplest cooking pots. But since women were not allowed to make pots at all until after they married, I assumed that Nasou was widowed or divorced, for she had a little girl about three years old.

Traditionally, this was a way of ensuring that a young potter married the man the elders chose for her, for before metal pots became common in Kalikaha about fifteen years ago, a potter could become quite wealthy through the sale of her pots. A woman who was economically independent may not have been willing to marry the man chosen for her, and so she was not allowed to begin a real apprenticeship until after her marriage.

But I was wrong about Nasou; she was neither widowed nor divorced. Nasou was in love with a mechanic's apprentice in Korhogo and had borne his child. When they said that they were going to marry her to a young man in the other potters' quarter, she balked, and the night before she would have been bathed and carried to his house, Nasou simply disappeared.

The rumors flew thick and fast, and in Kafongon the women talked of little else. Where was Nasou? Where could a young girl like that have gone alone? Word came that she was not in Korhogo. Even Ma, her mother, claimed she did not know. Ma looked worried all the time and had headaches for which I proffered aspirin and a blessing Adama had taught me which meant "May God lighten your troubles." Some people in the village proper said that Adama was in love with the beautiful young Nasou and wanted to take her for his second wife. These people claimed that Tom had taken Nasou away on our Honda in the night and hidden her in some village far away, for how else could a young girl have escaped like that, so quickly, so cleanly, and without a trace?

She could have walked away, I thought to myself. Now that their pots were fired, the potters walked all over the countryside to sell them. Whenever I went to Kafongon, one or two of the women would be gone, making the rounds of the villages that were within a radius of fifteen or twenty kilometers. The women went on foot, carrying their pots on their heads. Unlike the Senufo and Dyula women, the potters knew the trails in the bush around the village and felt comfortable traveling on foot along them. Several times a year they packed up their pots and set off, a long line of perhaps twenty women to make the arduous trek to the nearest large market town, nearly thirty kilometers away.

The wedding went on without Nasou. From the potters, I heard all the gossip. One of the two girls was virgin. The other was not. The one who was not admitted that she had slept with a young high school student from Kafongon, a young man I saw when he came home from Korhogo on vacations. Amends were made by his family, and the affair was considered settled. The one who was a virgin refused to sleep with her middle-aged groom the first night. But the next day, they closed the door and she gave in. Adama said that this was not uncommon, and that if the husband was a good man he would not force the girl but would let the older women come in the next day to reassure the girl and try to persuade her to submit. As for the marriage of a girl who was not a virgin, Adama shook his head sadly and said that this was the first time this had ever happened in the two potters' quarters. "When we were young," he told me, "we only played with the girls' breasts. But now, they do everything. And the young girls are not happy about that."

The case of beautiful young Nasou, who had fled, disturbed him even more. The men had gone on their mopeds to Nasou's relatives in nearby villages, but she had not been found.

265

In the past, adultery was severely punished. If a man slept with another man's wife—or with his unmarried daughter—he was severely beaten. But now times have changed, and these traditional laws are no longer enforced. Adultery has become just another aspect of the system of arranged marriages.

The way Adama described it, the village at two in the morning sounded like a game of musical huts. The favorite gift for a man to give his lover was a flashlight so that she could find her way to him on dark nights. "But what do you do," I asked Adama, "when everyone is going around the village at two in the morning with their flashlights? You must bump into one another."

"Oh, we do!"

"What do you do then?" I asked.

"Oh, well, we greet one another."

"Then what? Do you ask them where they're going?" People were always asking me where I was going.

"Oh, no," said Adama. "Because if I asked them, they'd ask me. Oh, no! We just greet one another politely and then we keep going!"

Meanwhile, although Nasou had not returned, I went with the potters to dance at the houses of the other two brides. The potters' quarters tended to be more traditional than Dyulaso, and instead of cassettes of Bob Marley, the women sang and we circled around and around the house while the bride and groom sat in the middle of the room on their bed. Afterward, the groom gave me fifty francs and a kola nut for my dancing. I gave Nawa, my shy shadow, a bit of kola, and she reciprocated with a ripe mango, for it was now mango season and the trees outside Kafongon were beginning to bear fruit.

The next day Nasou returned. She had walked alone

to a village where she had relatives, a village just a bit farther than those the men had searched for her. "See?" said the gossips in the village proper, "it must have been Tom who took her there on his Honda. She could never have walked so far alone." But they didn't know the potters very well. Nasou said she was ready to go through with the marriage, but the prospective husband refused. Yet, somehow it was resolved, and the next thing I knew, Nasou had been washed and given to her groom. I was hurt that the women had not sent word to me to come for the washing of Nasou.

I went to visit Nasou several days later at her groom's house. She looked rather disconsolate, sitting on her bed with her groom, far more beautiful than any of the other brides. I gave her an extravagant gift of money because I felt badly for her. She insisted I take a handful of the largest kola nuts, which were stored under the bed for guests. I think she appreciated my visit, but there was really nothing to say. In the end, despite her beauty and her three-year-old child, and despite the fact that she was already making pots, she had given in and married the husband chosen for her.

THE HOUSES IN HEAVEN

Tom usually took long detours to avoid passing through the Traore quarter because the elder of the Traore clan, El Hadji Traore, a marabout and Koranic teacher who had been to Mecca, was determined to convert him. When pressed to give an answer about his conversion, Tom said that he could not do such an important thing lightly and that he needed some time to think it over. The marabout nodded approvingly at this answer. After that, Tom avoided Traorera, especially the grove of mango trees under which the old man usually sat. However, one day Tom passed through Dyulaso and ended up at the mango trees in spite of himself. He greeted the old man, who sat under the trees studying his holy books. The old man, who was quite wealthy from the proceeds of his Koranic school, his *maraboutage,* and from the farm work of his unusually large family, was building an impressive house of concrete blocks. He invited Tom to take a tour of the partially completed building.

"Once the old man moves in here," his nephews told Tom as they showed him around, "he won't ever go back out again."

Tom found this hard to believe. "Not even to sit under the mango trees?" he asked.

They said not and showed Tom a graveyard behind the house. The old man, they said, wanted to spend the rest of his days near the ancestors.

When Tom's tour was complete, the old man called him over. "Now that you have seen the house," the elder solemnly asked Tom, "what part do you intend to finance for me?"

Tom, casting around for a way out of this dilemma, thought seriously for a long moment or two and then replied that he would finance the electric light fixtures. This was an exceptionally safe choice in a village without electricity. Tom's reply delighted Adama, who loved a joke, and it was he who recounted this story to me.

The old man was already thinking hard. There was nothing he would have liked better for his house than light bulbs. "How could we get electricity in Kalikaha?" he asked Tom.

"You will have to change all the alleys and paths into a grid pattern," Tom replied. This was a requirement of the Ivorian government. Before a Senufo village could be considered for electric power, it must do away with the thousands of tiny alleyways and build wide new streets, which must be laid out in a grid. One village we passed on our way to Korhogo was in the process of making this change. The destruction was a terrible thing to behold. Bulldozers came in and plowed down hundreds of houses in order to reorganize the village into square blocks. Not only did most of the houses have to be rebuilt, but the traditional pattern of round family compounds and organic growth based on lineages was lost. We knew an anthropologist who had studied Senufo villages and had formulated an alternative plan to regularize the villages while still respecting kinship patterns of residence. Unfortunately, the government, after commissioning his study, had ignored it.

"Oh, no," replied the old *marabout.* "We mustn't put a grid pattern in Kalikaha. Kalikaha is an old village. If they want square quarters, they can build new quarters outside the village, but not in Kalikaha itself. We can build a new quarter for you, too," the old man offered cheerfully, "and you can send for your relatives and stay on here."

Tom explained that he had no money to remain. He had to go back to America to finish school and get a job. "Why don't you build a second story onto your house for me?" Tom asked the old man by way of retort. "If you build a second story and buy rice for me every week," Tom said teasingly, "we'll move in up there and stay on in Kalikaha."

"Oh, no!" replied the old man in a horrified voice. "Absolutely not. I would never do that."

Tom wondered what it was about us that the old man found so objectionable.

"I would never have a second story," explained the pious old man. "The houses in Paradise have more than one story, so we can't have more than one story here on earth."

"What about the houses in Abidjan?" countered Tom. "They have lots of stories."

But the old man was not in the least taken aback. "Hmph!" he snorted contemptuously. "Abidjan! Those people in Abidjan *know* they're not going to Paradise. So they want to have it all now!" He, however, was willing to wait in his one-story house, next to the ancestors.

MANGO AFTERNOONS

Part of the pleasure of visiting the potters every afternoon was the walk from the village to Kafongon after lunch and the walk back in the red glow of sunset. On the way, I always took the path by the sacred grove, and through these passages, I learned a bit more about the comings and goings of people and masks in the grove.

Once, just as I was passing, a very sacred procession of masks left the grove to walk to a funeral in another village. For a moment, I was overcome by a desire to turn my face and run, as a young woman from the village would have done. Powerful beings were leaving the seat of their power. At this moment, they were at their strongest, and the air around them resonated. I overcame the temptation to flee and drew myself up at attention. "Good afternoon," I said as they passed, greeting them respectfully in Senufo. The masks did not reply, but after they had disappeared into the bush, the man at the end of the procession, who was wearing only an old trenchcoat, turned and waved at me gaily.

Once, on a rare occasion when I passed in the early morning, I met the *poro* initiates emerging from the sacred grove dressed only in loincloths, rubbing their arms and stretching their stiff legs after a cold night on the ground.

After it passed the sacred grove, the path crossed over a small stream, and then went along an open, grassy area where oxen grazed, watched over by small boys. Climbing a small hill, I entered the shade of a large mango grove that was just outside Kafongon. When I arrived at the mango grove, the young girls would start a chant. "Caro's come! Caro-na! Caro-way! Caro-na!" We would take their long sticks and knock down two or three ripe mangoes before they flocked around me and escorted me into the quarter. "Oh Carol," they always sighed with sticky adolescent admiration. They reminded me of my own adolescence when I too had admired everything that was foreign and exotic. Lonely as I was, their affection warmed me. When I look back on these afternoons, I think of the juicy, stringy sweetness of the mangoes we ate together. Finally I had a place in the village where I felt I belonged.

I would zigzag through the circle of houses, greeting all the women and seeing what sort of pots they were working on before I ended up in the open area between Sita's, Mawa's, and Namwa's houses. These three older women were the most patient with my language problems. The younger women, when I didn't understand their stories, would get impatient. But the older women were in no hurry, and they made sure I understood one thing before they went on to another. The younger women would come and sit near us while they nursed their babies or rested between tasks, and often a baby was thrust into my arms as I sat on a low little stool.

Mawa was fun, always joking and dancing. Sita was often quiet, her alert eyes watching everything. But it was Namwa, of all the women, whom I admired the most. Once, I was talking to Adama about the minute differences among the different women's pots. If the pots were all piled together, I couldn't distinguish one woman's work from another. Adama and the women could, however. "It's like handwriting," Adama said to me. "Before you can write, you think it all looks the same. But after you learn, you recognize the handwriting of everyone you know well."

"I think Namwa's pots are particularly well made," I told him. "They have a certain strength about them." Adama gave me an odd look, as if he were surprised that I saw that clearly. "You are right about Namwa," he said. "She is a woman with a great deal of courage and wisdom."

Courage and wisdom, the women had told me, were the two most important qualities a woman must have to be a good potter. The beauty of the pots, in their view, depended on the courage and wisdom of the woman who made them. Courage, in the way they meant it, didn't mean going out to slay lions barehanded. Courage, they explained to me, meant not giving up day after day. To keep on working, to persist, that was being courageous in the hard Senufo world. "You have courage," they said to me by way of explanation. "You never get tired of asking these questions."

As I burnished their pots Mawa and Namwa taught me the names of all the pottery techniques and recounted their marriages, for they were both widows, Namwa for the third time.

"There was another white woman who came to where I lived who was just like you," Namwa told me one day. "She asked questions and wrote things down all the time, just like you. You must know her. Her name is Zacharie. She lived with us for a long time. At first, she was alone, but then she got married. Now she lives in Abidjan and has two children."

Zacharie? What French name, for the woman was most likely French, could that be? Zacharie, Zacharie, I repeated over and over to myself. I opened my mind and let the name drift through, one syllable at a time. Zach-a-reee. Zach-a-ree. Only one name came to mind. Jacqueline. For the French pronounce it Jzach-a-leen.

"Was she named Jacqueline?" I asked Namwa.

"Yes," said Namwa. "That's right. Zach-a-ree."

I knew that Namwa had spent most of her adult life away from Kafongon; she had been married to a Logon in another village. As soon as I got home I asked Tom if he had ever heard of a researcher in the region named Jacqueline.

"Yes," he replied immediately. "Jacqueline Peltre-Wurtz. She did a long-term study on agriculture in Synofan. But how did you know about her?"

Synofan was the village where Namwa had lived. The mystery was solved. Perhaps her long acquaintance with Jacqueline explained in part Namwa's warmth and openness toward me.

Another day, Namwa asked me if I had been to Abidjan. I said that I had. "Then you have seen the ocean. The ocean sounds like this," she said quietly and began to imitate perfectly the soft swishing sound of surf breaking on shore. Her face had a look of deep concentration, as if all her being were focused on that memory.

"Then you've been to Abidjan, too, Namwa! I didn't know that. When did you go?"

"No," she said sadly. "I have never seen the ocean. But my second husband went and he came back and told me how it sounds." And she made the sound again, so perfectly, of one wave after another breaking, foaming, and subsiding on a shore she would never see.

To please the potters, I brought the camera with me one day, and they all dressed up with their children for portraits. Everyone came to watch while I took enormous old Tene. She went inside her house, and when she came out, she had donned a huge flowing dress with a design of blue and yellow clocks all over it. The clocks all said four o'clock. "Mo-ther! Mo-ther!" shouted the younger women in delight when they saw her, and they all clapped their hands in a fast, appreciative rhythm.

Three-year-old Salifou was too shy to be taken and hid behind a granary. But everyone else posed for their portrait. Even Nawa, that wild little creature, slid to a shy stop in front of her mother long enough for me to click the shutter and capture her, all arms and legs and big eyes.

The pictures were developed in a decrepit studio in Korhogo and came back looking like ancient family portraits, in sepia and gray tones and very very grainy. If you wanted color prints, you had to send them to France. But everyone in Kafongon was delighted when I handed them out, and the women compared pictures and laughed at their children and studied one another's images with real pleasure. All except Namwa and Salifou. Salifou now deeply regretted that he had not had the courage to come out from behind the granary. He looked so mournful that I let him wear my baseball cap.

Namwa sat looking at her portrait with visible disappointment. This seemed very unlike her. She never took part in the petty rivalries of the other women who were now comparing portraits. I asked her what was the matter.

The problem was that her headscarf, which had been piled magnificently high and was very well-wrapped, had come out exactly the same shade as the sky, so that you couldn't see it at all. It looked, because the turban blended into the sky, as if she were not wearing anything on her head.

"We know the headscarf is there," I began. "It is just difficult to see it because it looks the same as the sky. It's because the picture is made only in black and white."

"But the sky and the headscarf should not look the same," she said firmly. "Can't you fix it?"

I was about to say that I could not, to explain that the picture was already developed and could not be changed. Photographs are finished once they're developed, I opened my mouth to say. But something made me stop.

"Give it to me," I said. "I can fix it for you." And I took my pencil out of my bag and colored in the small rectangle of sky, so that the gray became one shade darker. I went around the wrapped headscarf carefully; I could just barely make out its outline. When I was done, the turban gleamed white against the gray sky, and it looked very tall on her head and very well-wrapped and very dignified.

I handed it back to Namwa, whose face changed as

277

soon as she saw it. The disappointment was gone, and she had the same look of rapt appreciation that I had seen on her face when she made the sound of the sea. "Thank you," she said happily.

Often, now, when I think about art, I think about that day when I colored the sky in for Namwa. My first response was to say no. The picture had come out a certain way and that was that. But what was the picture for, if not to please Namwa? And what sort of photographer was I, if I was too much in awe of my own creation to change it? Sometimes, when life seems difficult and art ineffectual, on those days when I wonder if what I do is worthwhile, or when the world seems particularly insulting, I remember Namwa, how proudly she stood for her portrait and how she refused to accept that the sky had obliterated her turban. Then I feel proud, too, for whatever else I may have failed to do, I didn't hesitate that day but took my pencil in hand. Whatever doubts may assail me, I know that once, in Kafongon, I changed the nature of things by coloring the sky a darker gray.

When sunset approached, my visit to the women drew to a close. It always ended formally with the same ritual. Since Nafini was my *jatigi-muso,* I always asked her for the road. This is an African custom of asking your host for permission to leave. "Nafini, I'm asking for the road."

"Oh, is it time already?"

"Yes," I would reply. "It's time."

"You're sure you have to go?"

"Yes, I have to leave. Night is falling."

"All right then, I'll take you and put you on the road," Nafini would say firmly, setting her work in order and gathering her children around her.

Salifou, her little boy, with a toddler's fat belly and

short stubby legs, would take my hand for the walk. Salifou acted so much like a lovestruck beau when I was around that we had taken to calling him my *kanbele,* my boyfriend. "Don't give away to Tom that you have a *kanbele* here at Kafongon," the women would tease me. "Then he wouldn't let you come to visit us in the afternoons!"

Yacouba would be tied on Nafini's back, and Nawa would skip circles around us as we walked. "Nawa, do you want to come and sleep at my house tonight?" I would ask her as she skipped near. Her eyes would light up with delight at the question, but she would skip away again, kicking up her heels, until she was even farther out of reach.

Often, one or two of the other women would join us. "Come on! We're putting Carol on the road," they would call to their children. And if they didn't have water to carry or rice to pound, my fan club of young girls would come, too. Against the brown-gold savanna and the dusty-rose sunset sky, our little procession of women and children flocked along together, with Nafini as my *jatigimuso* in the lead, and the children skipping now behind us, now to the side.

At a certain point, Nafini would step off the trail. The place where she stopped varied every day, and the logic for the choice was her own. At first, it seemed arbitrary to me. I did not understand that this gesture, too, was part of a language. Later I realized that the farther she walked me, the more she was saying that she appreciated my visit, and sometimes, we would be nearly at the village edge before she stepped off the path and turned back. This was the case whenever I brought snuff for Tene and Sita, or aspirin for Namwa's sore foot, or antiseptic soap for Yacouba's impetigo. "We are stopping here," she would say quietly. "See you tomorrow. May Allah give the village a good night."

"Amina," I replied and repeated the blessing to her.

"Ami . . ." she replied softly. Then each of us turned and went our separate ways.

I always went on with a light happy step, taking a different trail that curved through the tobacco gardens of the Dyula women and ended up at the well outside our quarter. The Dyula women grew tobacco in the dry season, harvested the leaves, dried them, and pounded them into snuff to sell. They irrigated the small fields themselves, using large gourds to carry the water from wells dug near the fields. In early morning and late afternoon, the tobacco gardens were full of women, swinging the gourd vessels skillfully so that the water sprayed out. The trail passed right by Mariam's plot. Mariam and I always stood talking for a few minutes, and I examined the progress of the hairy leaves that reminded me of floppy green rabbit ears. If I was later than usual, Mariam would hustle me away with the admonition to hurry home and cook dinner for my husband. "He'll beat you if you don't hurry!" she would tease me as I ambled away, determined to dawdle and enjoy the sunset.

Mariam was always coming by our house to give me little lectures. She found my lack of concern for Tom's welfare appalling and often told me so. This just made me act all the more unconcerned. If Tom and Mariam came in while I was typing or writing in my journal, I would greet them and go on working.

"That's very bad," she would scold me. "You should be here cooking so that when your husband comes in from the bush, you have food waiting for him."

"It's always like this at our house, Mariam," Tom would moan with comic resignation. "I have to cook for myself or I don't eat! And when she's writing or reading, she won't even answer me!" Tom's rendition of the suffering husband had benefitted tremendously from his study with that master of the genre, Yardjuma.

"A ma nyi!" Mariam said to me, wagging her finger. "That's not good."

One day it was very late when I passed Mariam's tobacco garden. "You had better get home and cook dinner for your husband," Mariam said to me. "Night is falling." She picked up her watering gourds. "Let's go together," she offered. "I am going home myself, and I will go your way and greet Tom."

"That will please him," I replied.

"Maybe by the time we get there," I said mischievously as we walked along the path, "Tom will have cooked dinner, and we can eat."

Mariam looked at me skeptically. She thought I was joking. "Maybe he will have made guinea fowl with rice or maybe, if we're lucky, he will have made fried plantains for us. Now that would please me! I'm very hungry."

Mariam obviously regarded these hopes of mine as a form of delusion. So imagine her surprise when we arrived at the house and found Tom with fork in hand, skillfully turning slices of plantain in a skillet of hot oil. He sat us both down and served us little plates of delicious fried plantains and refused to give Mariam the road until he had fried another cupful for her to take home with her.

I am not sure how Mariam viewed this spectacle. Perhaps, in her view, white people were so different that the most bizarre behavior was to be expected. Noupka and I turned our differences into jokes and pantomimes and laughed over them. But Noupka was an outcast anyway, someone who questioned her life long before she met me. Except for Noupka, the young women, caught up in marriage and child raising, did not seem to question how they lived. If they wanted to be friends, they pretended that I lived as they did. The older women like Namwa and Mariam were not threatened by difference; they had survived too much for that. They accepted my oddities with a wry smile. Even Mariam's lectures had the air of farce.

One afternoon, I was leaving Kafongon with Adama after a morning of interviewing the older potters about their lives. It was the heart of the dry season, and the sun beat down relentlessly on the red earth. "We'll have to walk the long way around through Dyulaso," Adama told me. "There is something going on in the sacred grove and you mustn't pass by." I was very tired and I didn't feel like walking twice as far in the midday sun.

"Let's take the path that goes the short way but isn't right next to the sacred grove," I countered.

Adama hesitated for a moment and then reluctantly said that he thought that would be all right. As we set off, his father called to us to come back. "Don't go that way today," said his father. "Go around through Dyulaso." Adama explained what we were going to do and that I was tired.

"All right," conceded his father. "But you walk between her and the sacred grove, and tell Carol to look away until you are well past. It is a powerful thing."

Adama and I walked away in silence. I was surprised that his father, a devout Moslem, had so much respect for the power of *poro*. Yet I knew that before the people of Kafongon converted to Islam in the fifties, their *poro* had the reputation of being the strongest in the area. And the old man had made sure that Adama, al-

though he was a practicing Moslem, had been initiated
into the *poro* of Kalikaha in a perfunctory initiation.

"You know that my father said that to protect
you," Adama said. His tone implied that I was acting
like a rebellious child. "If a woman who is not initiated
sees anything, she can die. No other woman would even
want to come this way. They would all be afraid."

When we got near the sacred grove, there was an
incredible hullabaloo coming out, loud yells and beastly
howls. Of course, I glanced over toward the grove. But I
couldn't see anything through the thick undergrowth.

NAWA
LEARNS TO WORK

Nawa was five, and in our culture, she would have had a long career ahead of her as a child, another several years at least, or until harshness from one quarter or another squelched her playful spirit. But in Kalikaha this was not to be. At five, Nawa had to be taught to accept the tasks a woman does in her society. As I watched them gentle her and reward her for obedience, I was reminded of the way a wild colt is trained, gently, one step at a time, with praise but always with firmness.

Here was Nawa, to my surprise one day, still dressed only in her brightly colored briefs and waist-beads, coming toward us with a small bucket of water on her head. She had to steady the bucket with her hand as she walked. And here was Sita, her grandmother, lifting down the bucket and praising Nawa with exaggerated admiration. *"I ni chay,* Nawa, *i ni chay. I ni baara.* May God bless you for your work."

"*I ni chay,* Nawa," echoed the other women admiringly. "You have really worked well!" Nawa bent her head under the praise and even before it was finished, bolted away through the granaries, kicking up her heels.

Soon I saw Nawa pounding rice and corn, and her little arms began to develop small muscles. Now she still ran between the granaries when I chased her, but she didn't run quite so fast, nor did she kick up her heels so high. And where before she had been deaf to her mother's warnings not to play wildly near the fragile pots drying in the sun, now she was attentive for the call of her mother or grandmother to come and help them, to pound, to go for water, to winnow rice.

Soon after I noticed this change in Nawa, she was excised along with the other girls of Kafongon. The girls slept in a separate house, and I would see Nawa there with the others, sitting glumly in the shade until she healed. Then, for another two weeks, the girls had a holiday and did as they pleased, spending their days mostly with long sticks under the mango trees. When this special period was over, the girls went back to their mothers and back to work.

I did not know beforehand that the girls would be excised. I simply arrived in the quarter one afternoon, and it had been done. Perhaps my face gave away my feelings. Or perhaps somehow, in that strange osmosis that brings ideas from our dominant culture even as far as Kalikaha, the women suspected that I disapproved. They watched me worriedly for a reaction. "What do you think?" they asked me. "Is it good to do this?"

What could I say in my limited Dyula? Without an interpreter, how could I explain my complicated feelings and ask them theirs? "We don't do this where I come from," I replied. "But, yes, it's all right with me."

285

I wasn't being honest, but I was lonely, and their friendship meant more to me than anything else at that moment. I knew they felt that the "maleness" had been removed and that their daughters were now wholly female. But beyond that, I knew very little, and I was too taken aback to phrase more questions.

When I asked Adama about it, he told me that when he was small, the girls who were excised were older than Nawa and they danced at night. He also told me how much he had paid for the excision of Nafini's little sister, who lived with them. But that was all he knew about it. I prepared long lists of questions I wanted to ask the women. "It's no use," Adama told me. "They will never speak about it."

"I will promise never to tell anyone. I just want to know for myself!"

"It's not you," Adama replied. "The women would speak to you about it. But they will never say a word in front of me." I put up my list of questions with a sigh. My vocabulary was too limited, and I did not know any women in the area who spoke French.

This was not the first time that Tom and I had encountered excision. One Sunday, just after the stormy firing of Yardjuma, Tom and I decided to take a trip for the day, just to get out of Kalikaha. We decided to go to the tiny Senufo village of Behvogo, where our friend the woodcarver Wangolo lived. Tom had ordered a stool from Wangolo and we wanted to pick it up.

When I came back from buying *baga,* the rice porridge that the Dyula girls made and sold for breakfast, flavored with ginger and red pepper, Donnisongui and Tom were drinking Nescafé together. "We're just going to relax today," Tom told Donni. "We're going to look at birds in the bush and then go to Behvogo."

"Oh?" replied Donni. "My mother just left for Beh-vogo."

"Why did she go?" we asked.

"She went to circumcise a child," he answered.

I felt a sinking in my stomach. "A boy or a girl?" I asked him.

"A girlchild. Kali, my little sister." Kali now worked for us because Fanta had become ill. She was a cheerful little girl of about ten, and she reminded me of Donnisongui himself, hard working, with the same compact muscular build and always in good spirits. I loved to watch her when she kicked off her rubber thongs, looped them over her fingers like gloves, and took her place in the circle of dancing women. Donnisongui had sent her to school along with his own daughter, but Kali had not liked it; she preferred to work alongside her grandmother, with whom she lived. She was really Donni's niece. Kali's mother, Donni's sister, had died just after Tom came to Kalikaha.

"Carol, do you know about it?" Donni asked me. I hesitated. Finally, I said that it wasn't done where we came from, but that I did know a little bit about it. He told us that he had paid one thousand CFA (African francs) plus a large basket of rice and a chicken to the woman who would do it. And last year he had paid for the excision of his future wife, Fatouma, since she was already promised to him.

Tom and I went on to Behvogo. It seemed fated in some way, and we set out exactly as we had planned. The birds in the marshes were bright and beautiful—a red Roller, first cousin to my Abyssinian Rollers, carmine bee-eaters, hawks, herons, a pair of green parrots, and an iridescent green bee-eater that we had never seen before and never saw again after that day.

We were walking through Behvogo when we came to a large shady clearing where there was an ancient, spreading mango tree. About twenty young girls were lying under the tree, each one covered with a dark blue cloth. A number of older women sat nearby, watching over them. The girls lying on the ground had expressions of pain-filled numbness. The ones waiting their turn sat silently.

The air felt dark and heavy and dangerous, and both Tom and I felt that we were trespassing. We walked through the area quickly. When we reached Wangolo's house, his wife told us that he had gone to the bush to cut wood for carving and wouldn't be home until dusk. We turned and made our way back through the small village. We reached the clearing under the large mango tree and greeted the old women. Somehow, we couldn't just leave. I felt that my face must give away the horror I felt and my pity for the girls in pain. The older women looked serious but matter-of-fact.

"I'm going to take a picture," Tom said to me quietly. He took out the camera, adjusted the light, and focused on the young girls' faces.

"You took a picture," said the woman to Tom.

"Here," said Tom, giving her some coins. "This is for you, so that you can all drink some corn beer." The woman smiled, and Tom continued taking pictures. Both he and I felt as if something terrible were going to happen to us at any moment, but he calmly finished taking pictures before we left. "Come back and give me one of the pictures," the woman called after us.

In leaving, we passed by one of the two houses where the old women were taking the girls. A girl came out with rags pressed tightly between her legs. I could see blood on the cloth as the old woman took it off and checked the girl's genitals. The old woman put the cloth back and fastened it to a rope that went around the girl's waist so that the cloth passed between her legs. Then the woman draped the indigo blue cloth around her and led her back to her place under the tree.

I looked back one more time, drawn by the scene yet terrified and wanting to flee it. I saw Kali lying on the ground, her little face set. None of the girls ever cried out or sobbed. I didn't feel safe again until we reached Kalikaha and were back inside our own house. Even then, I felt a cloud of darkness, as if the shade cast by the giant mango tree hung over me, too.

As for the child-sprite, Nawa, she still had an air of limber grace about her, but she had grown out of her wilfulness and her wildness. One day when I arrived, they had tressed her hair into lots of little plaits. "Nawa, you look so pretty!" I exclaimed. But Nawa's only reply was a deeper pout. "What's the matter, Nawa? Don't you like it?"

"It hurts. It hurts. It *hurts,*" was all she said to me, her dark eyes brimming with outrage and betrayal. I remembered my own childhood and the skin-tight ponytails that my mother called "neat" and how it used to hurt when she pulled and fastened them.

In a picture I have of us taken on my last day in Kalikaha, I am holding Yacouba. Nafini stands in the middle, smiling, and Nawa is on her other side, dressed for the first time ever in a woman's waistcloth and blouse. Her mother has one hand lightly on her wrist, as if to make sure she doesn't bolt as the picture is taken, and Nawa looks at the camera with tilted head and a question in her eyes. Gone is the sureness of her childhood gaze.

WAITING FOR RAIN

When the time came near for our departure, we could see that it weighed upon Donnisongui. He knew as well as we did that the three of us might never meet again. We hated to see the look of sadness cross Donni's face, so we avoided talking about our plans while he was visiting. He came into the house one day, looked at Tom sadly, and then burst out, with the air of someone unburdening himself. "I am really not happy that you are leaving for good in a month! This makes me very unhappy." I dusted off a chair and offered it to him. "No," he replied. "I won't sit down. I only came to tell you that. I had to say it." He turned and walked away.

It was the difficult time of year again. Everyone was waiting for rain so that they could work their fields, but the rains were late in coming. There was very little food left in the village, and the weather was excruciatingly hot by ten o'clock every morning, sultry and oppressive. I was glad that Tom was getting away to attend a conference on agriculture in Abidjan. He refused to slow down his work, working harder than ever in one last desperate attempt to fill every gap in his data, and the heat made him short-tempered and grouchy. I found myself praying again and again for rain, for the cool winds that came before each storm and for the water that was needed so that they could plow the parched land. Cruelly, we would see dark clouds in the distance, but the rain wouldn't fall. At other times, the clouds would release their small loads of rain on the village but not on the fields. Sometimes, after a shower, Donnisongui went hopefully out to his fields and came back downcast, to tell me that the rain had fallen near his fields but not on them. The Dyula went to the marabouts to purchase blessings for rain, and the Senufo put sacrifices before their household shrines and in the bush for the bush spirits. Everyone watched the sky constantly.

Noupka was a frequent visitor to our house during the dry season, since there was no work to be done in the fields. Sometimes I went into the bush with her to collect pods from *nere* trees, one of two trees that no one in Kalikaha ever cuts down. Although I couldn't stand the sauce that *nere* was made into (it smelled like rotten fish to me), I liked the raw pods, and, like the children, I would suck on the bright yellow insides, which looked like skinny neon-yellow bananas and had a delicate flavor.

Whenever Noupka came to visit me, she always announced her arrival with: "Carol, your girlchild has come!"

"How is my girlchild today?" I would ask.

"Your girlchild is very tired," Noupka would say. "She went to the pump early this morning, then to the bush to harvest *nere* all day, then she came home and had to carry wood and go to the pump again. She's so tired!"

"*I ni chay,* Mama!" I would say. "You've worked so hard."

In this way, I would hear all about Noupka's doings that day. Noupka found my concern for Mama very funny, since Mama had done all these things comfortably tied onto Noupka's back. Mama now grinned in delight at the sight of either Tom or me, and jumped out of Noupka's arms to come to us. Only Mama and very small babies would let us hold them. Toddlers, even though they had seen us daily for months, were still afraid. I suspect that some mothers, like Sibatia, may have been tempted by our presence, so convenient, to instill obedience in their children. The way Sibatia's little boy still squalled in terror at the sight of us, I thought he must have been told the night before, "If you don't stop crying and eat your rice, I'm going to feed you to the whites. They eat little children who misbehave!"

We saved our evaporated milk cans for Mama to play with, rolling them across the floor in front of her. No matter where I rolled the can, she would never turn over on all fours to crawl. Sitting upright with her plump little legs spread in front of her like a doll's, she would scoot along on her bottom to retrieve the can. I had always assumed that crawling was a necessary step in child development, but I suppose that even this is cultural, for in Kalikaha, children learned to walk without ever having crawled. The fathers encouraged their children to learn to walk because a cultural taboo forbade the parents to have sexual intercourse until the child walked well—not just a few steps, but well enough to cover distances on its own. If the parents slept together before this, they risked damaging the child's health. This ensured that a woman did not have another baby while she still had a child on her back and was one of the reasons why men said that you weren't *really* married until you had two wives.

Donnisongui was openly jealous of Noupka's visits and disapproved of the way she made herself at home. Unlike the other women, she always took a chair, and she didn't give it up willingly when a man arrived. At night, when she passed by on her way to the well, she asked to borrow either our flashlight or Donni's. If Donni said no, she taunted him until he gave in.

Late one afternoon, we were sitting on the porch with Donnisongui when there was an outcry of angry women's voices from the other side of the quarter. "It's about Noupka," Donni said after a moment. "She's been caught stealing food from another woman's house. That's very bad," Donnisongui kept saying over and over, shaking his head sadly. We both agreed. Noupka had taken one bouillon cube to make sauce.

For several days I didn't see Noupka, and I wondered what had happened. I couldn't keep from thinking about another time when some sweet potatoes had disappeared from our house. Only Noupka and Fanta had remarked on the sweet potatoes, and after they disappeared, I asked Fanta if she had taken them. She was very hurt and replied that if she wanted something from me like sweet potatoes, she would have asked, which was true. She often asked me for aspirin, for Nescafé, for empty bottles to trade at the market, for a pair of sandals from Korhogo. I didn't want to think that Noupka would have taken anything from me, so I dismissed the sweet potatoes as mysteriously lost.

I had always admired Noupka's brazenness, but now I felt really angry at her for stealing food. To steal from a neighbor was like stealing from your own kin, and to

293

the other woman the one bouillon cube was valuable. I didn't want the other women in the quarter to think that I condoned Noupka's actions or was protecting her, so I swore to myself that if Noupka came back, I wouldn't speak to her. I wished that she had come to me and asked me for something, rather than taking it, but I also knew that I got impatient with her constant requests.

When Noupka finally came back after a week, she had been beaten so badly that she could barely walk. Despite Donnisongui's lectures on village morality and my own resolves, when I saw her I couldn't maintain the stony silence I had planned. I gave in and returned her greetings.

We resumed our old relationship, but I was more aware than ever of how little trust existed between us and of how little I really understood Noupka's life. Only through Mama did I feel really connected to Noupka. I watched proudly as Mama ate her first bite of rice, hotly spiced with cayenne pepper, and agreed with Noupka that she was wonderfully smart. When Noupka pierced Mama's ears and outlined her glowing eyes with lines of blue kohl, I concurred that she was beautiful beyond belief. Even when Mama peed on my lap, which she always did, I conceded that it would bring me luck, for with me, as with Noupka, Mama could do no wrong.

One afternoon, I was sitting on the porch with Adama eating hot roasted peanuts. We roasted the peanuts in their shells by laying a pile on the ground, covering them with thatch, and lighting it. The smell of roasting peanuts usually pulled in a small crowd—Donnisongui, Beh, and a group of children usually joined us. Noupka came up to Adama and said something in Senufo that was obviously about me. Adama gave her a strange look and laughed nervously.

"Carol," she said to me in Dyula, "I'm hungry."

"We've got peanuts here," I said, holding out a handful. But Noupka turned and walked away without taking them.

"What did she say before?" I asked Adama.

He hesitated before he answered. "She said, 'How can Carol joke with me every day when her stomach is full and mine is empty?' " To this question, I had no reply. Once more, Noupka had put her long angular finger squarely upon the difference between us.

There was no doubt that this was the most difficult period of the year for the villagers. Once again, there were deaths and funerals. One night in the middle of a lavish funeral for a relative of Beh Tuo's, drums began to beat frantically from the sacred grove. I recognized the particular rhythm of a quarter on the other side of the village. Young initiates, *balafon* players, old women— everyone suddenly put down their instruments and ran at full speed toward the grove. Later, we learned that a middle-aged man had died suddenly, and his death was being announced. His funeral was held immediately after the first one was finished.

One day, while Tom was gone to Abidjan, Adama and I went to the compound of Lonala, Mariam's husband, because one of his children had come the day before and asked us to write a letter for him. Adama and I were the village scribes. The schoolteachers and extension agents who worked in the village refused to help the villagers read or write letters, and before we came, Adama had been the only one who was willing to do it. He was delighted that I helped him, for writing was still an arduous task for Adama. "You write so quickly!" he would say to me. "Just like that. I say it to you and it's already down on the paper. So neatly, too!" For myself, I liked writing the letters for I learned intimate bits of village dealings that people would not have spoken about other- wise—a mother writing to her son about his marriage prospects, a man writing to his brother to declare his in- nocence when he was accused of sorcery, an old man who sent a letter to a friend in another village just to say, "I am still alive." Our favorite letter was the one we had written for a very elderly Dyula man to his prospective bride in another village, a young maiden of fifteen. "Have no fear," dictated the shaky old groom to the young girl he had never seen, "I love you already." Adama and I barely escaped from the house before we collapsed in laughter. This became a favorite joke among the three of us, and we would lean over, raise our eye- brows, and whisper throatily to one another: *"N'aie pas peur. Je t'aime déjà."*

This must be the hottest day of our entire stay, I thought to myself as Adama and I walked listlessly across the village. I was glad that Tom had missed this heat. He broke out in rashes when it got this hot and turned into a human snapping turtle. When we walked into Lonala's compound, which was usually the nucleus of an extremely active and neighborly quarter full of women pounding and children playing, all was eerily quiet. Lonala's neighbors barely responded to our greet- ings. Even they are affected by this heat, I thought to myself.

But gradually, I became aware of labored, raspy breathing coming from the house next to Lonala's. When we reached the door, we saw that the house was full of older people, including Lonala and Mariam. Inside their circle, a man was lying on the floor. I recognized him as a relative of Lonala. With each breath, his whole body struggled, and his hands clenched and unclenched and clawed the air. What air he was able to draw in rasped and gurgled as it passed through his throat.

"God cure him. God help you with your troubles," Adama mumbled over and over, although it was clearly a death watch. I echoed his blessings weakly.

The next day, we heard that the man had died. We went once more to their compound to give Lonala and Mariam a contribution to the funeral expenses.

A week later, Lonala came all the way across the village to call on us, the only time he ever came to our house. I was honored because he was old and not in very good health. For the first time, he spoke about his experiences under French colonial rule. He was sent to the forest region and forced to work in the lumber camps. "All they did," Lonala said, "was give you a sheet when you arrived and put you to work. If you died working, there was a crew of four men who did nothing but bury the bodies. They wrapped you in the same sheet you had slept in and buried you in a shallow grave. If the sheet was ripped," Lonala said mournfully, "they wrapped you in it anyway."

This must have seemed barbaric to the Senufo and Dyula, who put so much importance on their funerals and who wash the body carefully and wrap it in as many as forty or fifty handwoven cloths. At that time, the Dyula had their own sacred grove and celebrated funerals with masks and dancing, much like the Senufo.

"Sometimes," Lonala said, "the trees were so huge that one hundred men would have to take hold of the ropes in order to pull the fallen tree out to the road. Working for the white men in the labor camps was terrible," he concluded. "They did not care if you died, and they did not bury you well or send your body home to your people. I would never have thought that I could live side by side with white people like this," he ended quietly. "You came when my relative died and brought money to help with the funeral. I would never have believed this could happen. It is a very great difference."

Tom returned from ten days of air-conditioned comfort at the apartment of American friends and told me rhapsodically, "You know something that's really wonderful, absolutely heavenly?"

"What?" I asked.

"Couches," sighed Tom. "And real chairs . . . aaah! They're so soft. You just sink down into them, and then you have a real light to read by. You can't imagine how wonderful it is!"

"*Baga* again for breakfast?" he asked me the second morning after his return.

"Of course," I said in surprise. "We always have *baga*."

"I guess we do," he sighed. "I'd forgotten."

INSIDE THE GROVE

THAT SAME WEEK, TOM AND I WERE INITIATED INTO THE *poro* of the quarter of Pempoho, the quarter where we lived. We had been waiting for Beh Tuo to return from a trip because we wanted him to be present. One day, the head of the sacred grove came to our door and said only that it was time for our initiation. Tom jumped on the motorcycle and rode off to find Adama, who had gone home to eat lunch. Adama was grinning from ear to ear when he arrived. The prospect of our doing the *poro* delighted him. *"Ça va, Carol? Ça va beaucoup?"* We had been told to bring a certain sum of money and that it must be in small coins, so Tom rode off again to Chez Mama for change. This would be distributed among the elders. When our change was ready, we sat in the house with Adama and Donnisongui, looking from one to the other in excitement. Finally, someone came for us.

We walked single file, Adama in front of us, Donni

behind. The noonday sun beat down, and a hot wind was blowing. I looked back and saw behind me a long line of men coming toward the sacred grove. At the second large tree, we stopped and took off our sandals. One always enters a sacred grove barefoot.

Inside, we were taken into a large round house with low walls and a pointed roof. The head of the sacred grove and most of our male neighbors were there, seated on logs worn to a smooth gray patina. Beh Tuo was there as well. Several young initiates stood guard in their loincloths just outside the door. There was a long discussion, and each man present gave his opinion. Finally, it seemed an agreement had been reached. Adama explained that they had asked the ancestors to excuse us for not undressing.

We were led back to the path that enters the grove. Tom was told to squat on his heels. "Why have you come?" they asked him. "To do the *poro*," he replied, as he had been taught. "Can you?" they asked. "Yes," he replied. One of the young initiates came up behind Tom with a bundle of green sticks and whacked it on the ground just behind Tom so that he jumped. Then it was my turn.

After I got up, they taught us the secret greeting that we must use inside the grove: "I greet you at the work of our grandmother."

We were taken on a tour of the grove and shown the house where they stored the drums, the place where food was prepared, and ritual altars built of earth. There was a round enclosure made of sticks with a small hut inside. Leading into this enclosure was a narrow, pointed tunnel made of sticks that leaned against one another. This was where the initiates had to enter, crawling through the small tunnel while they were pelted with stones and water. Adama told us that they were made to do it again and again until they were exhausted. All of them had to sleep inside the enclosure together every night for three months.

We were taught what to say and how to behave while we were inside the grove. There are certain things one must and must not do, and all the objects in the grove have secret names that we must memorize. After that was finished, we all sat down again inside the house, and we gave them our fee, which was distributed then and there among the elders according to their seniority. As this ended, the chief wandered in, just as he always did, after the real action was over.

"Why didn't anybody notify me?" he stormed petulantly. "No one ever tells me what's going on! Why wasn't I called? I'm the chief, aren't I? It's not right."

Everyone ignored him, as usual. Beh Tuo had told us that the elders would probably never give him the official red hat of chiefdom. Instead, they would give it to the head of the sacred grove, who was well-respected despite having converted to Islam. The head of the sacred grove would then, Beh Tuo predicted, be killed by the would-be chief via sorcery. I couldn't imagine that he was capable of killing anyone by sorcery, but Beh Tuo claimed that he had inherited powerful magical knowledge.

Donnisongui told us our secret *poro* names. "If anyone ever doubts that you have really done the *poro*," he said, "or if any Senufo ever tries to harm you, you have only to say these names, and any Senufo will let you pass unharmed. Any man who has done the *poro* will know what they mean."

Tom's name they translated for us as "you have already done good things," a reference to the dam he had

301

convinced the government livestock agency to build. Mine meant "a stranger who is good and kind." Never tell these names to anyone who has not done the *poro,* they admonished us, and we promised. They agreed to let us write down what we had been taught so that we could study it, as long as we did not show it to anyone. Then the head of the sacred grove, who was also the quarter chief of Pempoho and the land priest of all the land surrounding Kalikaha, made a formal speech.

"If any other strangers came to us," he said, "and wanted to be initiated into our sacred grove, we might initiate them into the *poro* of Sediunkaha or Peguedala or another quarter, but never into the *poro* of Pempoho, which is the *poro* of the founder of Kalikaha, of its chiefs, the head of the sacred grove and the land priest. It is only because you have lived together with us and because we have found you to be good people that we have decided to admit you into the *poro* of Pempoho. From now on," he ended, "whenever you see people going into the sacred grove, you can come, too, and you can ask questions about whatever you see."

Tom and I each made a speech in reply, saying that we were very honored to be allowed to sit with them in the place of their ancestors.

"Now," cried Donnisongui, the moment the speeches ended, "we are all related. We are all the same!"

Once again in the middle of the line of men, we walked single file out of the grove, along the levee built high like an earthen serpent to protect the grove from brush fires. We emerged from the shadows, and the bright sunshine and open spaces of the village seemed like another world. When we reached the funeral grounds, a crowd was assembling. On every path I could see women converging on the funeral grounds, carrying bowls of rice and sauce on their heads. In the center of the area, an enormous pot of meat stood cooking. As each woman arrived she sat her bowl down on the ground, and the children milled around expectantly, their eyes on the food. For one moment, I imagined that the entire village had come together in a celebration of our *poro* initiation, but Adama explained that the feast was in honor of the bush spirits so that they would send rain.

The meat, a rare luxury, was served out, and each Senufo quarter ate together, sitting on the ground in circles around the assembled pots of rice and sauce. The air resounded with the talk and laughter of the entire Senufo population of the village. Tom and I circulated through the groups as if at a carnival, chewing on proffered bits of meat and taking pictures of the children. The men who had been inside the grove smiled at us with knowing pleasure.

"Your initiation was exactly like mine," Adama said with satisfaction. "Not one thing was different, except that you wore clothes instead of a loincloth."

That night, for the first time ever, Tom told me the entire story of his initiation into the *poro* in Yardjuma's village before my arrival. Yardjuma's village was more traditional than Kalikaha, and Tom's initiation had reflected this. He had entered at night in a loincloth and had had to perform certain tasks and undergo symbolic hardships. He had also been shown many sacred objects. We were both a little sad that it had not been more like this in Kalikaha. When Tom asked about sacred objects, they told us that Kalikaha no longer had any. Rumor had it that the last chief had sold them to art dealers. Nevertheless, the initiation in Kalikaha meant something to us that a more dramatic initiation in another village never could. We knew the history of Kalikaha, and could recite a litany of its chiefs and their exploits. I knew now that I would never truly understand the "way of *poro*" and that the initiation was a gesture from our hosts to us, a gesture of trust and affection. But we now belonged to Kalikaha, in a certain sense, for life.

Contrary to what I had expected, the sacred grove was a very womanly place, full of cooking pots and winnowing baskets. These utensils had been given secret *poro* names to differentiate them from the ordinary ones used by women. Although men carry out most of the activities of *poro,* each sacred grove is actually founded by a woman, the oldest woman of the founding lineage. When a new village is built and a new grove is sanctified, the presence of this elder woman is indispensable, and she remains its titular head.

A Senufo legend recounted by Anita Glaze says that it was the women who first had *poro,* and the men who cooked. If the women came out of the grove dressed in *poro* gear, the men had to go into their houses and hide, leaving the food outside. "The men were too tired and thin. They had to hide while the women ate. Then the Creator God said, 'No, I cannot leave Poro with the women—they are too wicked and sinful.' So he seized the Poro and gave it to the men."

Inside the grove, I had felt the longing for the creative power that belongs innately to women. In this sense, the legend which says that men stole *poro* from women tells the truth.

 LEAVING

WE SPENT ONE OF OUR LAST MORNINGS IN THE VILLAGE
consulting the bush spirits through a diviner. The diviner was Beh Tuo's wife, a fiercely spirited old woman
who was always breaking out into wild little dances. Her
name was Nerewa. I had told her earlier in the week that
I would like to come for a consultation with her. "Fine,"
she said, "but since you aren't Senufo, you can't ask the
bush spirits anything directly. You will have to have a
Senufo sit in the divining house and ask your questions
for you." I went to see Donnisongui.

Donni gave me a long hard look. "You've asked me a
question," he said. "Now before I answer, let me ask you
one. If the diviner tells you that you have to do something, like sacrifice a chicken to the bush spirits or give a
gift, will you do it?"

Donni had me there. I hadn't even thought about it.
I just wanted to experience a divining session. I didn't

really believe that sacrificing chickens would help me finish my novel, which was what I wanted to consult the
bush spirits about. On the other hand, I had to admit
that Donni had a point. If I wanted to play the game, I
had to abide by the rules.

I sighed. "Okay, Donnisong. Whatever the diviner
says I have to do, I'll do it. I give my word."

"Then I'll be happy to sit in for you," Donni replied, smiling.

"She could say that we need to give a feast of
chicken and rice for the whole village!" worried Tom,
when he heard our plans. Our budget was already
strained. But despite his fears, he wanted to come, too.

Diviners have tiny houses, just large enough for two
people to sit in, where they do their work. Donnisongui
sat inside with Nerewa. Tom, Adama, and I sat just outside the door on stools. Nerewa took out her handful of
divining charms—nuts, seeds, and small brass miniatures—and called to the bush spirits to come by ringing a
small brass bell. Then she took Donni's hand in hers and
slapped it, over and over, against her thigh, once on the
outside of her thigh, once on the inside. She mentioned
different things that could be causing my problems, and
when the bush spirits heard the right one, they would
cause the slap to be louder. If a client comes to consult
about an illness, for example, the diviner determines
what has caused the illness—neglect of an ancestor, a
bush spirit who has been angered by some trespass, an
animal that has been killed unnecessarily.

Nerewa asked Donnisongui why we had come, and he
replied that we were concerned about finishing our work.
I was trying unsuccessfully to write a novel. The distrac-
tions of the village, heat, and illness had just about made
me give it up. I wondered if I would ever be able to fin-

ish it, if I would ever be able to call myself a writer. I wondered, too, what would happen now that we were leaving Kalikaha. For so long, the purpose of our lives had been to try to understand life in this strange adobe labyrinth and to adapt ourselves to it. What now? Tom would turn his data into a thesis. Would I be able to take home all that I had learned and integrate it into my life, to make use of it in some way?

Nerewa threw out her divining charms, caught them before they fell, and then slapped them down on the ground in front of her, spreading them out. She did this several times, studying the fall of the articles carefully each time.

Then she looked up at us and said, "You must not hesitate. You must go right ahead and finish what you have started. In your own country, there are very many people who do what you do, but you will be first among them, both of you. You must not hesitate. Just go ahead and finish your work."

And then she added, although we had not asked, "And when you want to have a child, you won't have any problems. When you want the child, it will come."

Donnisongui beamed to hear our future predicted so glowingly, and I realized that he had been genuinely worried about what she would see ahead for us.

The idea that *woman* is synonymous with *mother* had been an issue for me during my entire stay in the village. The daily wishes that I be blessed with a child and the constant questions of "Where are your children?" had sent me into whirlpools of confusion and rebellion. But there had also been another side to village life: the experience of holding babies only a few hours old and feeling the strong desire rise up in me, unbidden, to hold my own. Never before had we been around so many children.

They scrambled over our porch and sat on our laps; the older ones ran errands for us, plucked guinea fowl, and scavenged through our luxurious garbage to find materials with which to make toys. I liked it when I saw Tom stand talking to a woman and unconsciously fondle the baby's feet that stuck out on both sides of her hips. In Kalikaha we reached the decision that, God willing, we would in the not-too-distant future have a child of our own. Nerewa's words, although we hadn't asked for them, were welcome.

As we interviewed Mariam for the last time, she caught me gazing off into space. "Carol must be missing her home," she said to Adama.

"No, it's not that!" I said in surprise, remembering how often I had been homesick in Kalikaha. "I'm sad because soon I have to leave Kalikaha."

Mariam nodded. "You'll come back someday," she said with that warm, wry smile of hers.

Tom and I made lists of all our possessions—pots and pans, sheets, clothing, flashlights, kerosene lanterns, bed, tables, and chairs. All these things we divided up and gave to the members of Tom's farm study. I gave away my clothes and the pottery jars that I had made.

It seemed that there were a million things to be done before we could leave. Each family had to be visited, the gifts handed out, and farewell and thank-you speeches made. A hundred last-minute questions had to be asked, for there wouldn't be another chance. We had to pack up our boxes—all the books and papers we had collected, Tom's boxes of filled-out forms and other data, and gifts of fabric and baskets we had bought for friends at home. I hated leaving the pots the women had given me, but they were too big to fit into the boxes. I took only one with me. It is a very small pot, a miniature of the ones used for cooking. A pot like this is placed in every Senufo woman's grave, and my pot was made for me by old Tene.

We went into Korhogo to mail the cartons and had one last ecstatic pleasure. Our friend Alain took us up in a tiny plane and flew us over Kalikaha. There was the savanna greening under the first rains, the rivers, the fields, the village. We saw the mosque, the mango trees, even our house, which stood out because Donnisongui had recently rethatched the roof for us. I saw Kafongon, a little circle of houses off by itself in the bush. Alain circled and circled and he and another French technical advisor approved the site for the dam that was going to be built just outside Kalikaha. We had not been able to get a clinic built in the village, although we had spent hours trying to convince various administrators with our statistics. But the livestock agency had decided, based on Tom's findings, to build a dam. The villagers called it Tom's Dam, and all were pleased except Beh Tuo, who had to give up his rice fields.

When we asked Adama what he wanted in thanks for his help, he said that he wanted a salaried job in Korhogo. While we were there, Tom arranged for Adama to have an interview at the livestock extension agency.

After our return from Korhogo, I went to spend one last morning with the potters. "It was you in the airplane, wasn't it?" asked Namwa. I nodded in surprise. "We knew it was you because the plane circled and circled. A plane had never done that before."

The women were cooking corn *toh* to take to the fields where the men were already working. Everything at Kafongon suddenly seemed precious to me because I was leaving. Na and Salimata were both pregnant, and as we kidded them about what was inside their round bellies, I realized sadly that I would not be there to go into the dark houses and hold the babies and bless them in person.

Just before noon, the food they were preparing was ready. Some was set aside for the old women and children who would stay at Kafongon and the rest was loaded into enamel basins. I was still amazed at how much Nafini could carry—a bucket of water, several bowls of sauce, clothes, her hoe and grains of rice carefully wrapped in a cloth, to be planted—all this with Yacouba on her back. I walked with her and Namwa and Mawa and little Nawa out to the trail. "Are you coming to the fields with us?" they asked me.

"No, I can't. I have too much work to do at home to get ready to leave. But I want to put you on the road," I added, the way they had so often said it to me. We started down the trail with me bringing up the rear.

"You pass us," Namwa said to me.

"Why?" I asked as I went around and got in front of her.

"Because when you put someone on the road, you go first," she replied.

"Oh, so you're putting Namwa and Nafini on the road," said Mawa.

"You, too, Mawa," I replied.

"Well, get in front of me, too, then!" she replied, laughing. Although I didn't know the way at all, I led into the bush for a long time until finally I stopped and stepped off the trail. We exchanged blessings, and I stood and watched until they disappeared into the savanna.

The last day, some American friends came with a car to take us to Abidjan. The courtyard in front of our house was full of people saying good-bye, as it had been for the last two weeks. Tom ran in and out of the house, watching over his cartons of data like a nervous mother. When we reached Abidjan, he would have to send them off alone to Berkeley, and he was consumed by the thought of the many perils that might befall them on the way.

Mariam came up to me and stood, gently looking at me. She began to cry. Mariam always cries, I told myself. The least little thing sets her off. She's always the first one at a wedding. But I couldn't stop the tears from flowing down my face. Mariam and I stood for a few moments, our hands on each other's shoulders, until I finally turned away to finish packing.

For the rest of the time we were loading the car, she stood under a mango tree and watched me from a distance, a guardian figure in flowing white. Her protective presence was comforting. When it was clear that we would soon be leaving, she came up to me at a moment when no one else was near. "I'm going home now," she said firmly and quietly. Then she disappeared.

Suddenly, there was nothing more to do, and Tom climbed into the backseat. I looked once more for Noupka and Mama, but they were not there. Donnisongui's eyes filled with tears, and I clasped his hand over and over. Nothing I could say would be enough. The real good-bye had been exchanged on our porch several nights earlier.

"You know," he said to us, "we say that if a man takes in a guest and the guest is ungrateful and makes trouble, that man will become inhospitable and refuse to take in any more guests. But if a man takes in a guest and it turns out well, the next time he sees a stranger, he will be kind to him. Now I have had two very good guests, and I feel as if I will be kind to every stranger for the rest of my life."

"We could have had a *jatigi* who simply gave us a house," we replied. "But we had a *jatigi* who gave us much much more. We have had the best possible *jatigi*," we said and we meant it. "Tell us what we can do for you in return."

"Someday," he replied, "perhaps my children will be strangers in a strange land. I may not be able to care for them and they may be in need of help. If someone cares for them, that is how I will be rewarded." I wondered if he was thinking of his daughter, who will be able to go out into the literate, French-speaking world outside the village.

Our last stop before leaving the village was in Kafongon, so that I could say one last good-bye. It was afternoon by the time we arrived, but the women had not gone to the fields. They were waiting, all dressed in their best clothes, for us to come. I sat on a stool one last time with the potters in a circle around me.

"Carol," they announced happily. "We found the pot you were looking for! Look!"

Salifou appeared from around a granary dramatically carrying a pot nearly as big as he was. It was a form that was rarely made anymore, a beautiful old specimen of a portable heater, in which small fires were built during the cold harmattan nights. I had been arguing with them about this pot for weeks, for I clearly remembered seeing it on my first day there, when the children paraded all the pots past me. But they had told me none like it were left.

"You were right, Carol! We found it in old Sirabe's house. Now your work will be complete."

I had gifts for all of them, even a little baseball cap for Salifou, my *kanbele,* and plastic containers with lids for the women's trading trips. We posed for last pictures together, and then flocking around me, they escorted us out to the car with many blessings. Our last glimpse of Kalikaha was the lane of mango trees leading to the village, the ones that had first enticed Tom to turn in there.

 EPILOGUE

Six years have passed since I left Kalikaha. We still hear news of Kalikaha through Adama's letters. He writes of births and deaths and funerals.

Donnisongui, who told us that he wouldn't feel really married until he had two wives, now has his second wife living in the house next to ours.

The man who was acting chief, who always arrived too late and asked why no one had called him, has been given the red hat of chiefdom by the elders after all. The *balafons* played all night, wrote Adama, and the villagers danced until dawn.

The first rainy season after our departure brought little rain and a poor harvest, the year after that, almost no rain fell at all. The women did not even plant their swamp rice fields. It was no use. "Too many funerals here," wrote Adama grimly. "Everyone is in debt." In nearly every letter, we lost someone we had known. Gentle Beh, our next door neighbor, who taught me so many Dyula phrases, finally succumbed to his disease. Lonala, Mariam's pious old husband, is also dead, as is Menergay, the Senufo elder who fell out of the tree trying to collect medicinal leaves for his dying baby. Beh Tuo married his daughter to a wealthy Dyula merchant in Korhogo, converted to Islam, and went to Mecca on an airplane.

Mariam was right. I have been back twice. In the summer of 1984, I was in Ivory Coast teaching a class of American potters who had come to Africa to study African ceramics. After the class left, I went to Kalikaha for five days, stayed in the same house as Donni's guest, and made the rounds of the village to greet old friends and to give my condolences to the families that had lost members. It was the children who reminded me that I had been away for two years. They had grown so much that I mistook them for their older brothers and sisters. When Noupka walked up with a baby that looked like Mama on her back, I asked, "Is that Mama?" and Noupka laughed at me. "Here comes Mama," she said, pointing to a little girl who was just catching up with her. With Donnisongui, I felt the same old camaraderie and the same comfortable feeling. At Kafongon, we still gathered our stools in a circle during the afternoons to talk and laugh.

The granaries had long been empty, but rain was falling, and the farmers were hopeful for a good harvest, the first in two years. Everywhere I looked, I saw signs of the two hard years that had passed since I left the village. Everyone was thin, gaunt. People were eating sauces made from wild fruits and nuts that I had never tasted before. The Saturday market was full of sacks of imported rice, and no one was buying the luxuries that the traders displayed. The bright cloths, headscarves, perfume, and canned food went untouched.

"If it wasn't for the dam," many people told me, "our animals would have died and we might have died, too. It was the only water we had."

The moment that I arrived and looked into Donni's eyes, I saw that something had changed with my arrival, something I had not foreseen, not intended. I had done what African custom demands: I had returned to greet my friends and family. Our stay in Kalikaha was no longer a fluke, a once-in-a-lifetime experience. By returning, even for a few days, I had validated our commitment to these relationships and strengthened them immeasurably.

Two years later, in the summer of 1986, Tom and I again returned to Kalikaha, this time for a month so that Tom could do a follow-up study. We set up a portable crib in Donni's house, for we brought our one-year-old son, Nicholas, with us. We had thought that it would be the rainy season, with its comfortably overcast skies. Instead, the rains were late that year, and we got the hot, oppressive, sultry weather that comes just before the rains. It's so hot here, Tom and I said to each other. It's so difficult. How in the world, we asked ourselves, did we ever live here for a year? We could only conclude that we had been so committed to living in Kalikaha that we hadn't really noticed the discomfort.

Tom's follow-up study went quickly and well. People were more cooperative than they had ever been, for we had proven ourselves and returned. Adama has grown sophisticated and knows about Xerox machines and the intricacies of Korhogo bureaucracies, but he hasn't lost his warmth or his sense of humor.

The women potters still hadn't done the last firing of the season when I arrived, so I once more found myself around a mountain of pots, laying sticks down carefully, and watching as the thatch burst into wild flames. Nafini now lives in Korhogo with Adama and the children, but she was back in Kalikaha to help with the farm work while we were there. Sita and Mariam were pleased that I finally have a child, for now, they said, "You will have someone to care for you in your old age." When I sat next to them and nursed Nicholas, I could feel their warmth and approval. I was finally a grown woman on their terms as well as my own.

Adama's last letter says that the rains are scarce this year and Donnisongui has hurt his arm and cannot work his fields.

ABOUT THE AUTHOR

CAROL SPINDEL WAS BORN IN MEMPHIS, TENNES-
see, and received a B.F.A. in art from the University of Iowa in 1977. She received an M.A.
in art history, with an emphasis on African art,
in 1988 from the University of Illinois. In between, she traveled in North and East Africa,
worked as a coordinator of "Women's Voices,"
a creative writing workshop at the University
of California at Santa Cruz, lived in a village in
northern Ivory Coast, taught African ceramics
through Parsons School of Design's "Parsons
in West Africa" program, and had two children. She lives in Urbana, Illinois, where she is
currently teaching creative nonfiction at the
University of Illinois.